MERRY MEN

MERRY MEN

written by
Robert Rodi

illustrated
by Jackie Lewis

colored by
Marissa Louise
with
Shari Chankhamma

lettered by
Jon Cairns

chapter 1-8, chapter 9 pages 2-5, 8 colored by marissa louise
chapter 9 pages 1, 6-7, 9-12 and chapter 10 colored by shari chankhamma

designed by hilary thompson and sonja synak

Published by Oni Press, Inc.

Joe Nozemack, founder & chief financial officer
James Lucas Jones, publisher
Charlie Chu, v.p. of creative & business development
Brad Rooks, director of operations
Melissa Meszaros, director of publicity
Margot Wood, director of sales
Sandy Tanaka, marketing design manager
Amber O'Neill, special projects manager
Troy Look, director of design & production
Hilary Thompson, senior graphic designer
Kate Z. Stone, graphic designer
Sonja Synak, junior graphic designer
Angie Knowles, digital prepress lead
Ari Yarwood, executive editor
Sarah Gaydos, editorial director of licensed publishing
Robin Herrera, senior editor
Desiree Wilson, associate editor
Alissa Sallah, administrative assistant
Jung Lee, logistics associate
Scott Sharkey, warehouse assistant

facebook.com/onipress
twitter.com/onipress
onipress.tumblr.com
instagram.com/onipress

First Edition: July 2018

ISBN 978-1-62010-547-4
eISBN 978-1-62010-548-1

Printed in China.

Library of Congress Control Number: 2018946792
1 2 3 4 5 6 7 8 9 10

Chapter
1

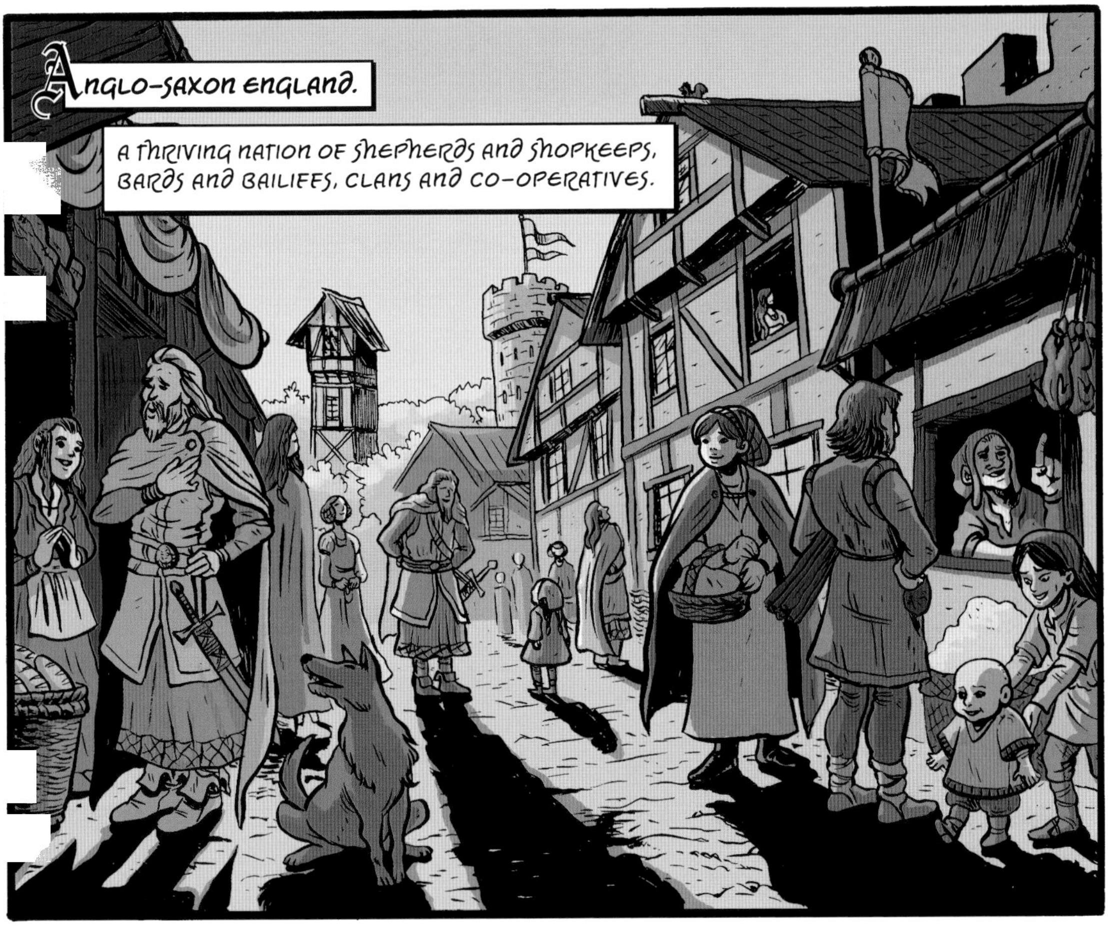
Anglo-saxon england.
a thriving nation of shepherds and shopkeeps, bards and bailiffs, clans and co-operatives.

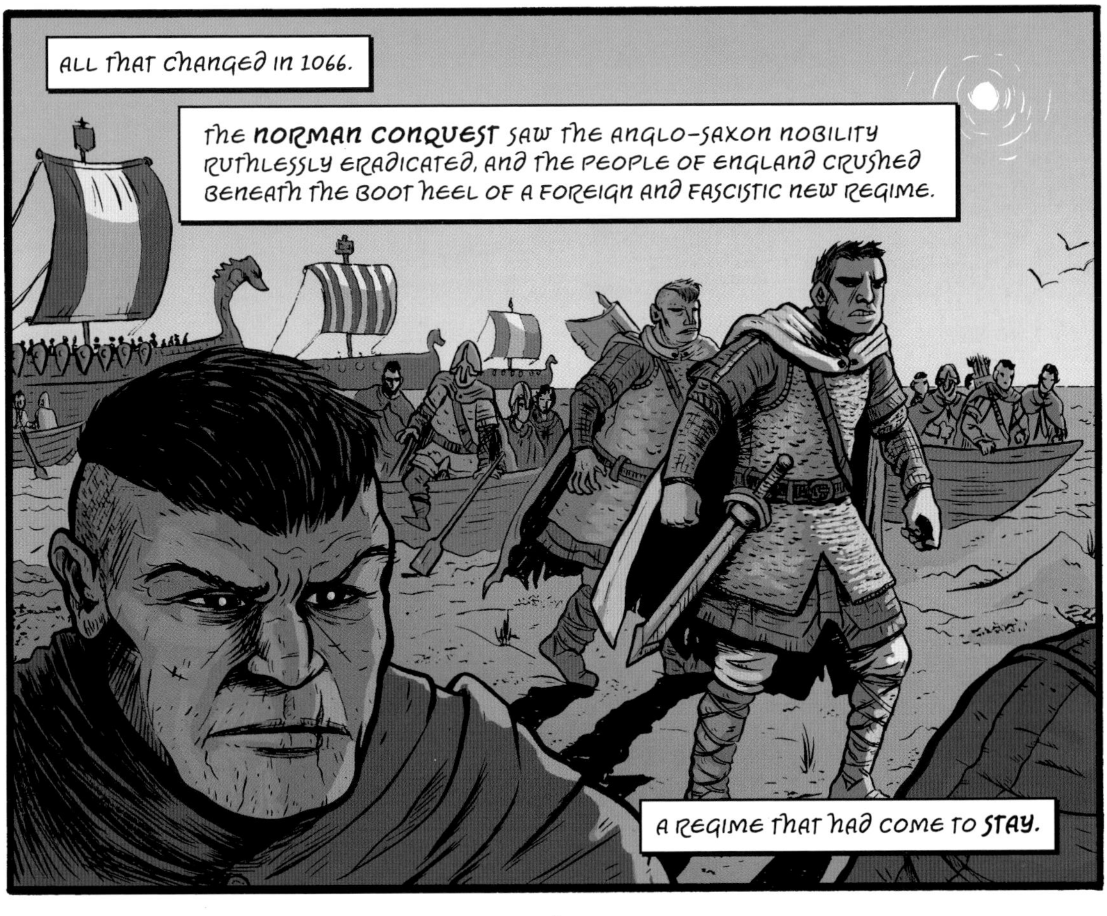
all that changed in 1066.
the **norman conquest** saw the anglo-saxon nobility ruthlessly eradicated, and the people of england crushed beneath the boot heel of a foreign and fascistic new regime.
a regime that had come to **stay.**

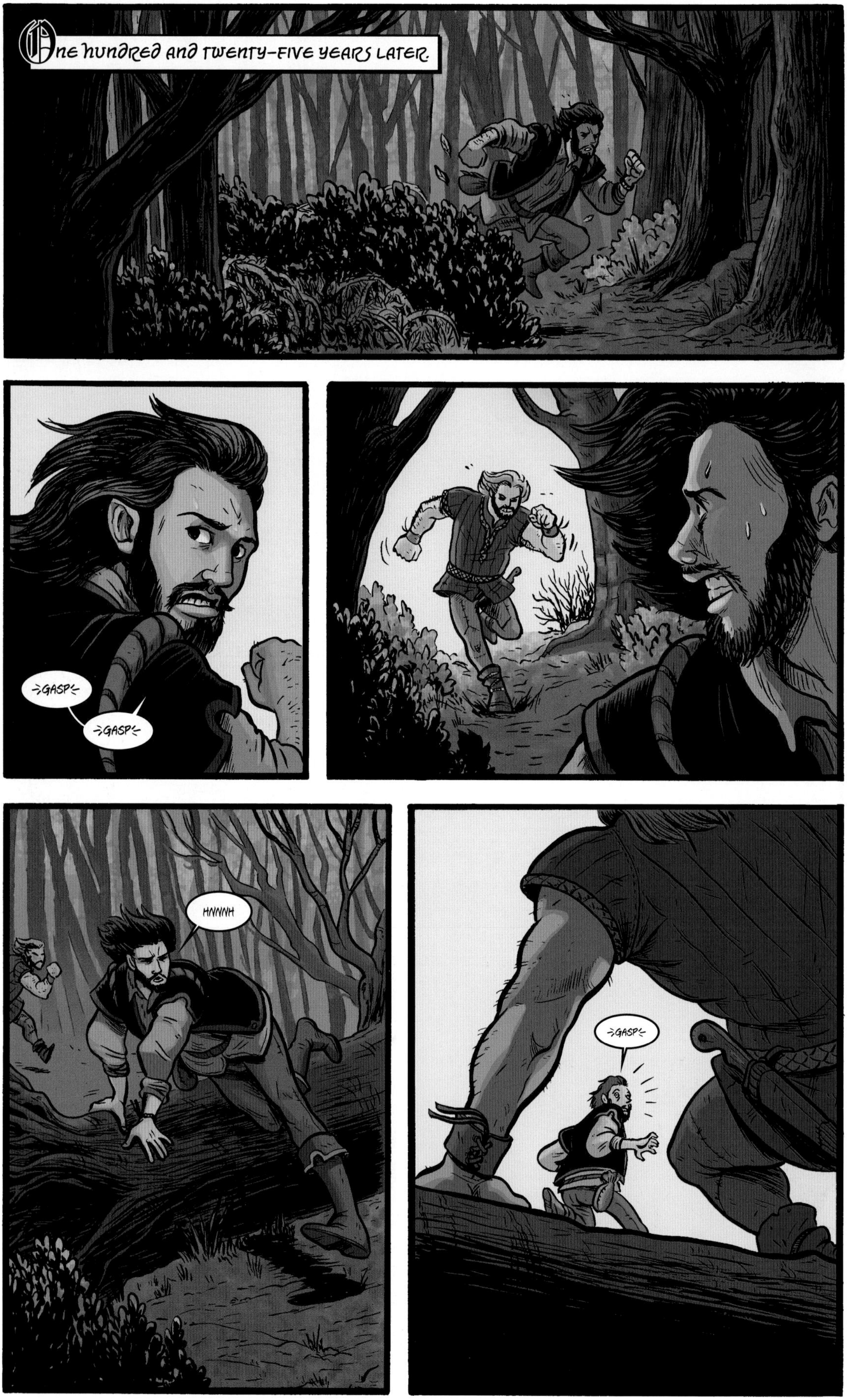
One hundred and twenty-five years later.
-GASP-
-GASP-
HNNNH
-GASP-

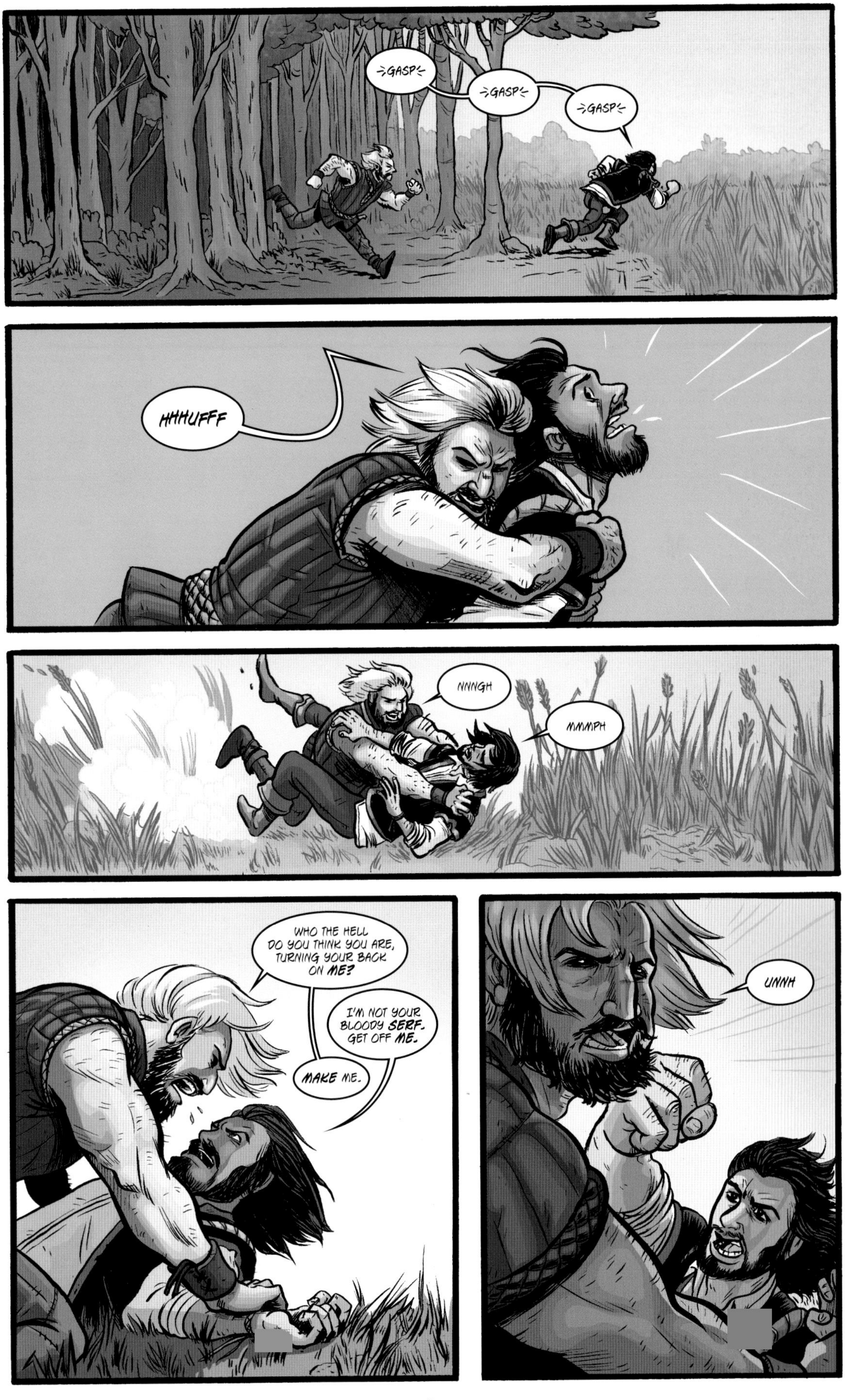

GASP
GASP
GASP
HHHUFFF
NNNGH
MMMPH
WHO THE HELL DO YOU THINK YOU ARE, TURNING YOUR BACK ON ME?
I'M NOT YOUR BLOODY SERF. GET OFF ME.
MAKE ME.
UNNH

WHY YOU FILTHY LITTLE...
MMM
OHHH
WHAT'S GOING ON?
NOTHING.
JUST ALAN AND ARTHUR
THE USUAL.

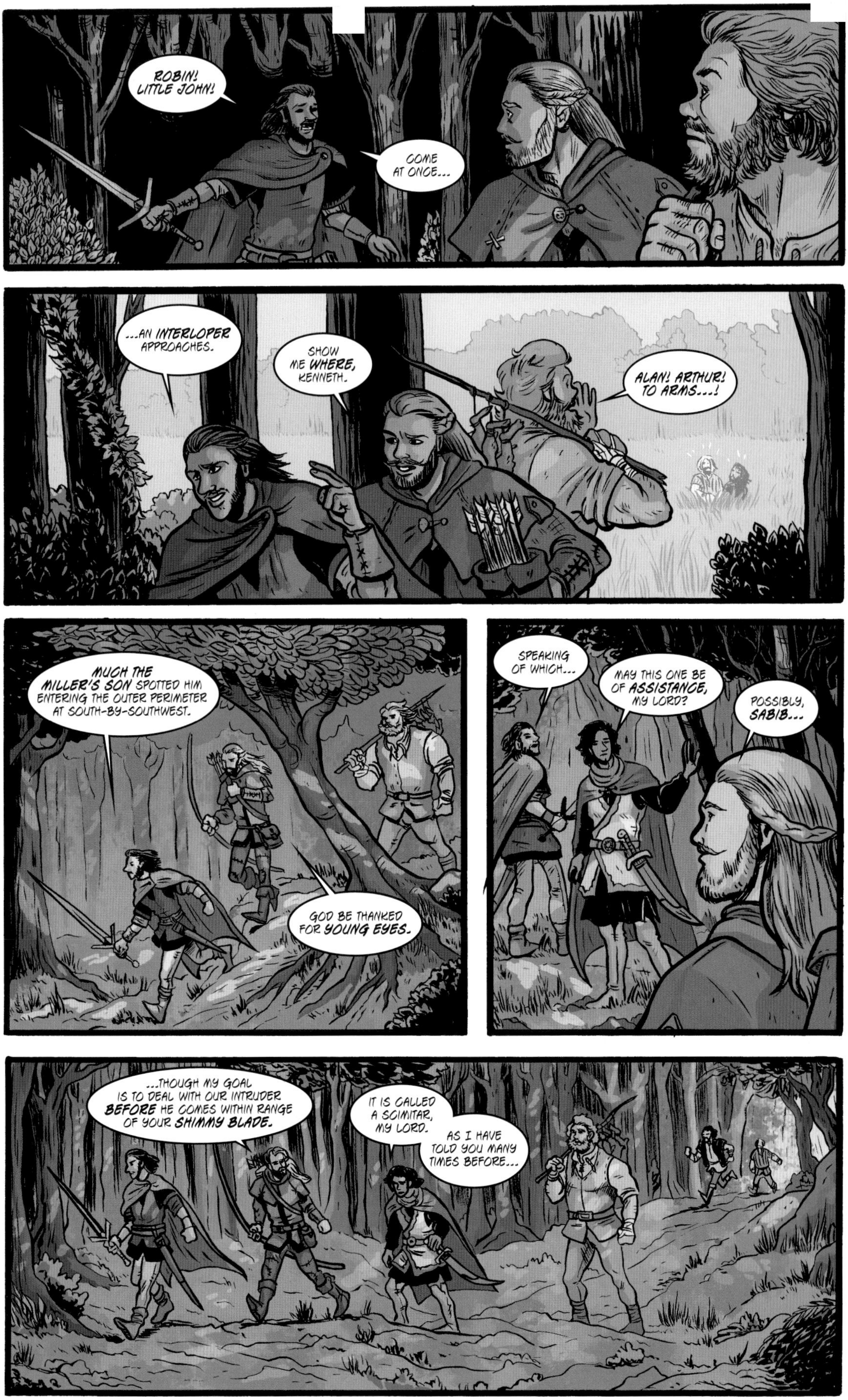
ROBIN! LITTLE JOHN!
COME AT ONCE...
...AN INTERLOPER APPROACHES.
SHOW ME WHERE, KENNETH.
ALAN! ARTHUR! TO ARMS...!
MUCH THE MILLER'S SON SPOTTED HIM ENTERING THE OUTER PERIMETER AT SOUTH-BY-SOUTHWEST.
GOD BE THANKED FOR YOUNG EYES.
SPEAKING OF WHICH...
MAY THIS ONE BE OF ASSISTANCE, MY LORD?
POSSIBLY, SABIB...
...THOUGH MY GOAL IS TO DEAL WITH OUR INTRUDER BEFORE HE COMES WITHIN RANGE OF YOUR SHIMMY BLADE.
IT IS CALLED A SCIMITAR, MY LORD.
AS I HAVE TOLD YOU MANY TIMES BEFORE...

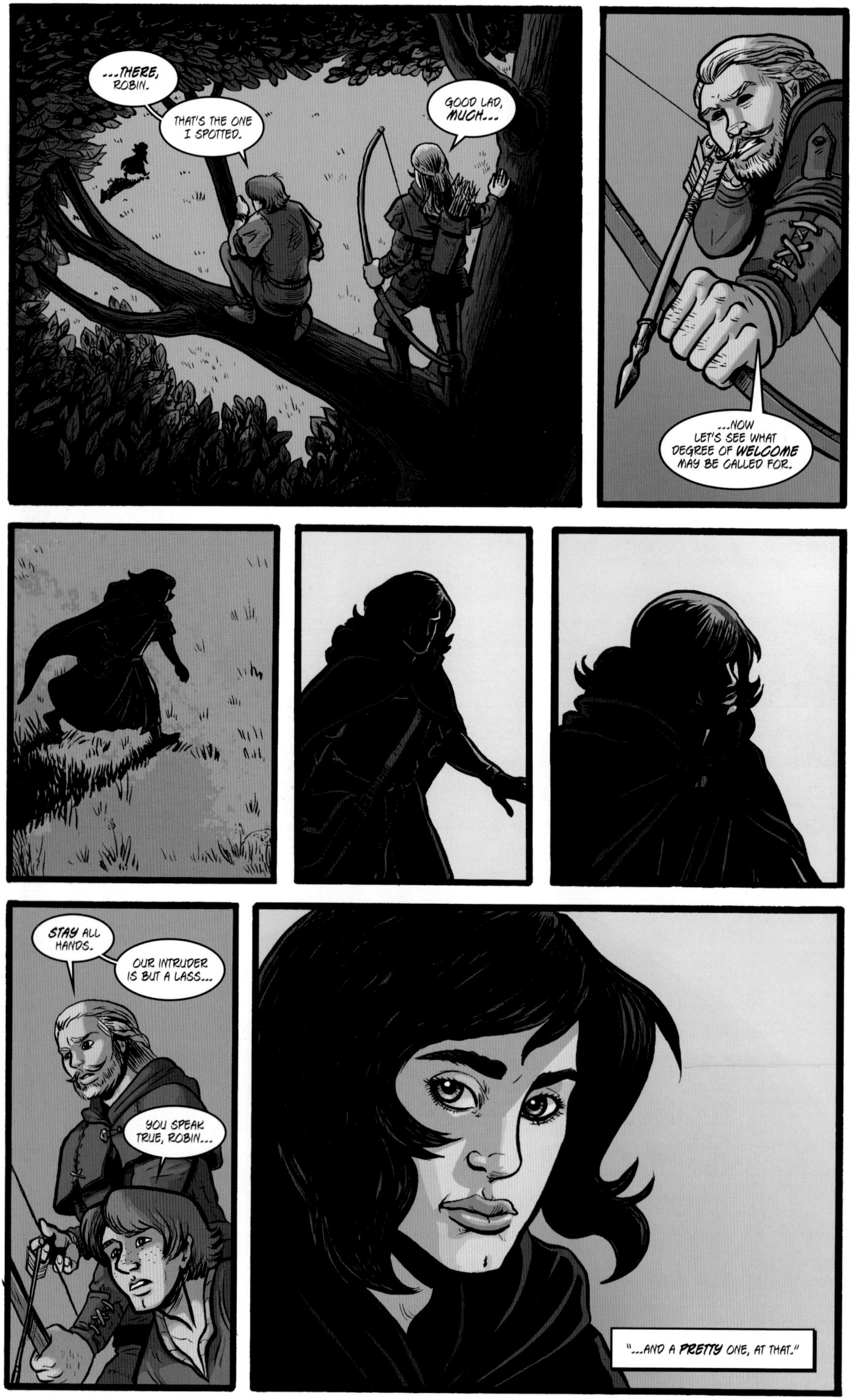
...THERE, ROBIN.
THAT'S THE ONE I SPOTTED.
GOOD LAD, MUCH...
...NOW LET'S SEE WHAT DEGREE OF WELCOME MAY BE CALLED FOR.
STAY ALL HANDS.
OUR INTRUDER IS BUT A LASS...
YOU SPEAK TRUE, ROBIN...
"...AND A PRETTY ONE, AT THAT."

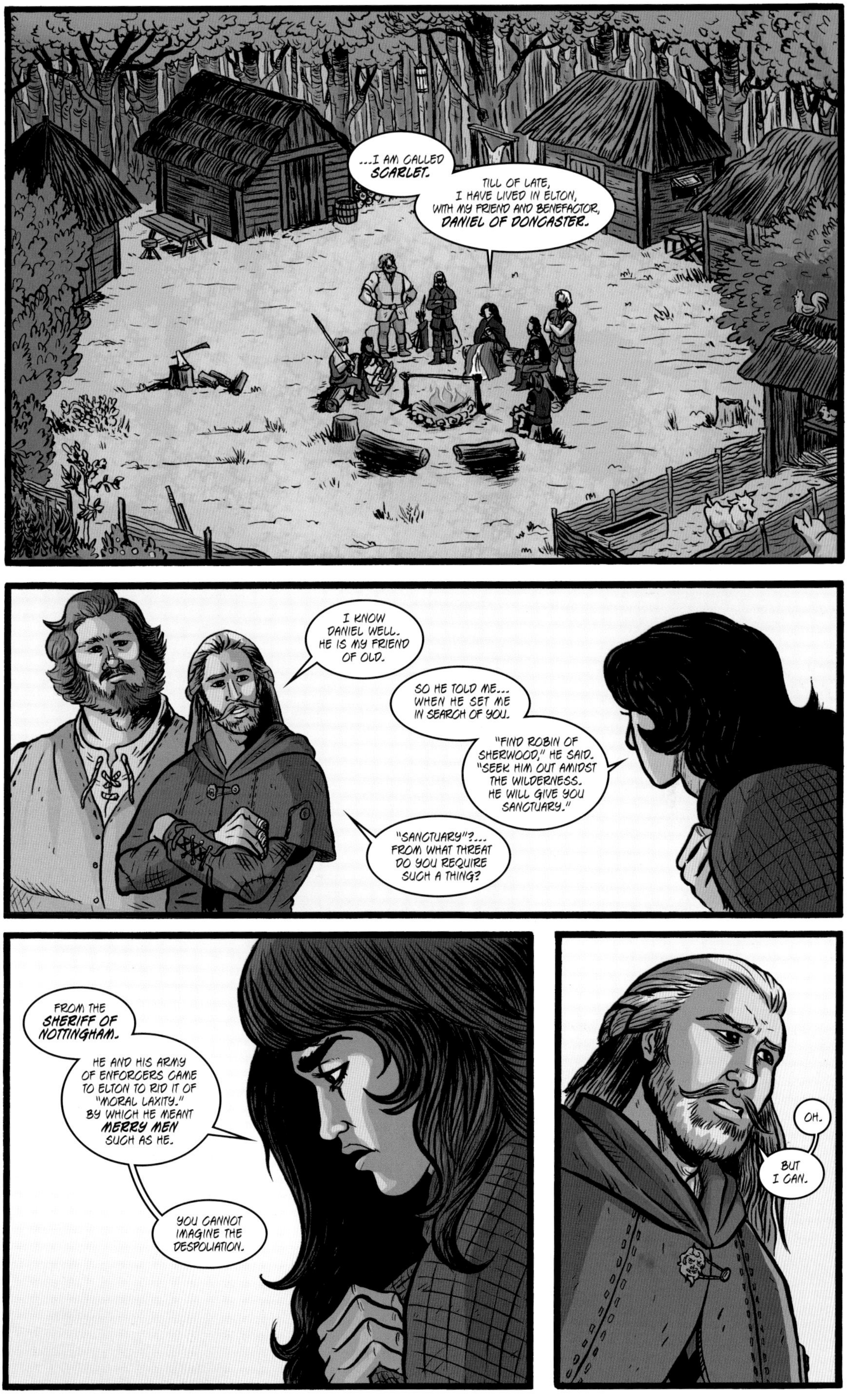
...I AM CALLED SCARLET.
TILL OF LATE, I HAVE LIVED IN ELTON, WITH MY FRIEND AND BENEFACTOR, DANIEL OF DONCASTER.
I KNOW DANIEL WELL. HE IS MY FRIEND OF OLD.
SO HE TOLD ME... WHEN HE SET ME IN SEARCH OF YOU.
"FIND ROBIN OF SHERWOOD," HE SAID. "SEEK HIM OUT AMIDST THE WILDERNESS. HE WILL GIVE YOU SANCTUARY."
"SANCTUARY"?... FROM WHAT THREAT DO YOU REQUIRE SUCH A THING?
FROM THE SHERIFF OF NOTTINGHAM.
HE AND HIS ARMY OF ENFORCERS CAME TO ELTON TO RID IT OF "MORAL LAXITY." BY WHICH HE MEANT MERRY MEN SUCH AS HE.
YOU CANNOT IMAGINE THE DESPOLIATION.
OH.
BUT I CAN.

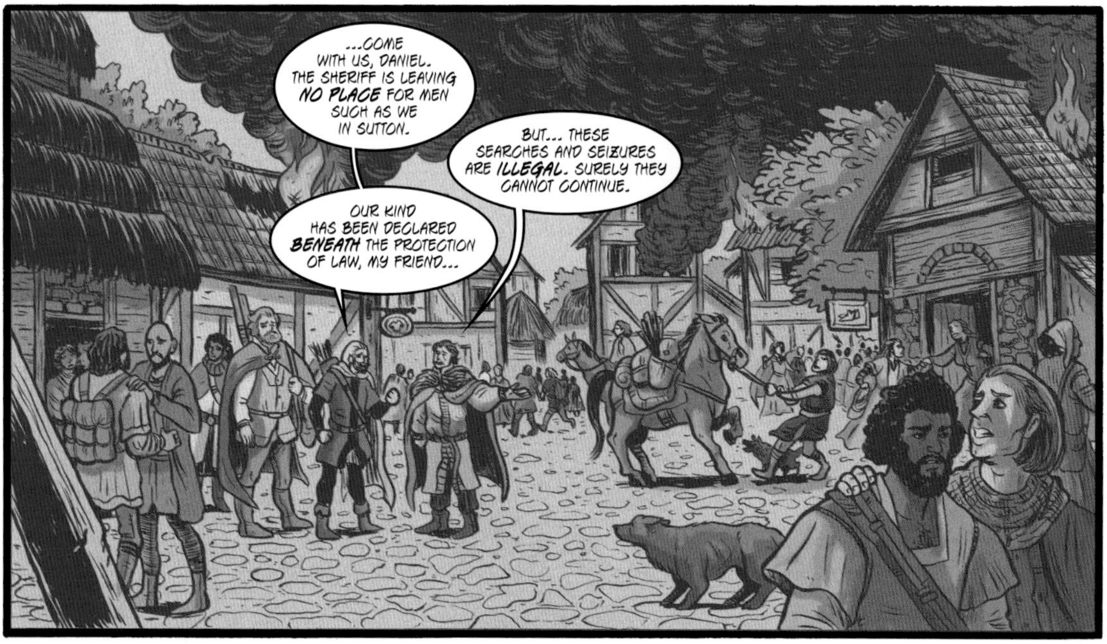
...COME WITH US, DANIEL. THE SHERIFF IS LEAVING NO PLACE FOR MEN SUCH AS WE IN SUTTON.
OUR KIND HAS BEEN DECLARED BENEATH THE PROTECTION OF LAW, MY FRIEND...
BUT... THESE SEARCHES AND SEIZURES ARE ILLEGAL. SURELY THEY CANNOT CONTINUE.

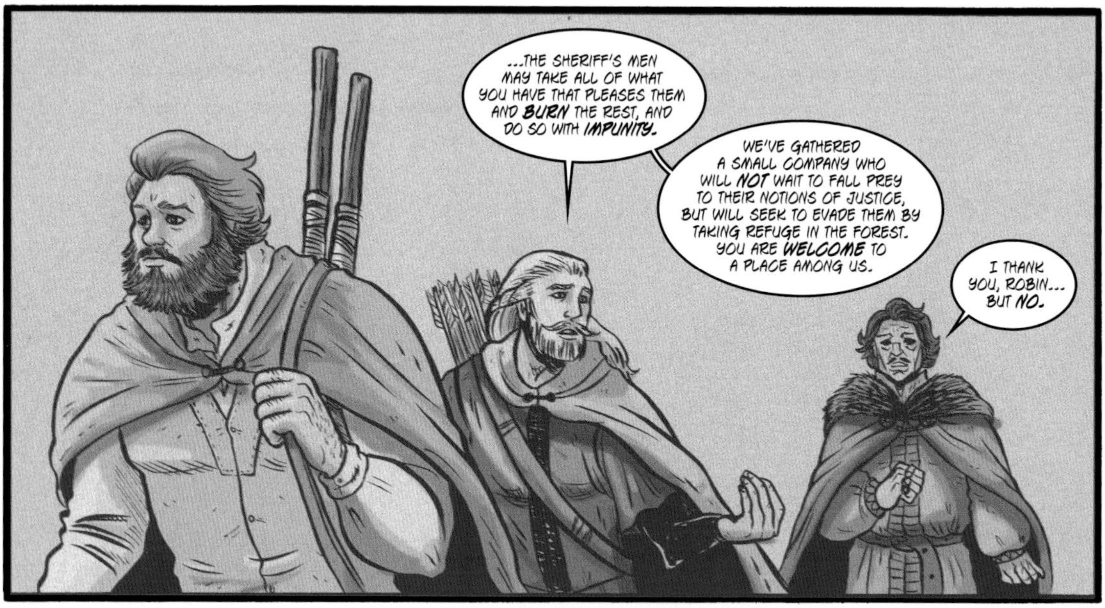
...THE SHERIFF'S MEN MAY TAKE ALL OF WHAT YOU HAVE THAT PLEASES THEM AND BURN THE REST, AND DO SO WITH IMPUNITY.
WE'VE GATHERED A SMALL COMPANY WHO WILL NOT WAIT TO FALL PREY TO THEIR NOTIONS OF JUSTICE, BUT WILL SEEK TO EVADE THEM BY TAKING REFUGE IN THE FOREST. YOU ARE WELCOME TO A PLACE AMONG US.
I THANK YOU, ROBIN... BUT NO.

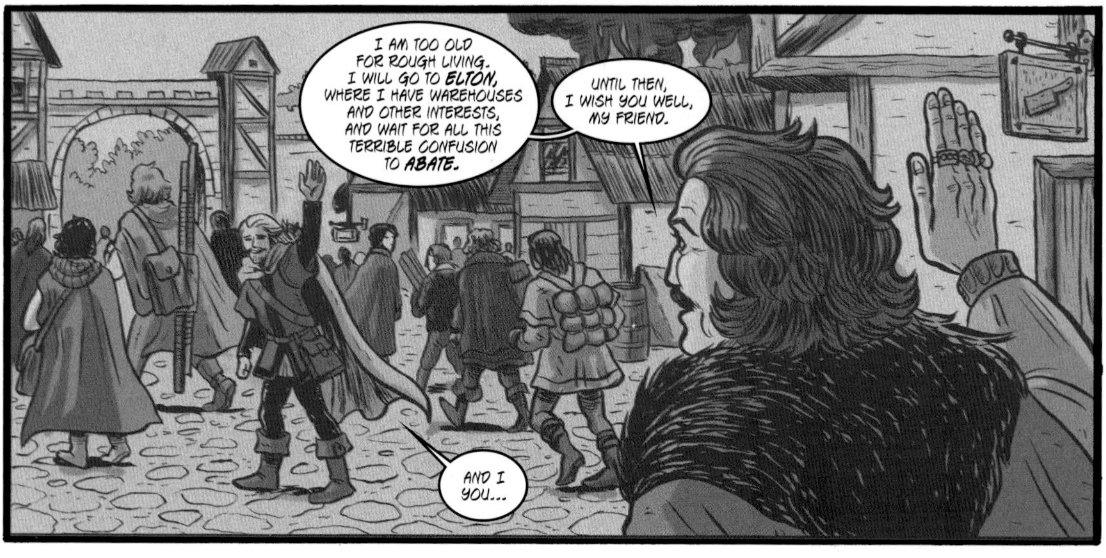
I AM TOO OLD FOR ROUGH LIVING. I WILL GO TO ELTON, WHERE I HAVE WAREHOUSES AND OTHER INTERESTS, AND WAIT FOR ALL THIS TERRIBLE CONFUSION TO ABATE.
UNTIL THEN, I WISH YOU WELL, MY FRIEND.
AND I YOU...

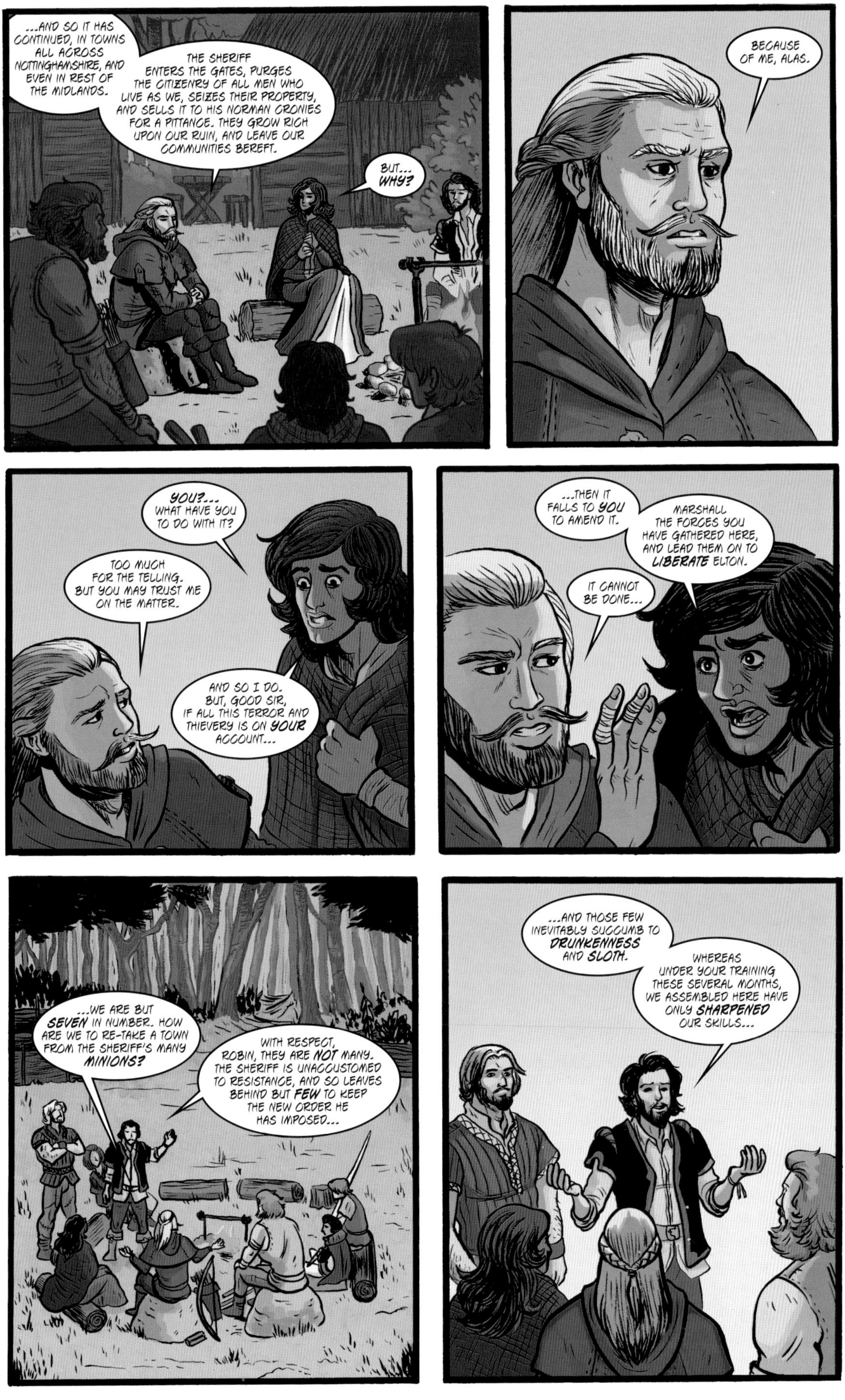
...AND SO IT HAS CONTINUED, IN TOWNS ALL ACROSS NOTTINGHAMSHIRE, AND EVEN IN REST OF THE MIDLANDS.
THE SHERIFF ENTERS THE GATES, PURGES THE CITIZENRY OF ALL MEN WHO LIVE AS WE, SEIZES THEIR PROPERTY, AND SELLS IT TO HIS NORMAN CRONIES FOR A PITTANCE. THEY GROW RICH UPON OUR RUIN, AND LEAVE OUR COMMUNITIES BEREFT.
BUT... WHY?
BECAUSE OF ME, ALAS.
YOU?... WHAT HAVE YOU TO DO WITH IT?
TOO MUCH FOR THE TELLING. BUT YOU MAY TRUST ME ON THE MATTER.
AND SO I DO. BUT, GOOD SIR, IF ALL THIS TERROR AND THIEVERY IS ON YOUR ACCOUNT...
...THEN IT FALLS TO YOU TO AMEND IT.
MARSHALL THE FORCES YOU HAVE GATHERED HERE, AND LEAD THEM ON TO LIBERATE ELTON.
IT CANNOT BE DONE...
...WE ARE BUT SEVEN IN NUMBER. HOW ARE WE TO RE-TAKE A TOWN FROM THE SHERIFF'S MANY MINIONS?
WITH RESPECT, ROBIN, THEY ARE NOT MANY. THE SHERIFF IS UNACCUSTOMED TO RESISTANCE, AND SO LEAVES BEHIND BUT FEW TO KEEP THE NEW ORDER HE HAS IMPOSED...
...AND THOSE FEW INEVITABLY SUCCUMB TO DRUNKENNESS AND SLOTH.
WHEREAS UNDER YOUR TRAINING THESE SEVERAL MONTHS, WE ASSEMBLED HERE HAVE ONLY SHARPENED OUR SKILLS...

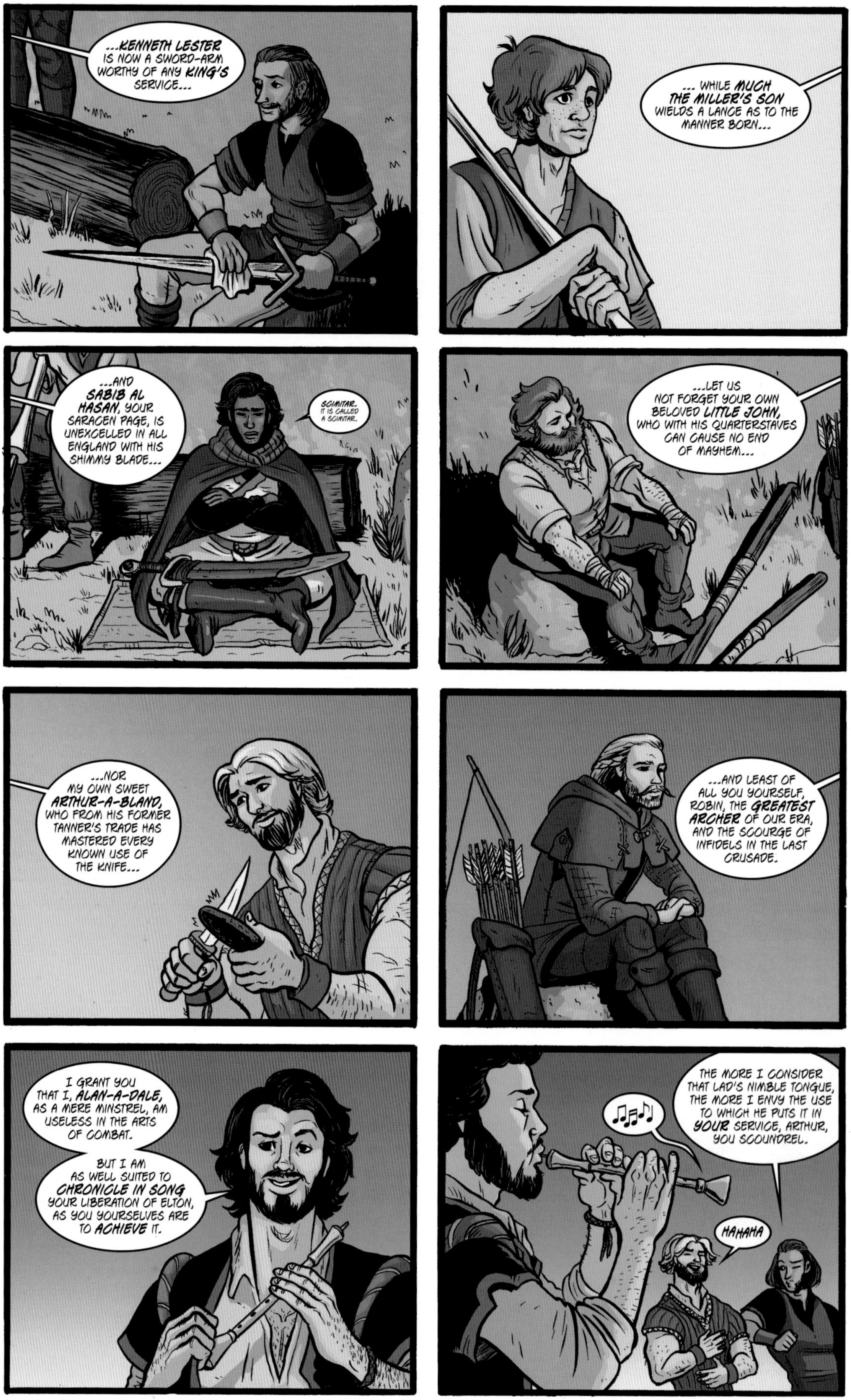
...KENNETH LESTER IS NOW A SWORD-ARM WORTHY OF ANY KING'S SERVICE...
... WHILE MUCH THE MILLER'S SON WIELDS A LANCE AS TO THE MANNER BORN...
...AND SABIB AL HASAN, YOUR SARACEN PAGE, IS UNEXCELLED IN ALL ENGLAND WITH HIS SHIMMY BLADE...
SCIMITAR. IT IS CALLED A SCIMITAR.
...LET US NOT FORGET YOUR OWN BELOVED LITTLE JOHN, WHO WITH HIS QUARTERSTAVES CAN CAUSE NO END OF MAYHEM...
...NOR MY OWN SWEET ARTHUR-A-BLAND, WHO FROM HIS FORMER TANNER'S TRADE HAS MASTERED EVERY KNOWN USE OF THE KNIFE...
...AND LEAST OF ALL YOU YOURSELF, ROBIN, THE GREATEST ARCHER OF OUR ERA, AND THE SCOURGE OF INFIDELS IN THE LAST CRUSADE.
I GRANT YOU THAT I, ALAN-A-DALE, AS A MERE MINSTREL, AM USELESS IN THE ARTS OF COMBAT.
BUT I AM AS WELL SUITED TO CHRONICLE IN SONG YOUR LIBERATION OF ELTON, AS YOU YOURSELVES ARE TO ACHIEVE IT.
♫♬♪
THE MORE I CONSIDER THAT LAD'S NIMBLE TONGUE, THE MORE I ENVY THE USE TO WHICH HE PUTS IT IN YOUR SERVICE, ARTHUR, YOU SCOUNDREL.
HAHAHA

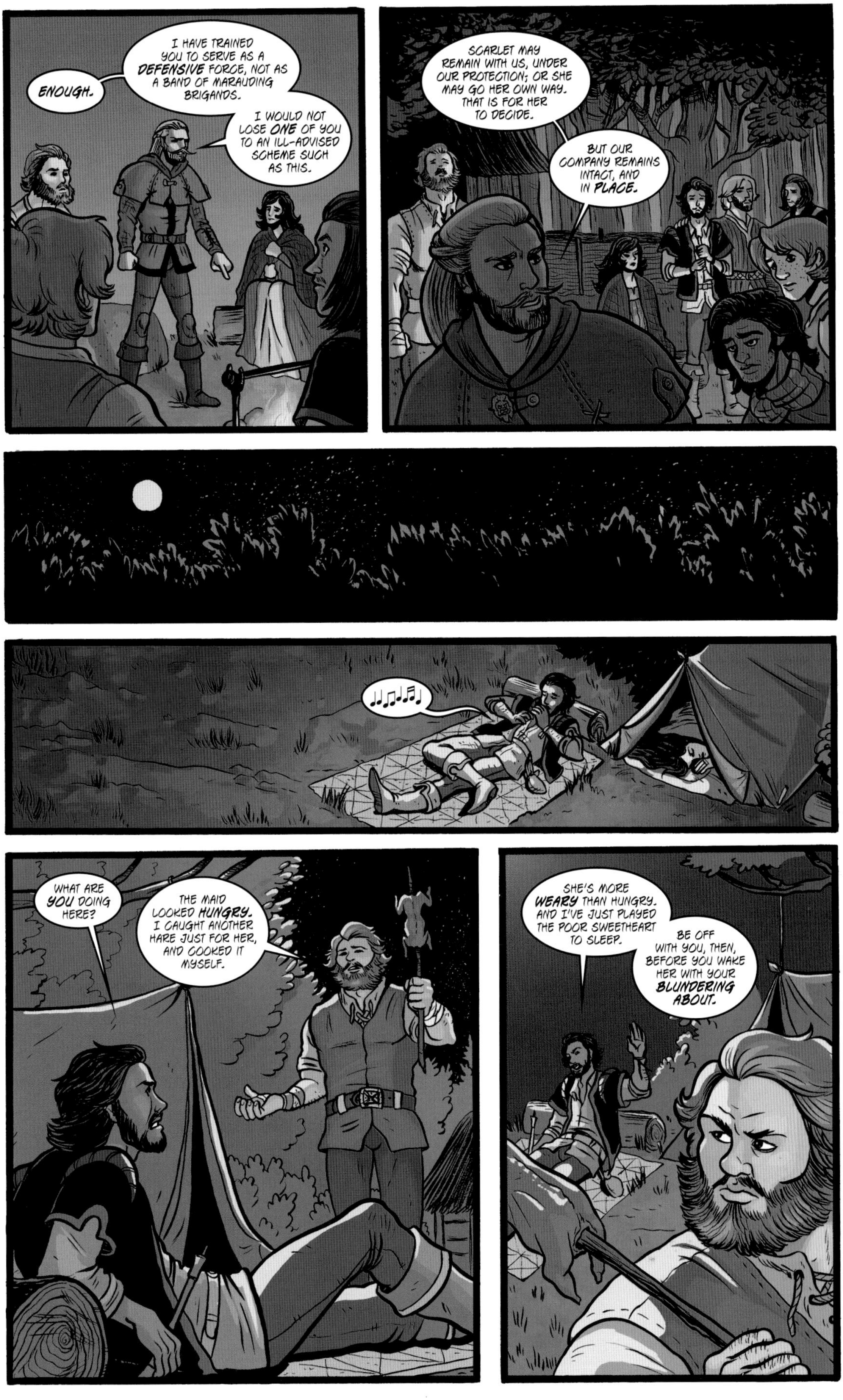
ENOUGH.
I HAVE TRAINED YOU TO SERVE AS A DEFENSIVE FORCE, NOT AS A BAND OF MARAUDING BRIGANDS.
I WOULD NOT LOSE ONE OF YOU TO AN ILL-ADVISED SCHEME SUCH AS THIS.
SCARLET MAY REMAIN WITH US, UNDER OUR PROTECTION; OR SHE MAY GO HER OWN WAY. THAT IS FOR HER TO DECIDE.
BUT OUR COMPANY REMAINS INTACT, AND IN PLACE.
WHAT ARE YOU DOING HERE?
THE MAID LOOKED HUNGRY. I CAUGHT ANOTHER HARE JUST FOR HER, AND COOKED IT MYSELF.
SHE'S MORE WEARY THAN HUNGRY. AND I'VE JUST PLAYED THE POOR SWEETHEART TO SLEEP.
BE OFF WITH YOU, THEN, BEFORE YOU WAKE HER WITH YOUR BLUNDERING ABOUT.

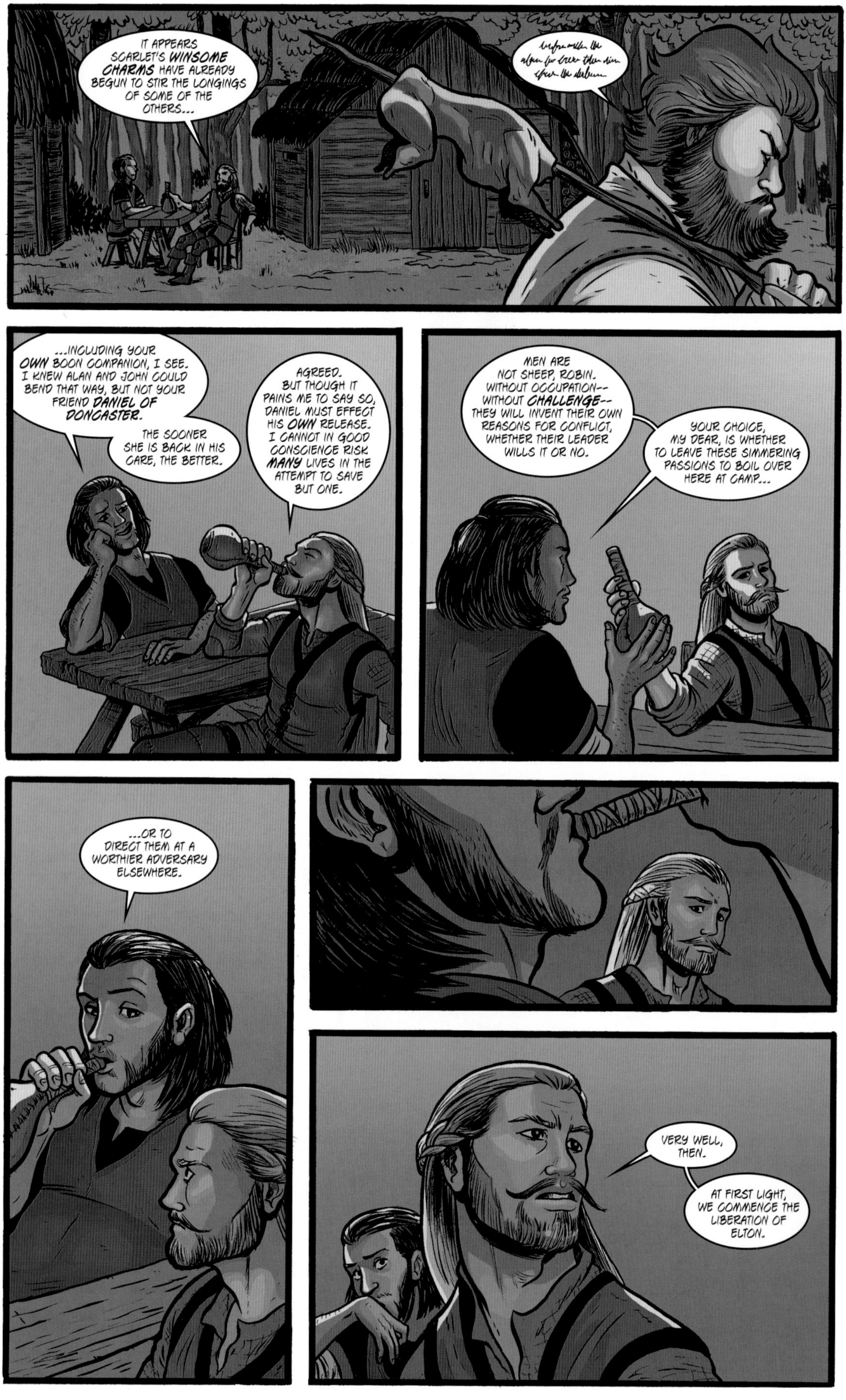
IT APPEARS SCARLET'S WINSOME CHARMS HAVE ALREADY BEGUN TO STIR THE LONGINGS OF SOME OF THE OTHERS...
...INCLUDING YOUR OWN BOON COMPANION, I SEE. I KNEW ALAN AND JOHN COULD BEND THAT WAY, BUT NOT YOUR FRIEND DANIEL OF DONCASTER.
THE SOONER SHE IS BACK IN HIS CARE, THE BETTER.
AGREED. BUT THOUGH IT PAINS ME TO SAY SO, DANIEL MUST EFFECT HIS OWN RELEASE. I CANNOT IN GOOD CONSCIENCE RISK MANY LIVES IN THE ATTEMPT TO SAVE BUT ONE.
MEN ARE NOT SHEEP, ROBIN. WITHOUT OCCUPATION-- WITHOUT CHALLENGE-- THEY WILL INVENT THEIR OWN REASONS FOR CONFLICT, WHETHER THEIR LEADER WILLS IT OR NO.
YOUR CHOICE, MY DEAR, IS WHETHER TO LEAVE THESE SIMMERING PASSIONS TO BOIL OVER HERE AT CAMP...
...OR TO DIRECT THEM AT A WORTHIER ADVERSARY ELSEWHERE.
VERY WELL, THEN.
AT FIRST LIGHT, WE COMMENCE THE LIBERATION OF ELTON.

Chapter
2

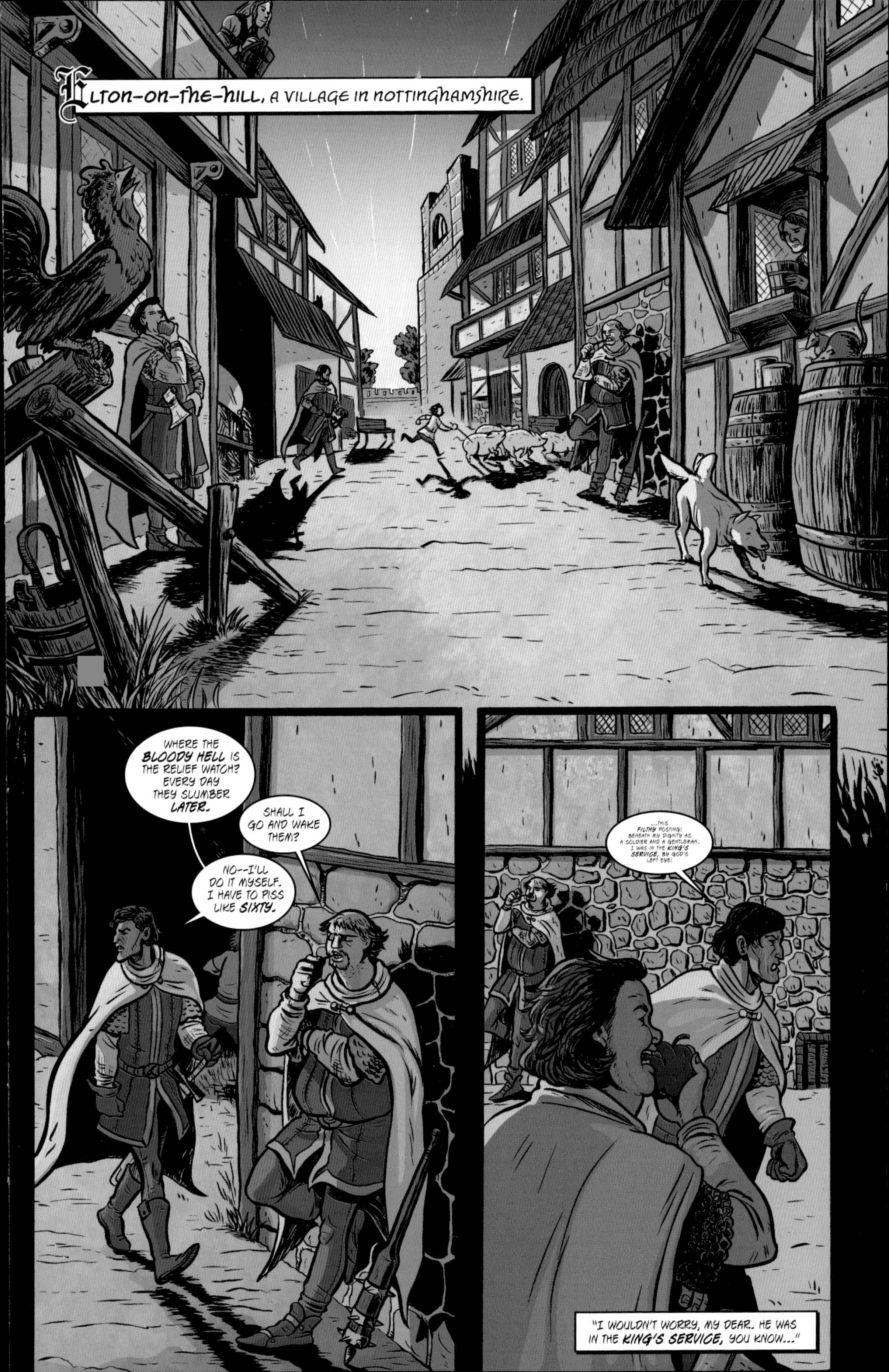
Elton-on-the-hill, a village in nottinghamshire.
Where the BLOODY HELL is the relief watch? Every day they slumber LATER.
Shall I go and wake them?
No--I'll do it myself. I have to piss like SIXTY.
...This FILTHY posting! Beneath my dignity as a soldier and a gentleman. I was in the KING'S SERVICE, by God's left eye!
"I wouldn't worry, my dear. He was in the KING'S SERVICE, you know..."

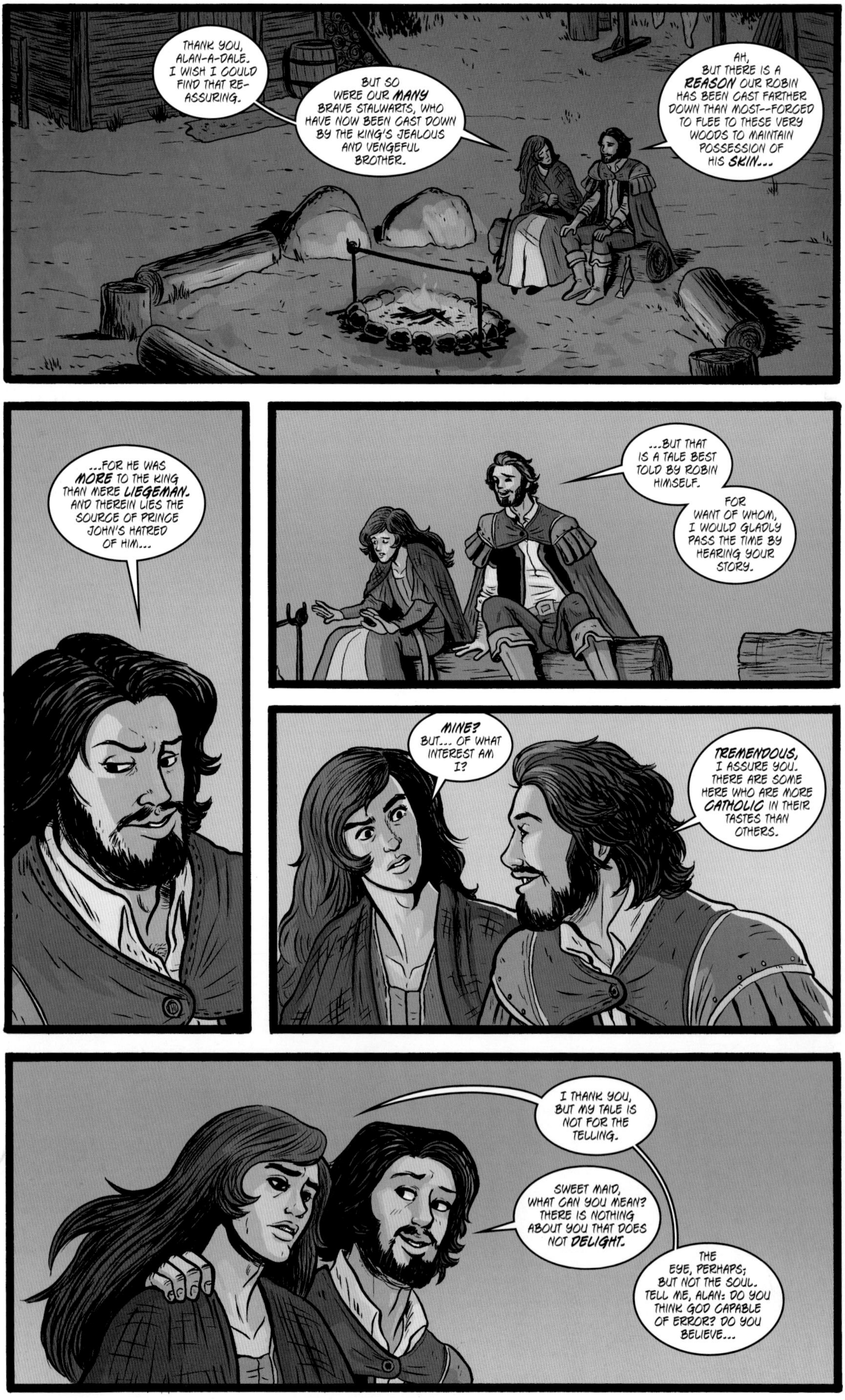
THANK YOU, ALAN-A-DALE. I WISH I COULD FIND THAT RE-ASSURING.
BUT SO WERE OUR MANY BRAVE STALWARTS, WHO HAVE NOW BEEN CAST DOWN BY THE KING'S JEALOUS AND VENGEFUL BROTHER.
AH, BUT THERE IS A REASON OUR ROBIN HAS BEEN CAST FARTHER DOWN THAN MOST--FORCED TO FLEE TO THESE VERY WOODS TO MAINTAIN POSSESSION OF HIS SKIN...
...FOR HE WAS MORE TO THE KING THAN MERE LIEGEMAN. AND THEREIN LIES THE SOURCE OF PRINCE JOHN'S HATRED OF HIM...
...BUT THAT IS A TALE BEST TOLD BY ROBIN HIMSELF.
FOR WANT OF WHOM, I WOULD GLADLY PASS THE TIME BY HEARING YOUR STORY.
MINE? BUT... OF WHAT INTEREST AM I?
TREMENDOUS, I ASSURE YOU. THERE ARE SOME HERE WHO ARE MORE CATHOLIC IN THEIR TASTES THAN OTHERS.
I THANK YOU, BUT MY TALE IS NOT FOR THE TELLING.
SWEET MAID, WHAT CAN YOU MEAN? THERE IS NOTHING ABOUT YOU THAT DOES NOT DELIGHT.
THE EYE, PERHAPS; BUT NOT THE SOUL. TELL ME, ALAN: DO YOU THINK GOD CAPABLE OF ERROR? DO YOU BELIEVE...

"...A CHILD CAN BE BORN WHO IS FROM HIS FIRST BREATH A *MISTAKE?*"

YOU MIS-BEGOTTEN WHELPS-- *SHITE AND PISS FROM* YOUR MOTHERS' BELLIES...

...GET UP ON YOUR FEET AND TAKE YOUR TURN AT THE *WATCH,* OR I'LL HAVE THE WHOLE LAZY LOT OF YOU TAKEN OUT BACK...

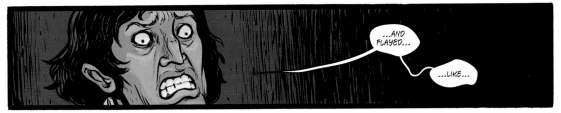

...AND FLAYED...

...LIKE...

...DOGS...

OHHH... OHHHH...

BOO.

AAAAGGGH

"YOU'RE BEGINNING TO FRIGHTEN ME, YOUNG MISS..."

23

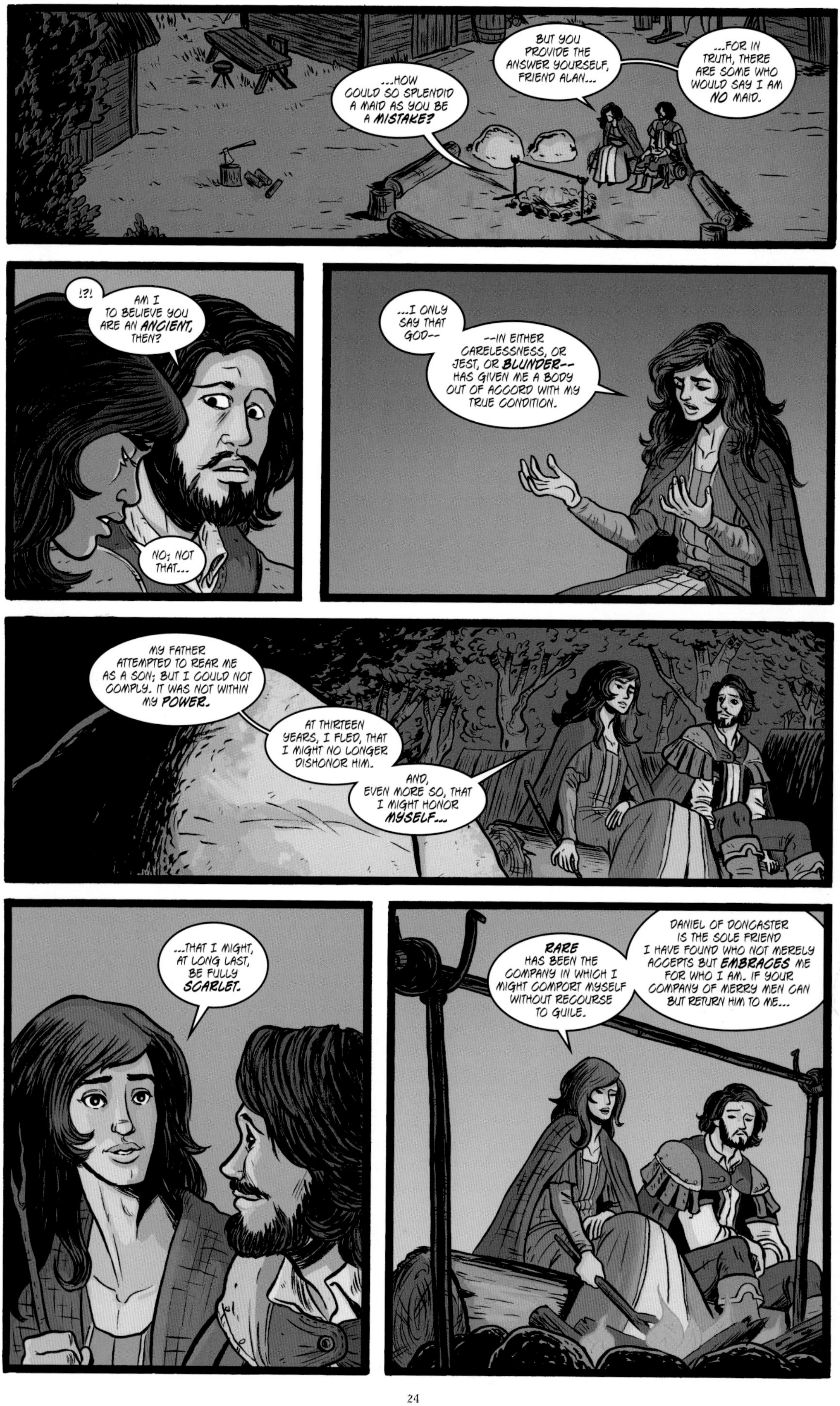
...HOW COULD SO SPLENDID A MAID AS YOU BE A MISTAKE?
BUT YOU PROVIDE THE ANSWER YOURSELF, FRIEND ALAN...
...FOR IN TRUTH, THERE ARE SOME WHO WOULD SAY I AM NO MAID.
!?!
AM I TO BELIEVE YOU ARE AN ANCIENT, THEN?
NO; NOT THAT...
...I ONLY SAY THAT GOD--
--IN EITHER CARELESSNESS, OR JEST, OR BLUNDER-- HAS GIVEN ME A BODY OUT OF ACCORD WITH MY TRUE CONDITION.
MY FATHER ATTEMPTED TO REAR ME AS A SON; BUT I COULD NOT COMPLY. IT WAS NOT WITHIN MY POWER.
AT THIRTEEN YEARS, I FLED, THAT I MIGHT NO LONGER DISHONOR HIM.
AND, EVEN MORE SO, THAT I MIGHT HONOR MYSELF...
...THAT I MIGHT, AT LONG LAST, BE FULLY SCARLET.
RARE HAS BEEN THE COMPANY IN WHICH I MIGHT COMPORT MYSELF WITHOUT RECOURSE TO GUILE.
DANIEL OF DONCASTER IS THE SOLE FRIEND I HAVE FOUND WHO NOT MERELY ACCEPTS BUT EMBRACES ME FOR WHO I AM. IF YOUR COMPANY OF MERRY MEN CAN BUT RETURN HIM TO ME...

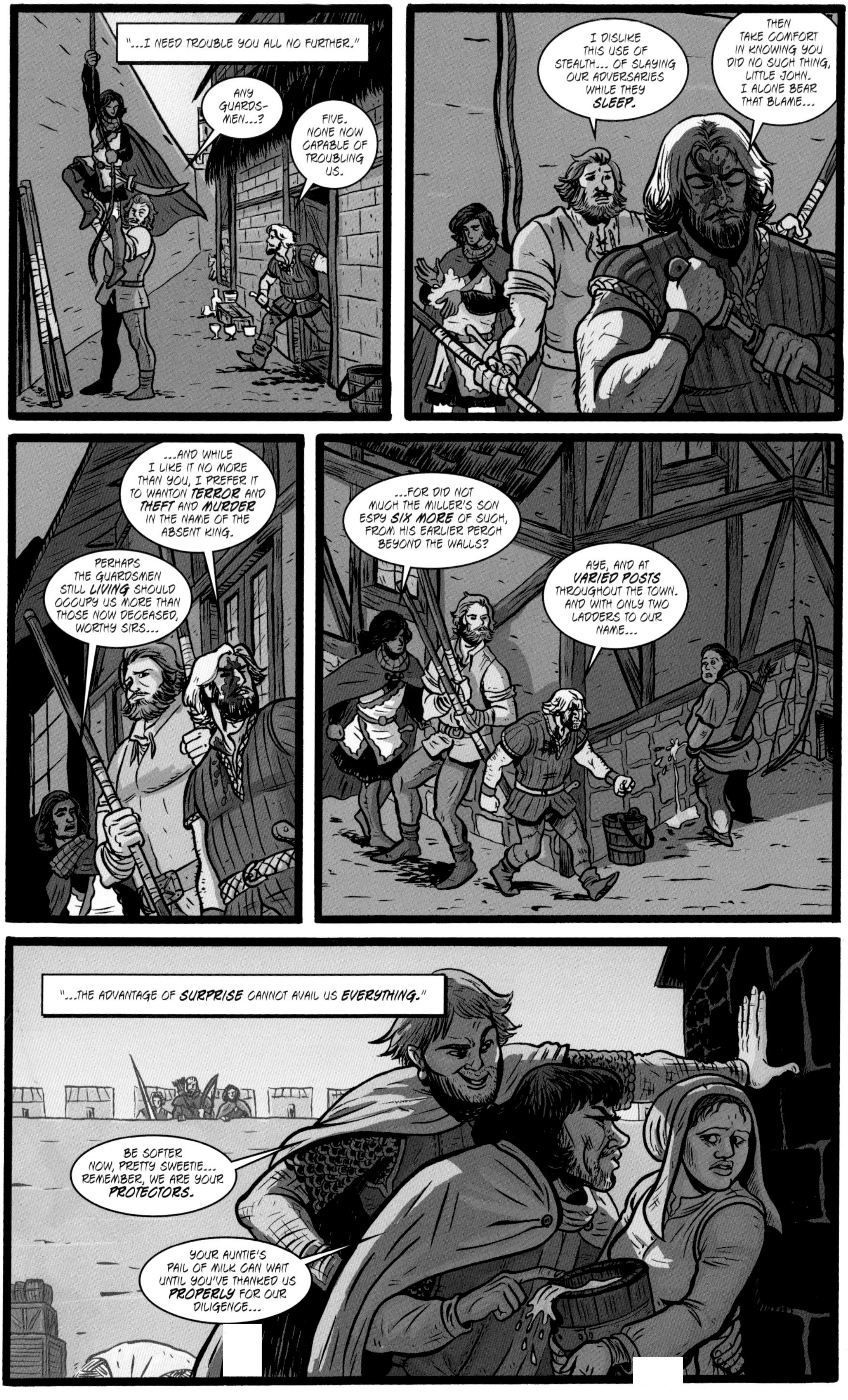
"...I NEED TROUBLE YOU ALL NO FURTHER."
ANY GUARDS-MEN...?
FIVE. NONE NOW CAPABLE OF TROUBLING US.
I DISLIKE THIS USE OF STEALTH... OF SLAYING OUR ADVERSARIES WHILE THEY SLEEP.
THEN TAKE COMFORT IN KNOWING YOU DID NO SUCH THING, LITTLE JOHN. I ALONE BEAR THAT BLAME...
...AND WHILE I LIKE IT NO MORE THAN YOU, I PREFER IT TO WANTON TERROR AND THEFT AND MURDER IN THE NAME OF THE ABSENT KING.
PERHAPS THE GUARDSMEN STILL LIVING SHOULD OCCUPY US MORE THAN THOSE NOW DECEASED, WORTHY SIRS...
...FOR DID NOT MUCH THE MILLER'S SON ESPY SIX MORE OF SUCH, FROM HIS EARLIER PERCH BEYOND THE WALLS?
AYE, AND AT VARIED POSTS THROUGHOUT THE TOWN. AND WITH ONLY TWO LADDERS TO OUR NAME...
"...THE ADVANTAGE OF SURPRISE CANNOT AVAIL US EVERYTHING."
BE SOFTER NOW, PRETTY SWEETIE... REMEMBER, WE ARE YOUR PROTECTORS.
YOUR AUNTIE'S PAIL OF MILK CAN WAIT UNTIL YOU'VE THANKED US PROPERLY FOR OUR DILIGENCE...

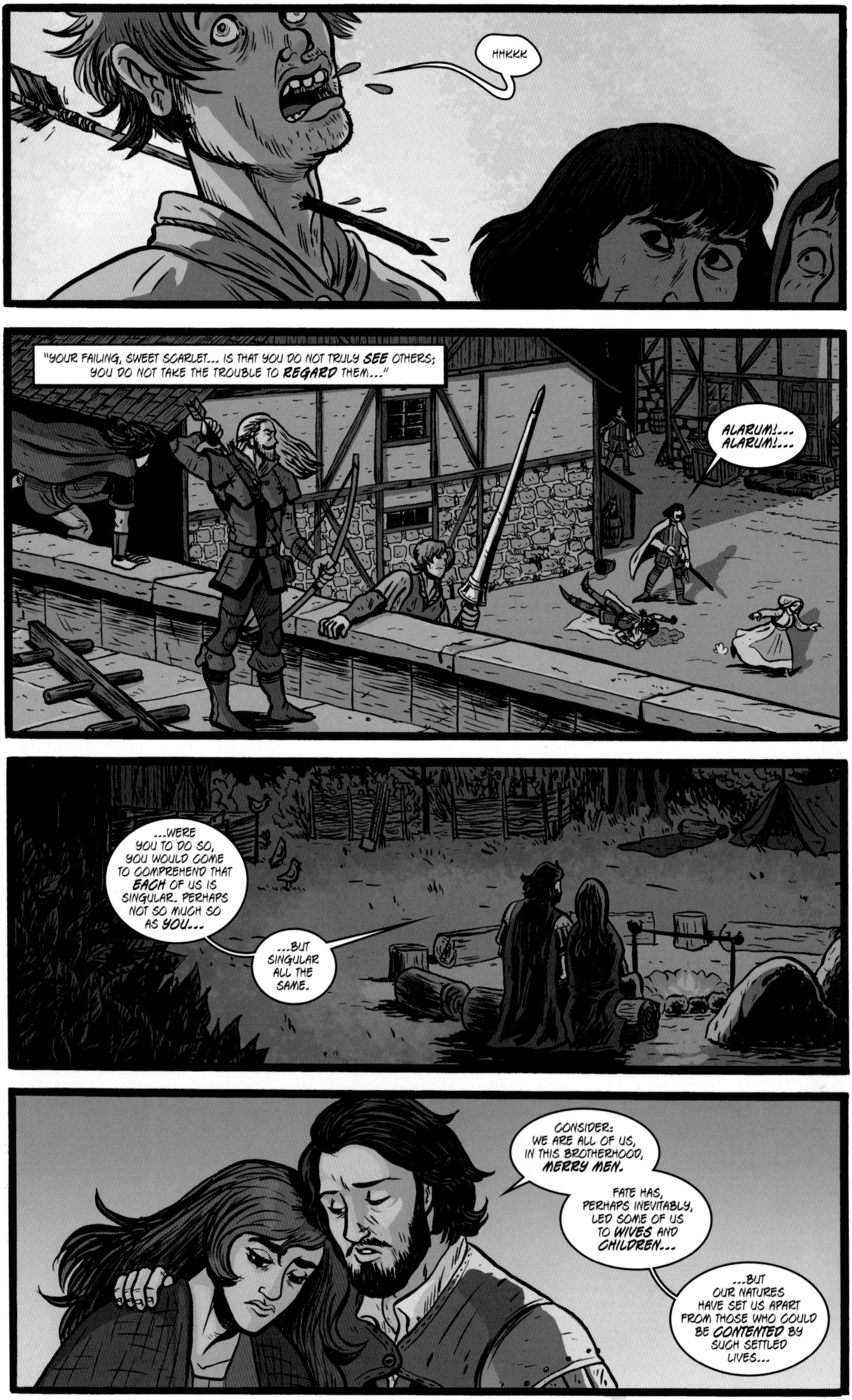
HHKKK
"YOUR FAILING, SWEET SCARLET... IS THAT YOU DO NOT TRULY SEE OTHERS; YOU DO NOT TAKE THE TROUBLE TO REGARD THEM..."
ALARUM!... ALARUM!...
...WERE YOU TO DO SO, YOU WOULD COME TO COMPREHEND THAT EACH OF US IS SINGULAR. PERHAPS NOT SO MUCH SO AS YOU...
...BUT SINGULAR ALL THE SAME.
CONSIDER: WE ARE ALL OF US, IN THIS BROTHERHOOD, MERRY MEN.
FATE HAS, PERHAPS INEVITABLY, LED SOME OF US TO WIVES AND CHILDREN...
...BUT OUR NATURES HAVE SET US APART FROM THOSE WHO COULD BE CONTENTED BY SUCH SETTLED LIVES...

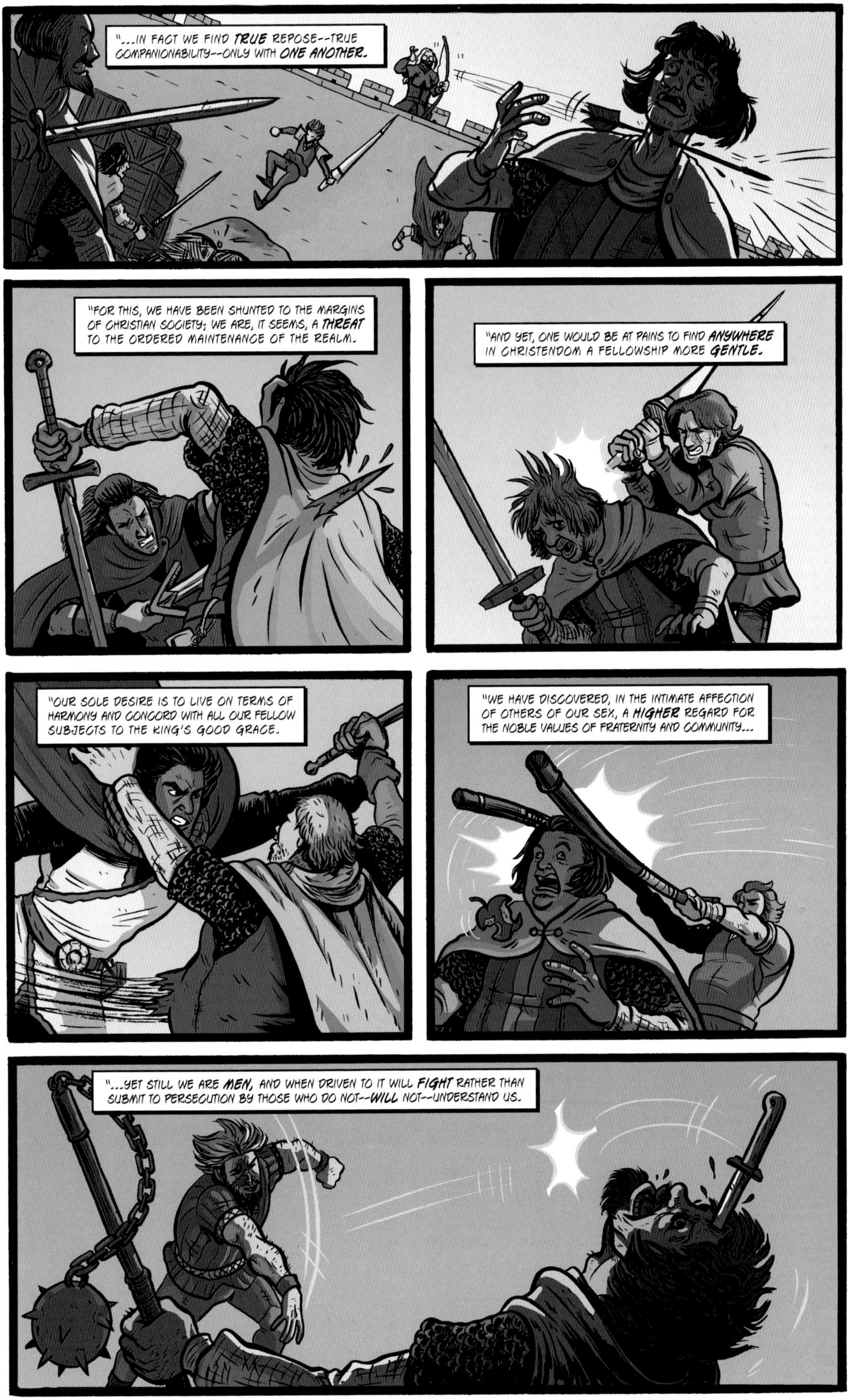
"...IN FACT WE FIND TRUE REPOSE--TRUE COMPANIONABILITY--ONLY WITH ONE ANOTHER.
"FOR THIS, WE HAVE BEEN SHUNTED TO THE MARGINS OF CHRISTIAN SOCIETY; WE ARE, IT SEEMS, A THREAT TO THE ORDERED MAINTENANCE OF THE REALM.
"AND YET, ONE WOULD BE AT PAINS TO FIND ANYWHERE IN CHRISTENDOM A FELLOWSHIP MORE GENTLE.
"OUR SOLE DESIRE IS TO LIVE ON TERMS OF HARMONY AND CONCORD WITH ALL OUR FELLOW SUBJECTS TO THE KING'S GOOD GRACE.
"WE HAVE DISCOVERED, IN THE INTIMATE AFFECTION OF OTHERS OF OUR SEX, A HIGHER REGARD FOR THE NOBLE VALUES OF FRATERNITY AND COMMUNITY...
"...YET STILL WE ARE MEN, AND WHEN DRIVEN TO IT WILL FIGHT RATHER THAN SUBMIT TO PERSECUTION BY THOSE WHO DO NOT--WILL NOT--UNDERSTAND US.

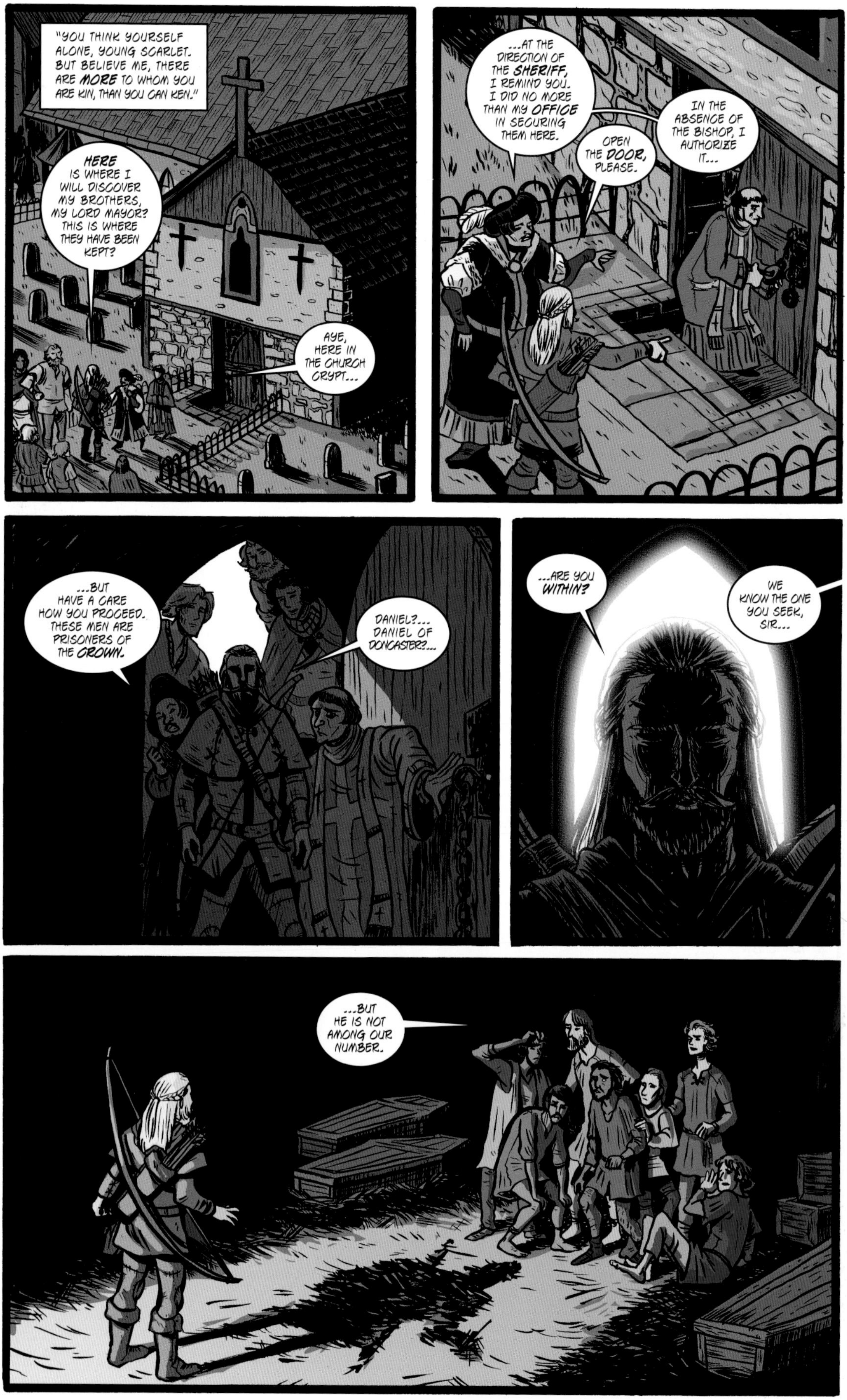
"YOU THINK YOURSELF ALONE, YOUNG SCARLET. BUT BELIEVE ME, THERE ARE MORE TO WHOM YOU ARE KIN, THAN YOU CAN KEN."
HERE IS WHERE I WILL DISCOVER MY BROTHERS, MY LORD MAYOR? THIS IS WHERE THEY HAVE BEEN KEPT?
AYE, HERE IN THE CHURCH CRYPT...
...AT THE DIRECTION OF THE SHERIFF, I REMIND YOU. I DID NO MORE THAN MY OFFICE IN SECURING THEM HERE.
IN THE ABSENCE OF THE BISHOP, I AUTHORIZE IT...
OPEN THE DOOR, PLEASE.
...BUT HAVE A CARE HOW YOU PROCEED. THESE MEN ARE PRISONERS OF THE CROWN.
DANIEL?... DANIEL OF DONCASTER?...
...ARE YOU WITHIN?
WE KNOW THE ONE YOU SEEK, SIR...
...BUT HE IS NOT AMONG OUR NUMBER.

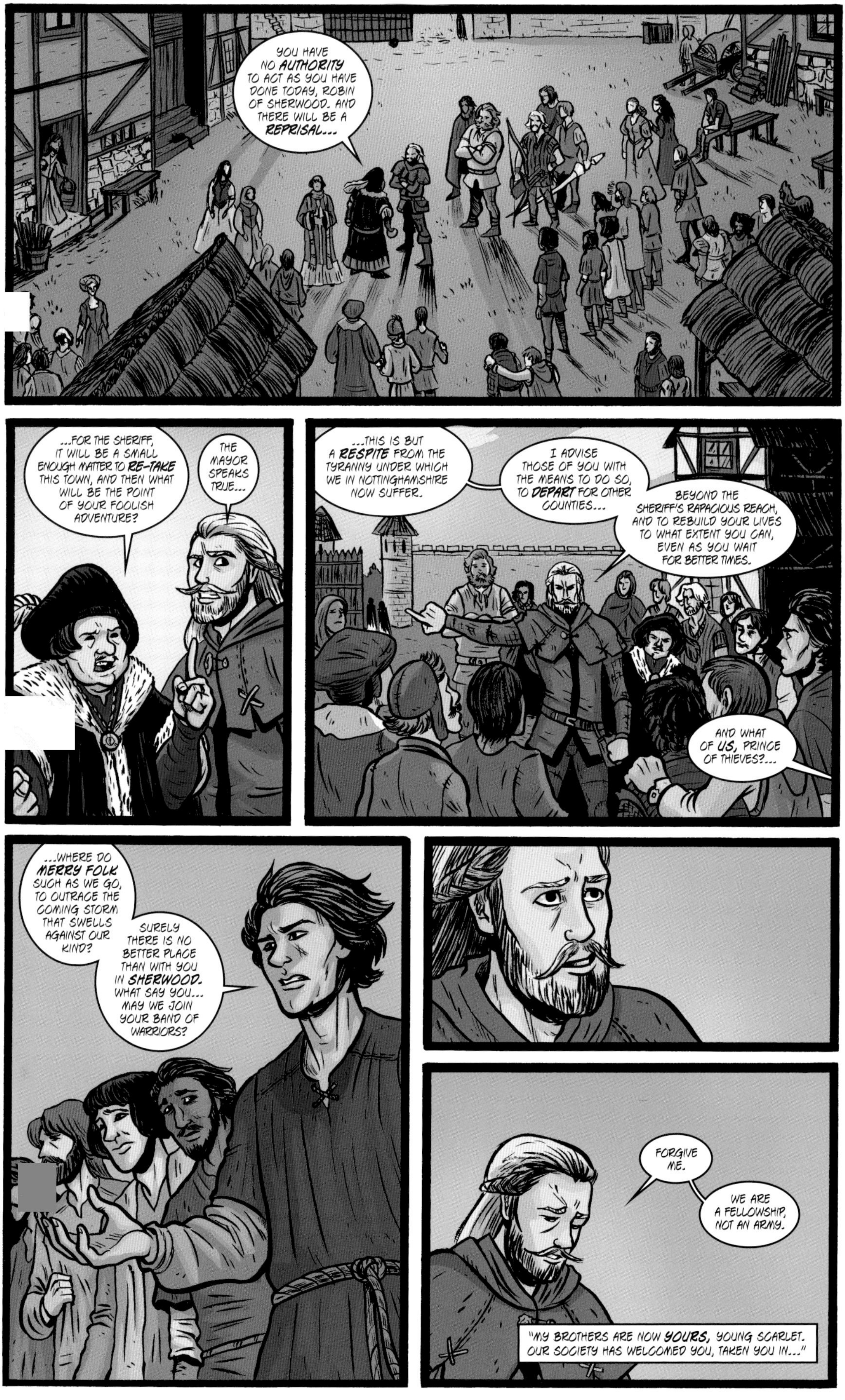

YOU HAVE NO AUTHORITY TO ACT AS YOU HAVE DONE TODAY, ROBIN OF SHERWOOD. AND THERE WILL BE A REPRISAL...
...FOR THE SHERIFF, IT WILL BE A SMALL ENOUGH MATTER TO RE-TAKE THIS TOWN, AND THEN WHAT WILL BE THE POINT OF YOUR FOOLISH ADVENTURE?
THE MAYOR SPEAKS TRUE...
...THIS IS BUT A RESPITE FROM THE TYRANNY UNDER WHICH WE IN NOTTINGHAMSHIRE NOW SUFFER.
I ADVISE THOSE OF YOU WITH THE MEANS TO DO SO, TO DEPART FOR OTHER COUNTIES...
BEYOND THE SHERIFF'S RAPACIOUS REACH, AND TO REBUILD YOUR LIVES TO WHAT EXTENT YOU CAN, EVEN AS YOU WAIT FOR BETTER TIMES.
AND WHAT OF US, PRINCE OF THIEVES?...
...WHERE DO MERRY FOLK SUCH AS WE GO, TO OUTRACE THE COMING STORM THAT SWELLS AGAINST OUR KIND?
SURELY THERE IS NO BETTER PLACE THAN WITH YOU IN SHERWOOD. WHAT SAY YOU... MAY WE JOIN YOUR BAND OF WARRIORS?
FORGIVE ME.
WE ARE A FELLOWSHIP, NOT AN ARMY.
"MY BROTHERS ARE NOW YOURS, YOUNG SCARLET. OUR SOCIETY HAS WELCOMED YOU, TAKEN YOU IN..."

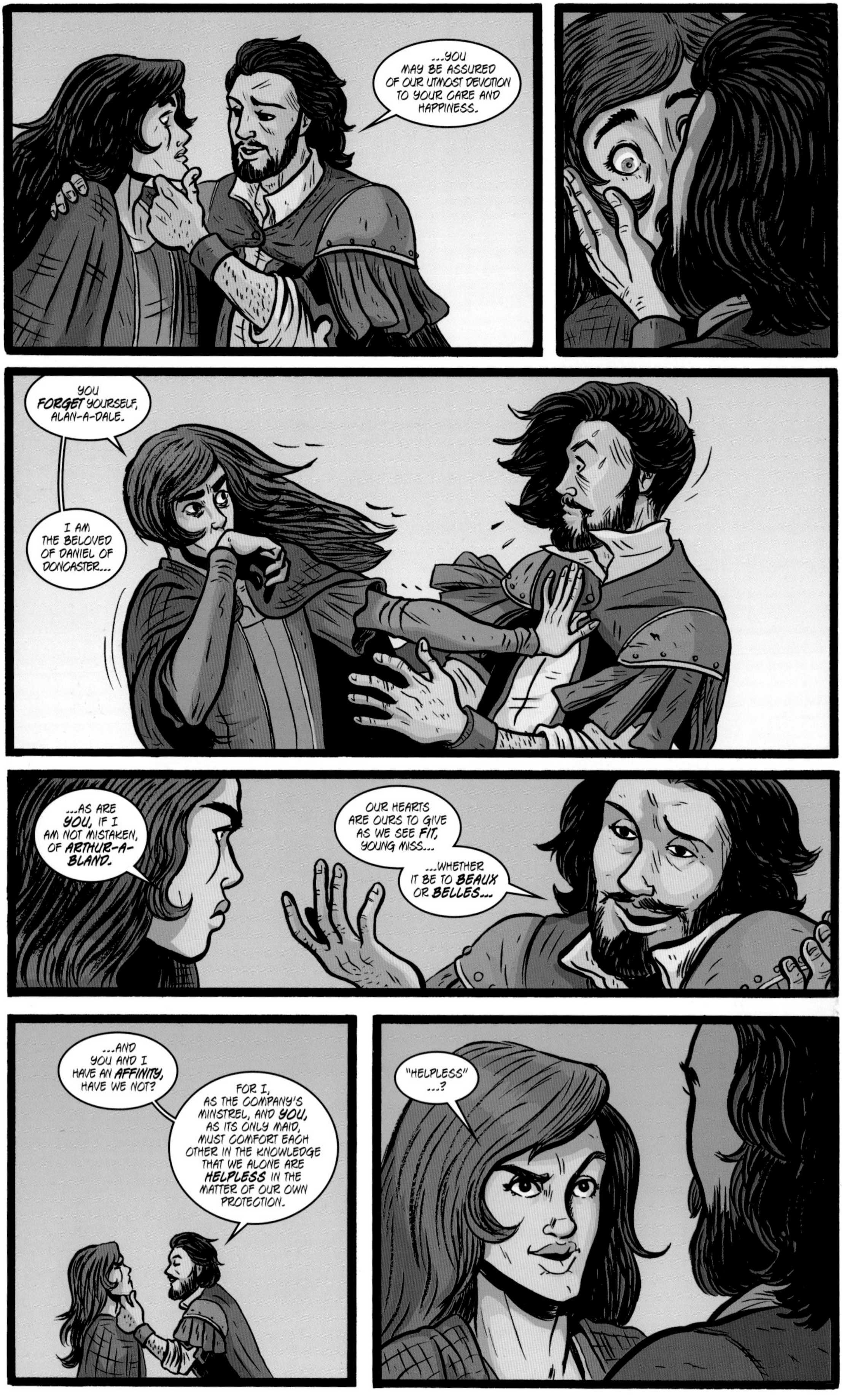
...YOU MAY BE ASSURED OF OUR UTMOST DEVOTION TO YOUR CARE AND HAPPINESS.
YOU FORGET YOURSELF, ALAN-A-DALE.
I AM THE BELOVED OF DANIEL OF DONCASTER...
...AS ARE YOU, IF I AM NOT MISTAKEN, OF ARTHUR-A-BLAND.
OUR HEARTS ARE OURS TO GIVE AS WE SEE FIT, YOUNG MISS...
...WHETHER IT BE TO BEAUX OR BELLES...
...AND YOU AND I HAVE AN AFFINITY, HAVE WE NOT?
FOR I, AS THE COMPANY'S MINSTREL, AND YOU, AS ITS ONLY MAID, MUST COMFORT EACH OTHER IN THE KNOWLEDGE THAT WE ALONE ARE HELPLESS IN THE MATTER OF OUR OWN PROTECTION.
"HELPLESS" ...?

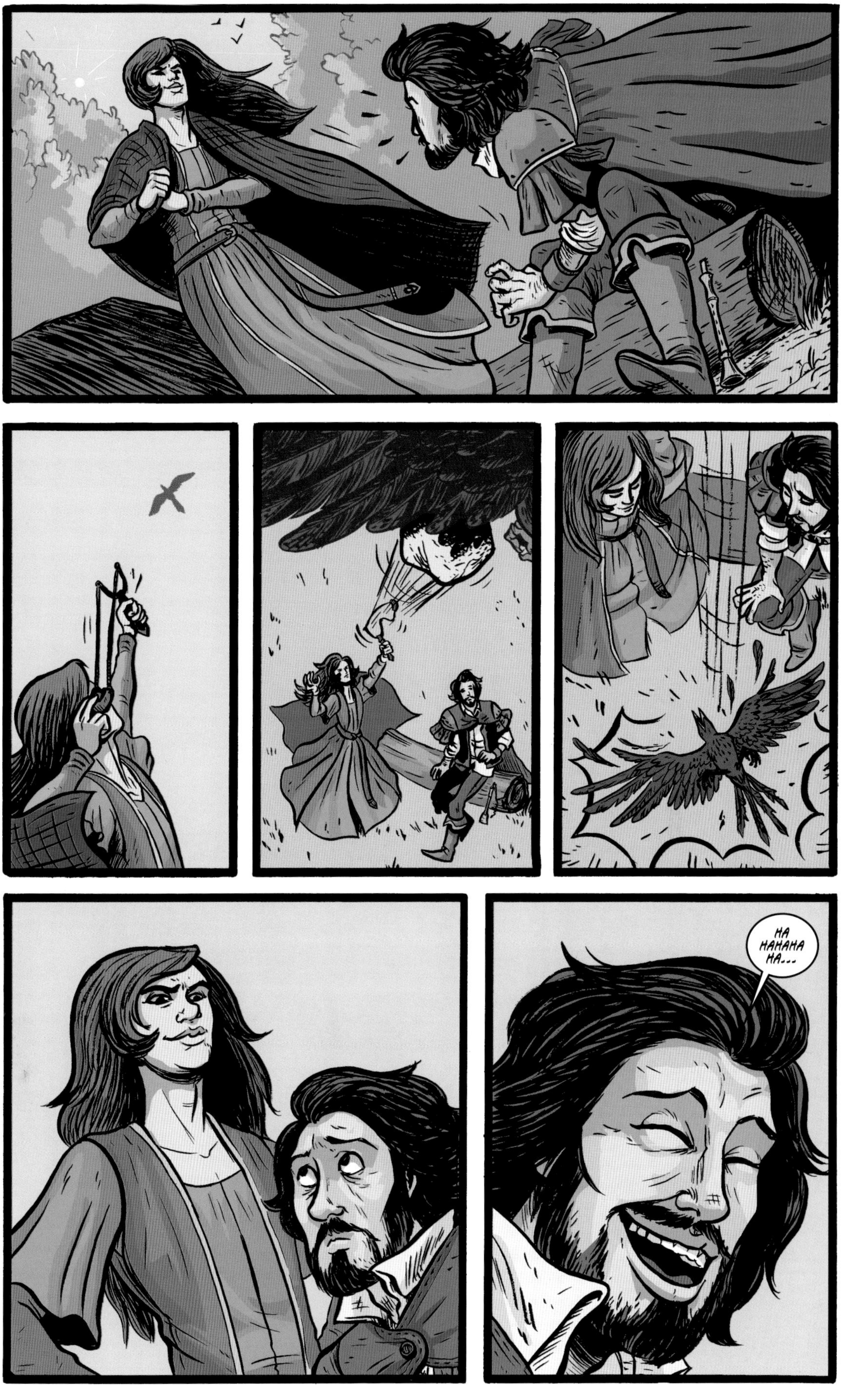
HA
HAHAHA
HA...

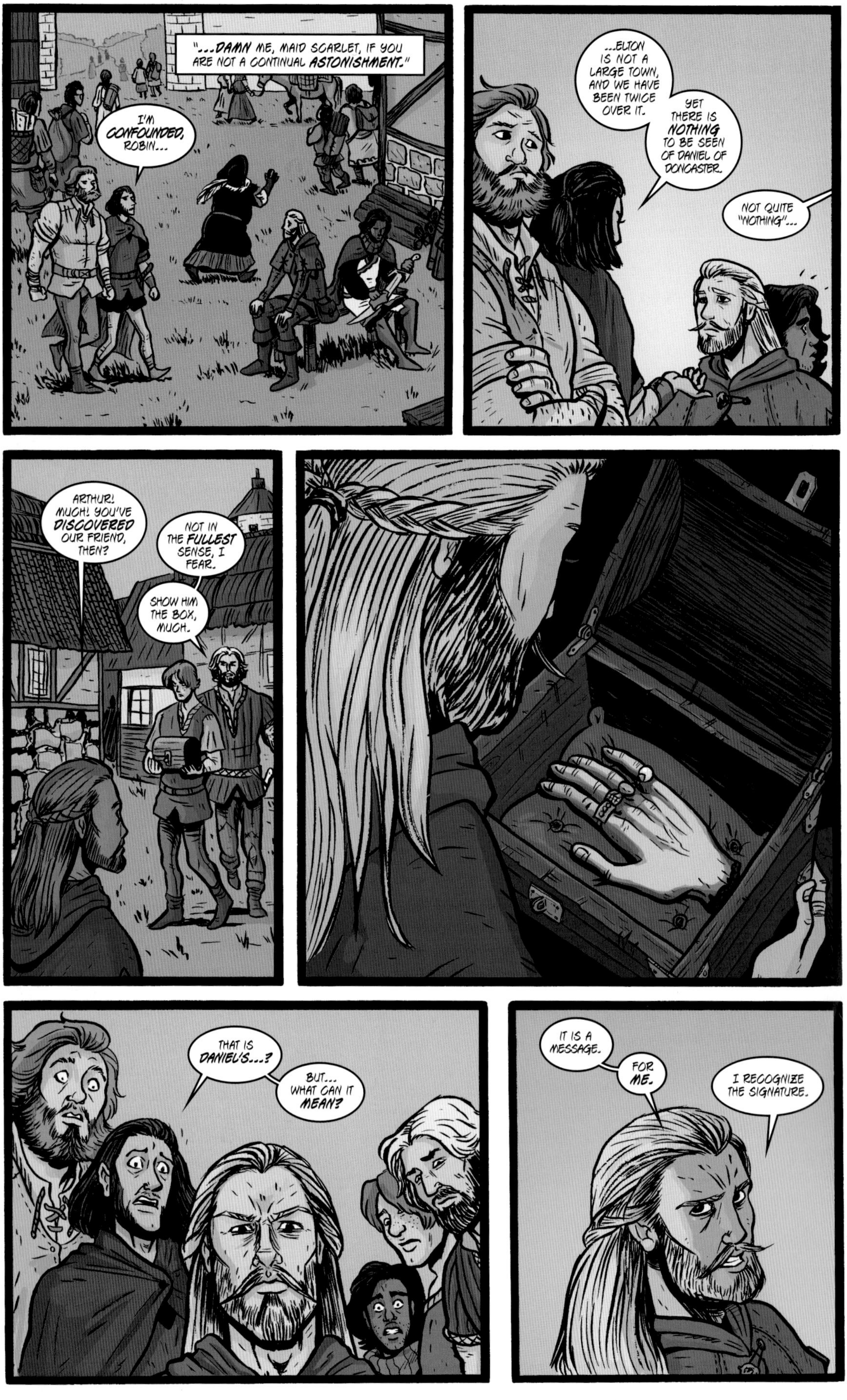
"...DAMN ME, MAID SCARLET, IF YOU ARE NOT A CONTINUAL ASTONISHMENT."
I'M CONFOUNDED, ROBIN...
...ELTON IS NOT A LARGE TOWN, AND WE HAVE BEEN TWICE OVER IT.
YET THERE IS NOTHING TO BE SEEN OF DANIEL OF DONCASTER.
NOT QUITE "NOTHING"...
ARTHUR! MUCH! YOU'VE DISCOVERED OUR FRIEND, THEN?
NOT IN THE FULLEST SENSE, I FEAR.
SHOW HIM THE BOX, MUCH.
THAT IS DANIEL'S...?
BUT... WHAT CAN IT MEAN?
IT IS A MESSAGE.
FOR ME.
I RECOGNIZE THE SIGNATURE.

Chapter 3

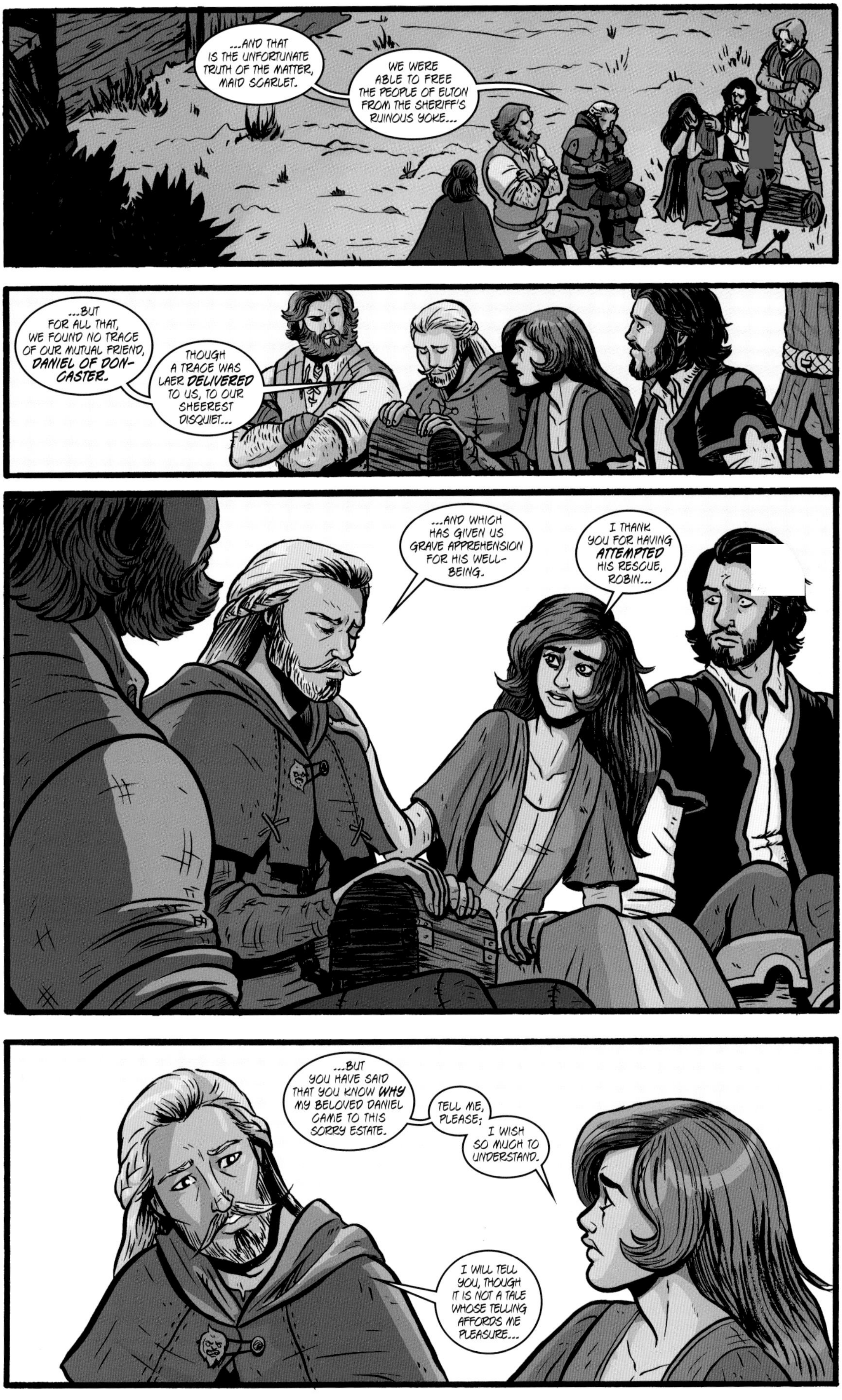
...AND THAT IS THE UNFORTUNATE TRUTH OF THE MATTER, MAID SCARLET.
WE WERE ABLE TO FREE THE PEOPLE OF ELTON FROM THE SHERIFF'S RUINOUS YOKE...
...BUT FOR ALL THAT, WE FOUND NO TRACE OF OUR MUTUAL FRIEND, DANIEL OF DON-CASTER.
THOUGH A TRACE WAS LAER DELIVERED TO US, TO OUR SHEEREST DISQUIET...
...AND WHICH HAS GIVEN US GRAVE APPREHENSION FOR HIS WELL-BEING.
I THANK YOU FOR HAVING ATTEMPTED HIS RESCUE, ROBIN...
...BUT YOU HAVE SAID THAT YOU KNOW WHY MY BELOVED DANIEL CAME TO THIS SORRY ESTATE.
TELL ME, PLEASE; I WISH SO MUCH TO UNDERSTAND.
I WILL TELL YOU, THOUGH IT IS NOT A TALE WHOSE TELLING AFFORDS ME PLEASURE...

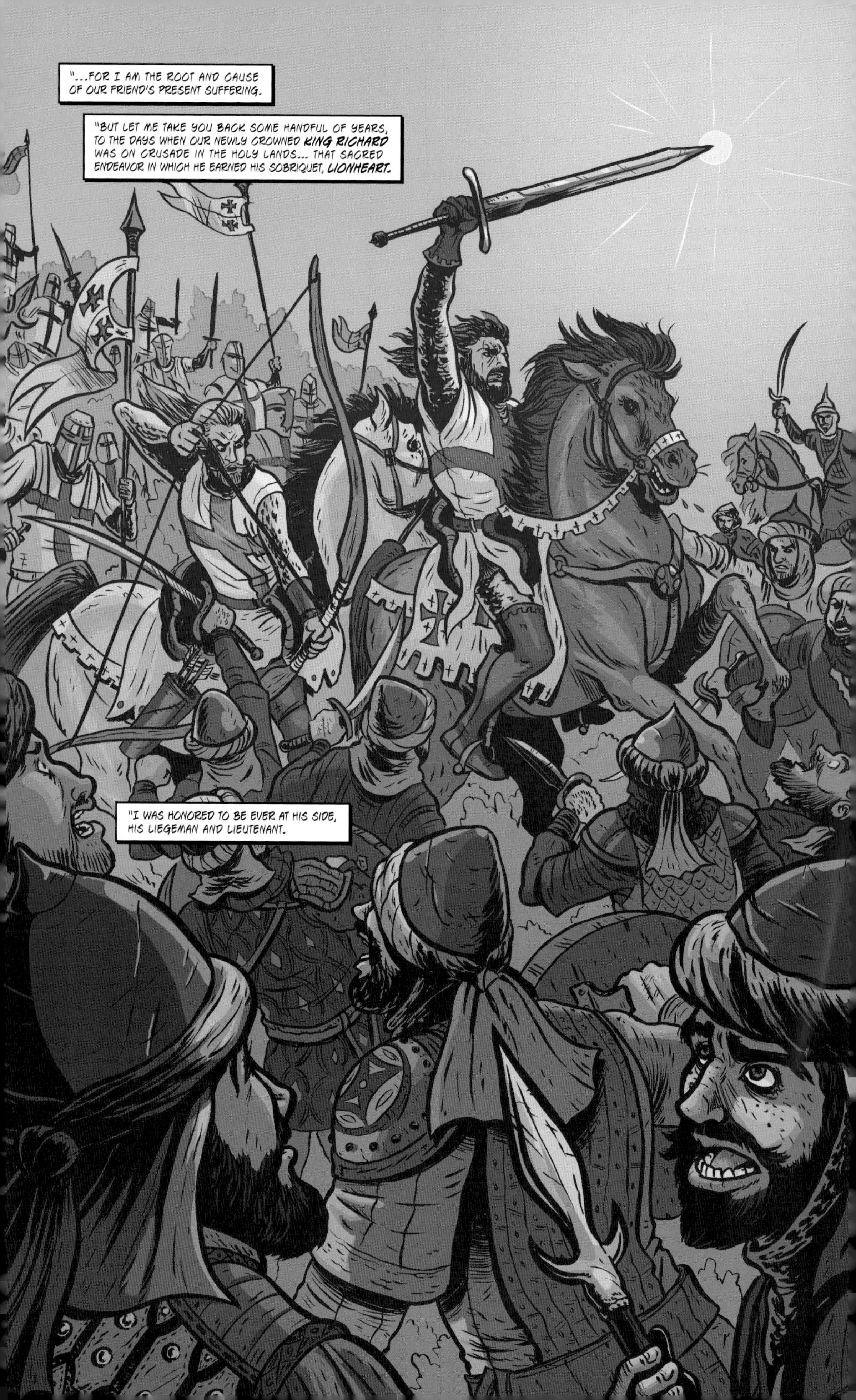
"...FOR I AM THE ROOT AND CAUSE OF OUR FRIEND'S PRESENT SUFFERING.
"BUT LET ME TAKE YOU BACK SOME HANDFUL OF YEARS, TO THE DAYS WHEN OUR NEWLY CROWNED KING RICHARD WAS ON CRUSADE IN THE HOLY LANDS... THAT SACRED ENDEAVOR IN WHICH HE EARNED HIS SOBRIQUET, LIONHEART.
"I WAS HONORED TO BE EVER AT HIS SIDE, HIS LIEGEMAN AND LIEUTENANT.

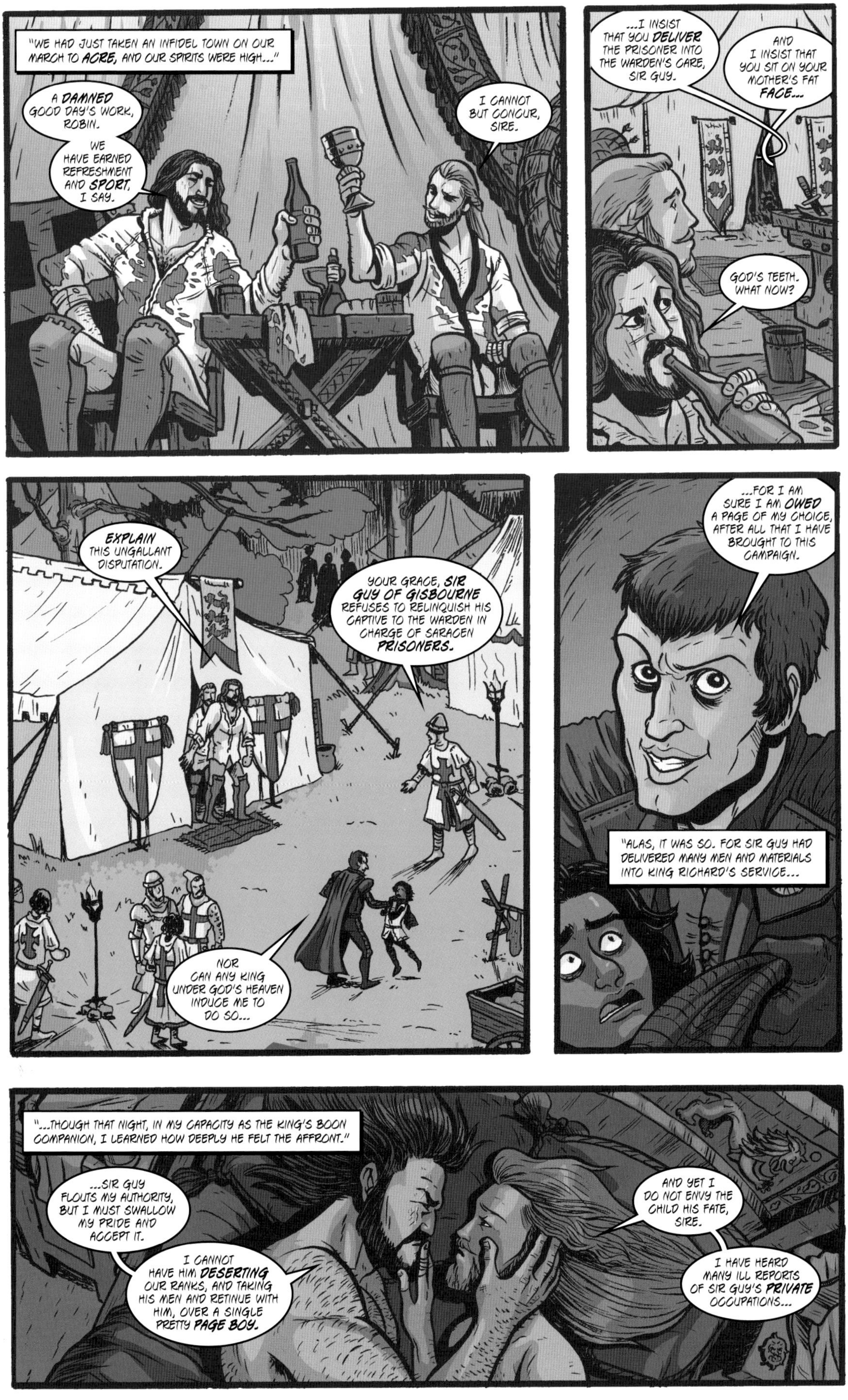
"WE HAD JUST TAKEN AN INFIDEL TOWN ON OUR MARCH TO ACRE, AND OUR SPIRITS WERE HIGH..."
A DAMNED GOOD DAY'S WORK, ROBIN.
WE HAVE EARNED REFRESHMENT AND SPORT, I SAY.
I CANNOT BUT CONCUR, SIRE.
...I INSIST THAT YOU DELIVER THE PRISONER INTO THE WARDEN'S CARE, SIR GUY.
AND I INSIST THAT YOU SIT ON YOUR MOTHER'S FAT FACE...
GOD'S TEETH. WHAT NOW?
EXPLAIN THIS UNGALLANT DISPUTATION.
YOUR GRACE, SIR GUY OF GISBOURNE REFUSES TO RELINQUISH HIS CAPTIVE TO THE WARDEN IN CHARGE OF SARACEN PRISONERS.
NOR CAN ANY KING UNDER GOD'S HEAVEN INDUCE ME TO DO SO...
...FOR I AM SURE I AM OWED A PAGE OF MY CHOICE, AFTER ALL THAT I HAVE BROUGHT TO THIS CAMPAIGN.
"ALAS, IT WAS SO. FOR SIR GUY HAD DELIVERED MANY MEN AND MATERIALS INTO KING RICHARD'S SERVICE...
"...THOUGH THAT NIGHT, IN MY CAPACITY AS THE KING'S BOON COMPANION, I LEARNED HOW DEEPLY HE FELT THE AFFRONT."
...SIR GUY FLOUTS MY AUTHORITY, BUT I MUST SWALLOW MY PRIDE AND ACCEPT IT.
I CANNOT HAVE HIM DESERTING OUR RANKS, AND TAKING HIS MEN AND RETINUE WITH HIM, OVER A SINGLE PRETTY PAGE BOY.
AND YET I DO NOT ENVY THE CHILD HIS FATE, SIRE.
I HAVE HEARD MANY ILL REPORTS OF SIR GUY'S PRIVATE OCCUPATIONS...

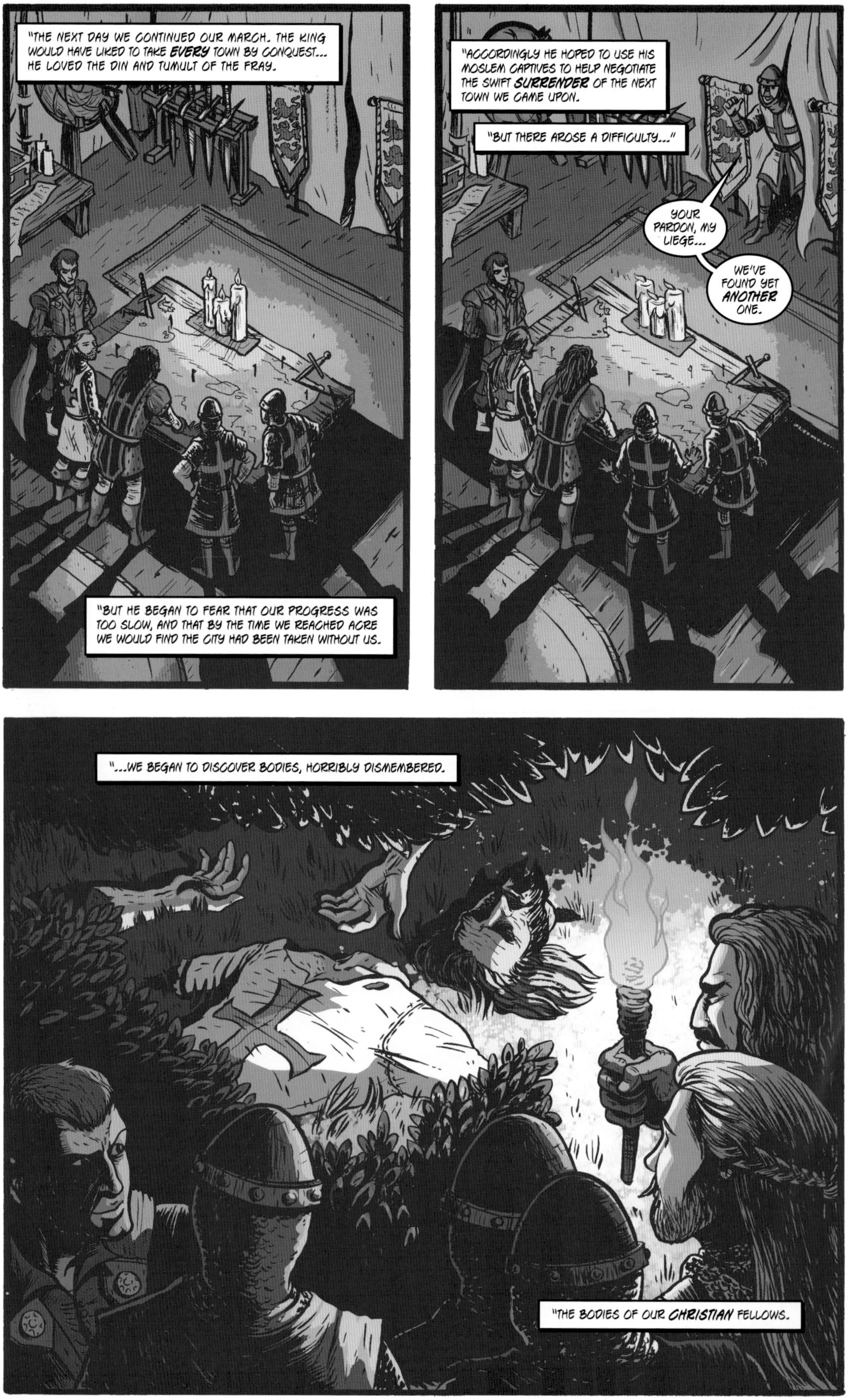
"THE NEXT DAY WE CONTINUED OUR MARCH. THE KING WOULD HAVE LIKED TO TAKE EVERY TOWN BY CONQUEST... HE LOVED THE DIN AND TUMULT OF THE FRAY.
"BUT HE BEGAN TO FEAR THAT OUR PROGRESS WAS TOO SLOW, AND THAT BY THE TIME WE REACHED ACRE WE WOULD FIND THE CITY HAD BEEN TAKEN WITHOUT US.
"ACCORDINGLY HE HOPED TO USE HIS MOSLEM CAPTIVES TO HELP NEGOTIATE THE SWIFT SURRENDER OF THE NEXT TOWN WE CAME UPON.
"BUT THERE AROSE A DIFFICULTY..."
YOUR PARDON, MY LIEGE...
WE'VE FOUND YET ANOTHER ONE.
"...WE BEGAN TO DISCOVER BODIES, HORRIBLY DISMEMBERED.
"THE BODIES OF OUR CHRISTIAN FELLOWS.

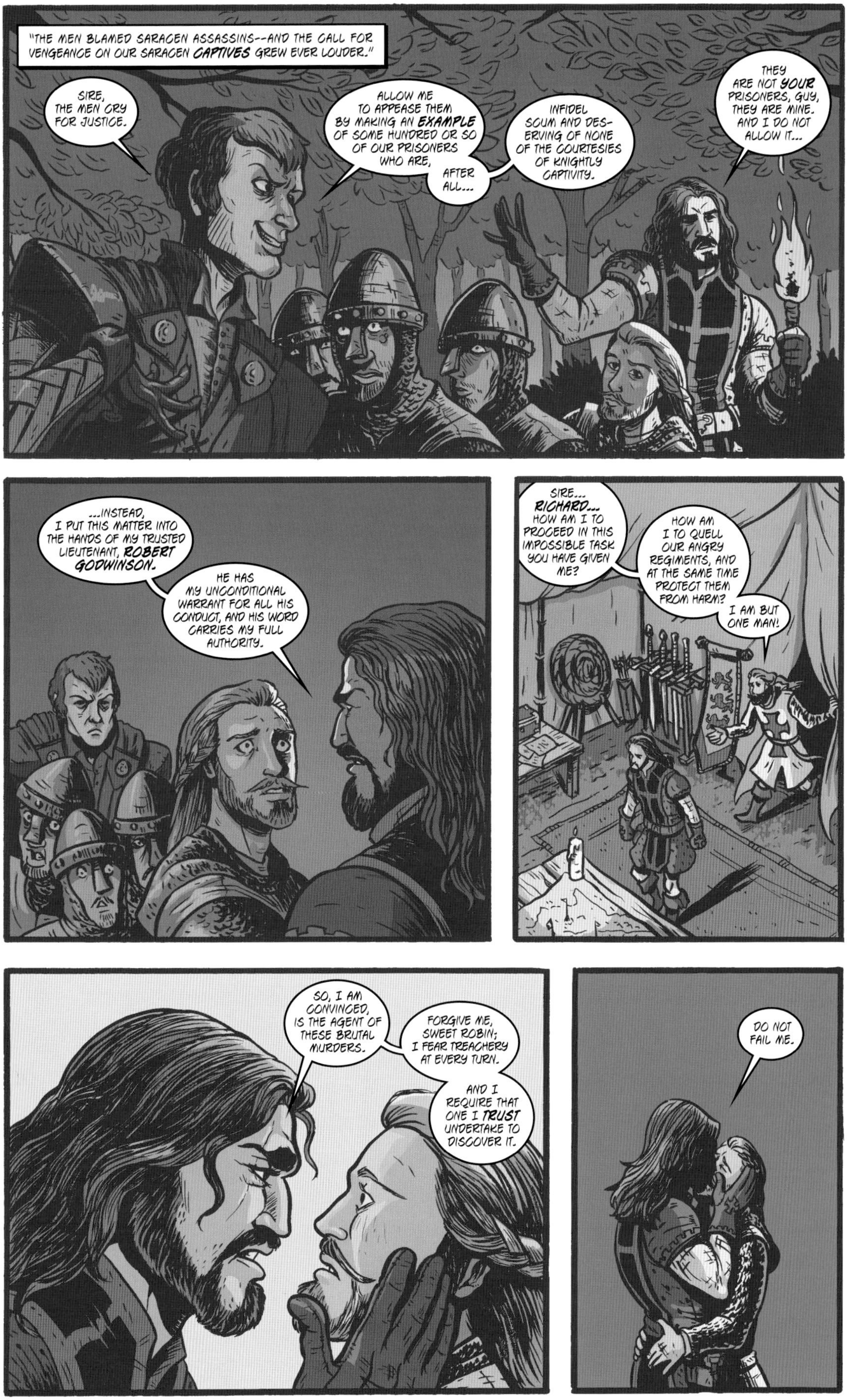
"THE MEN BLAMED SARACEN ASSASSINS--AND THE CALL FOR VENGEANCE ON OUR SARACEN CAPTIVES GREW EVER LOUDER."
SIRE, THE MEN CRY FOR JUSTICE.
ALLOW ME TO APPEASE THEM BY MAKING AN EXAMPLE OF SOME HUNDRED OR SO OF OUR PRISONERS WHO ARE,
AFTER ALL...
INFIDEL SCUM AND DESERVING OF NONE OF THE COURTESIES OF KNIGHTLY CAPTIVITY.
THEY ARE NOT YOUR PRISONERS, GUY, THEY ARE MINE. AND I DO NOT ALLOW IT...
...INSTEAD, I PUT THIS MATTER INTO THE HANDS OF MY TRUSTED LIEUTENANT, ROBERT GODWINSON.
HE HAS MY UNCONDITIONAL WARRANT FOR ALL HIS CONDUCT, AND HIS WORD CARRIES MY FULL AUTHORITY.
SIRE... RICHARD... HOW AM I TO PROCEED IN THIS IMPOSSIBLE TASK YOU HAVE GIVEN ME?
HOW AM I TO QUELL OUR ANGRY REGIMENTS, AND AT THE SAME TIME PROTECT THEM FROM HARM?
I AM BUT ONE MAN!
SO, I AM CONVINCED, IS THE AGENT OF THESE BRUTAL MURDERS.
FORGIVE ME, SWEET ROBIN; I FEAR TREACHERY AT EVERY TURN.
AND I REQUIRE THAT ONE I TRUST UNDERTAKE TO DISCOVER IT.
DO NOT FAIL ME.

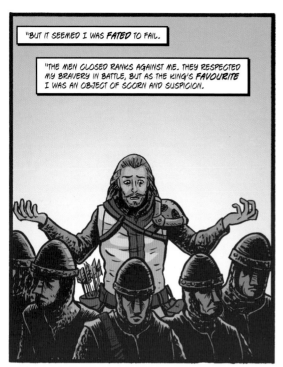

"BUT IT SEEMED I WAS **FATED** TO FAIL."

"THE MEN CLOSED RANKS AGAINST ME. THEY RESPECTED MY BRAVERY IN BATTLE, BUT AS THE KING'S **FAVOURITE** I WAS AN OBJECT OF SCORN AND SUSPICION."

"IT WAS ONLY LATER THAT I LEARNED GUY OF GISBOURNE HAD DONE MUCH TO STOKE THE FIRES OF THIS RESENTMENT."

...ARE WE TO SUFFER THIS? THE KING'S **BUM BOY**, TO HOLD SWAY OVER US?

THE MAN'S AN **UPSTART**... BEFORE HE TOOK UP ARMS HE WAS A MERE **MERCHANT** IN NOTTINGHAM-SHIRE.

THE ARMY IS SUCH A BOON TO THESE AMBITIOUS PROVINCIALS...

BUT THEY WON'T VAULT OVER **MY** HEAD SO EASILY AS THAT.

"THE KING GREW RESTLESS WITH MY LACK OF PROGRESS...."

I WANT NO **EXCUSES** FROM YOU, ROBIN!

ANOTHER BODY TODAY-- AND YOU CANNOT YET TELL ME OF A CERTAINTY WHETHER THE ASSASSIN IS FROM **WITHIN** OR **WITHOUT**!

I WILL NOT SUFFER A **MUTINY** BECAUSE OF YOUR LACK OF **ZEAL**!

"RICHARD HAD RAISED ME HIGH BECAUSE OF MY SERVICE TO HIM, IN BED AND IN BATTLE.

"NOW IT SEEMED THAT HE MIGHT CAST ME DOWN AGAIN, FOR MY INABILITY TO SERVICE HIM IN A CAPACITY FOR WHICH MY TALENTS DID NOT **RECOMMEND** ME."

"BUT WHERE MY TALENTS FAILED ME, MY INNATE KINDNESS AND CHRISTIAN FELLOWSHIP SERVED ME IN GOOD STEAD."

WHAT--? OH, IT'S YOU, LITTLE SARACEN... APOLOGIES.

MY MIND WAS VERY FAR FROM THE TREAD OF MY FEET.

HERE, WITH WHAT INFAMY DOES THAT VILLAIN GUY OF GISBOURNE TORMENT YOU NOW...?

...NEVER MIND. LET ME SHOULDER YOUR BURDEN FOR YOU.

I CAN BUT WISH YOU COULD AS EASILY SHOULDER **MINE**...

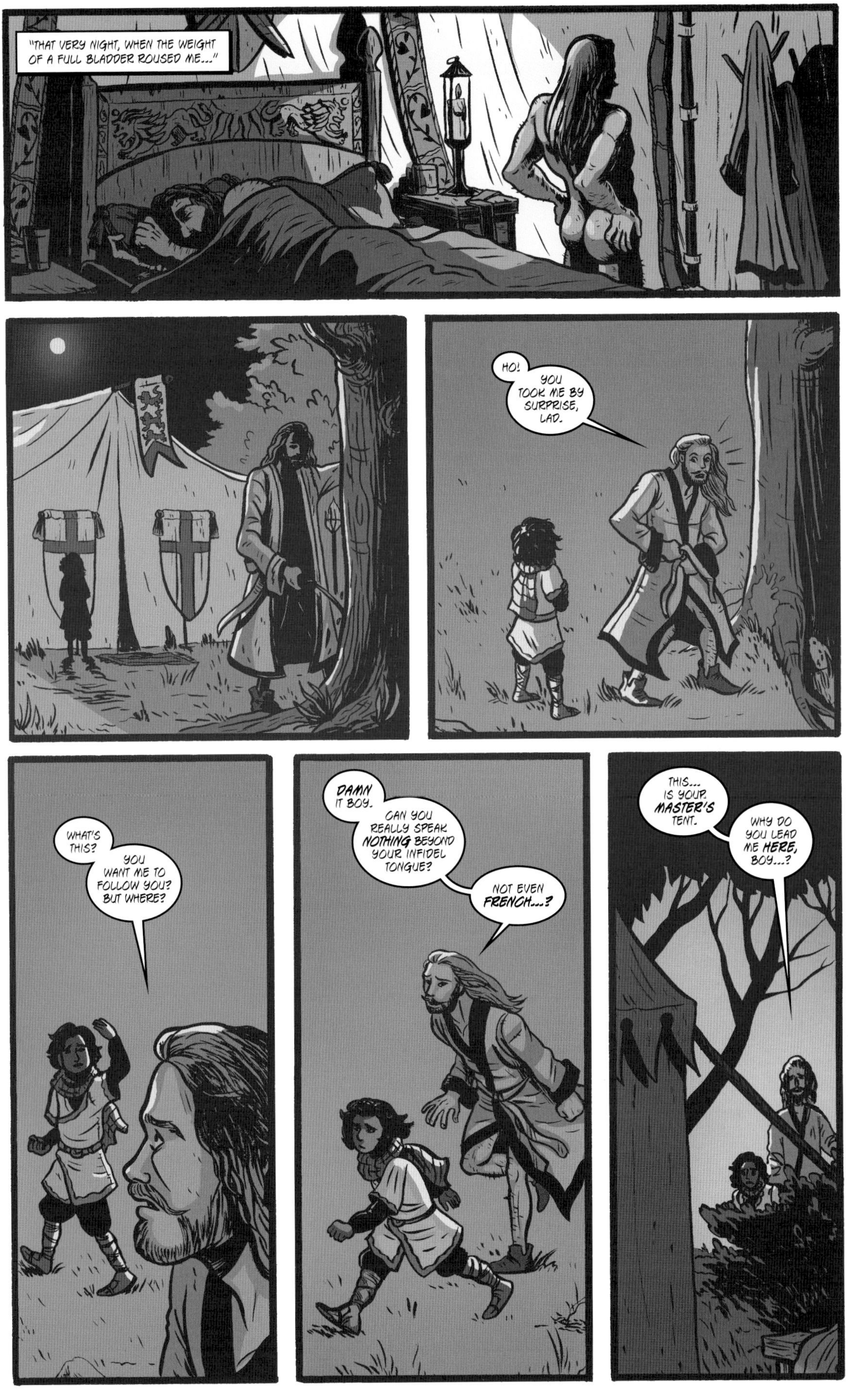
"THAT VERY NIGHT, WHEN THE WEIGHT OF A FULL BLADDER ROUSED ME..."
HO!
YOU TOOK ME BY SURPRISE, LAD.
WHAT'S THIS?
YOU WANT ME TO FOLLOW YOU? BUT WHERE?
DAMN IT BOY.
CAN YOU REALLY SPEAK NOTHING BEYOND YOUR INFIDEL TONGUE?
NOT EVEN FRENCH...?
THIS... IS YOUR MASTER'S TENT.
WHY DO YOU LEAD ME HERE, BOY...?

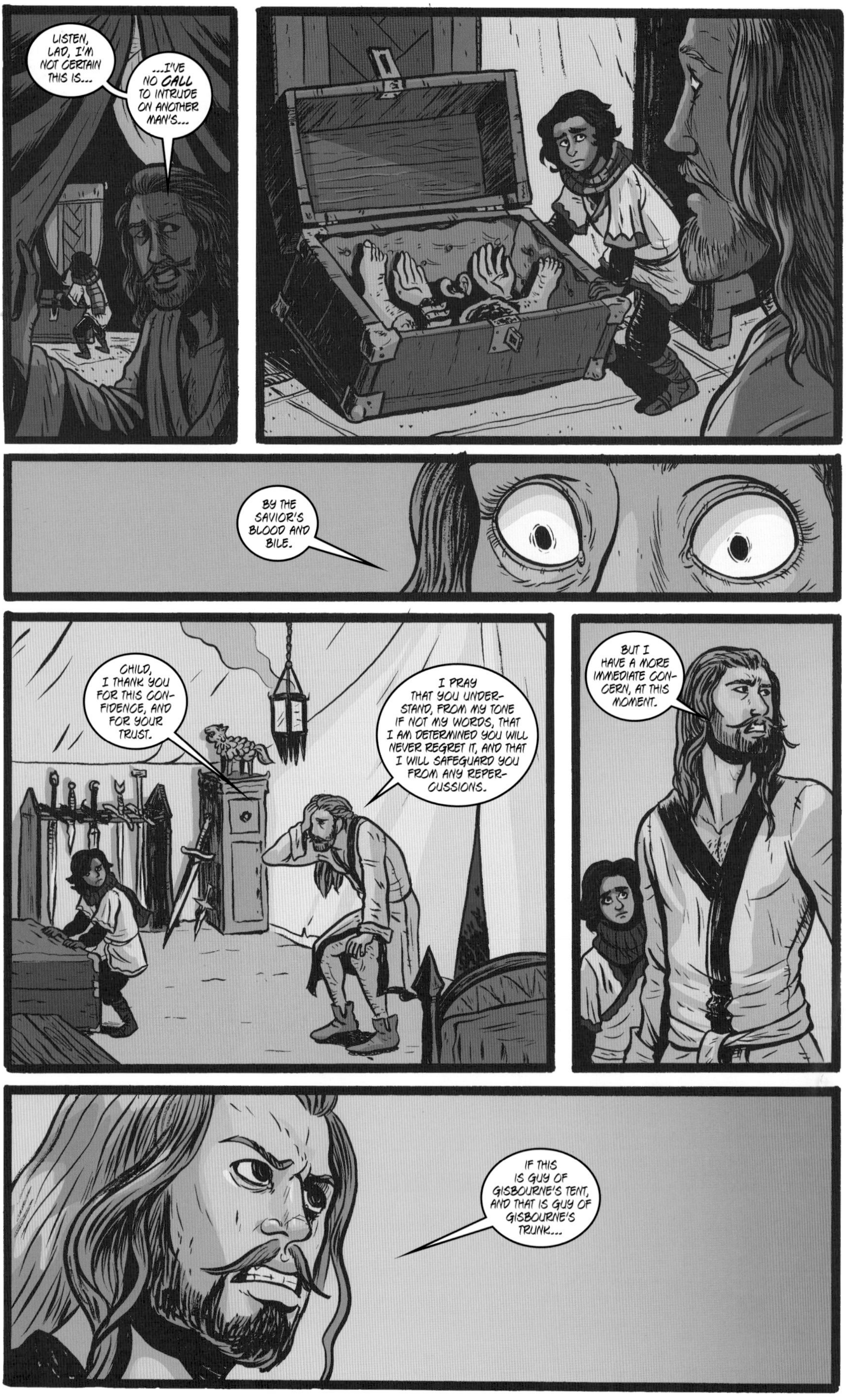
LISTEN, LAD, I'M NOT CERTAIN THIS IS...
...I'VE NO CALL TO INTRUDE ON ANOTHER MAN'S...
BY THE SAVIOR'S BLOOD AND BILE.
CHILD, I THANK YOU FOR THIS CONFIDENCE, AND FOR YOUR TRUST.
I PRAY THAT YOU UNDERSTAND, FROM MY TONE IF NOT MY WORDS, THAT I AM DETERMINED YOU WILL NEVER REGRET IT, AND THAT I WILL SAFEGUARD YOU FROM ANY REPERCUSSIONS.
BUT I HAVE A MORE IMMEDIATE CONCERN, AT THIS MOMENT.
IF THIS IS GUY OF GISBOURNE'S TENT, AND THAT IS GUY OF GISBOURNE'S TRUNK...

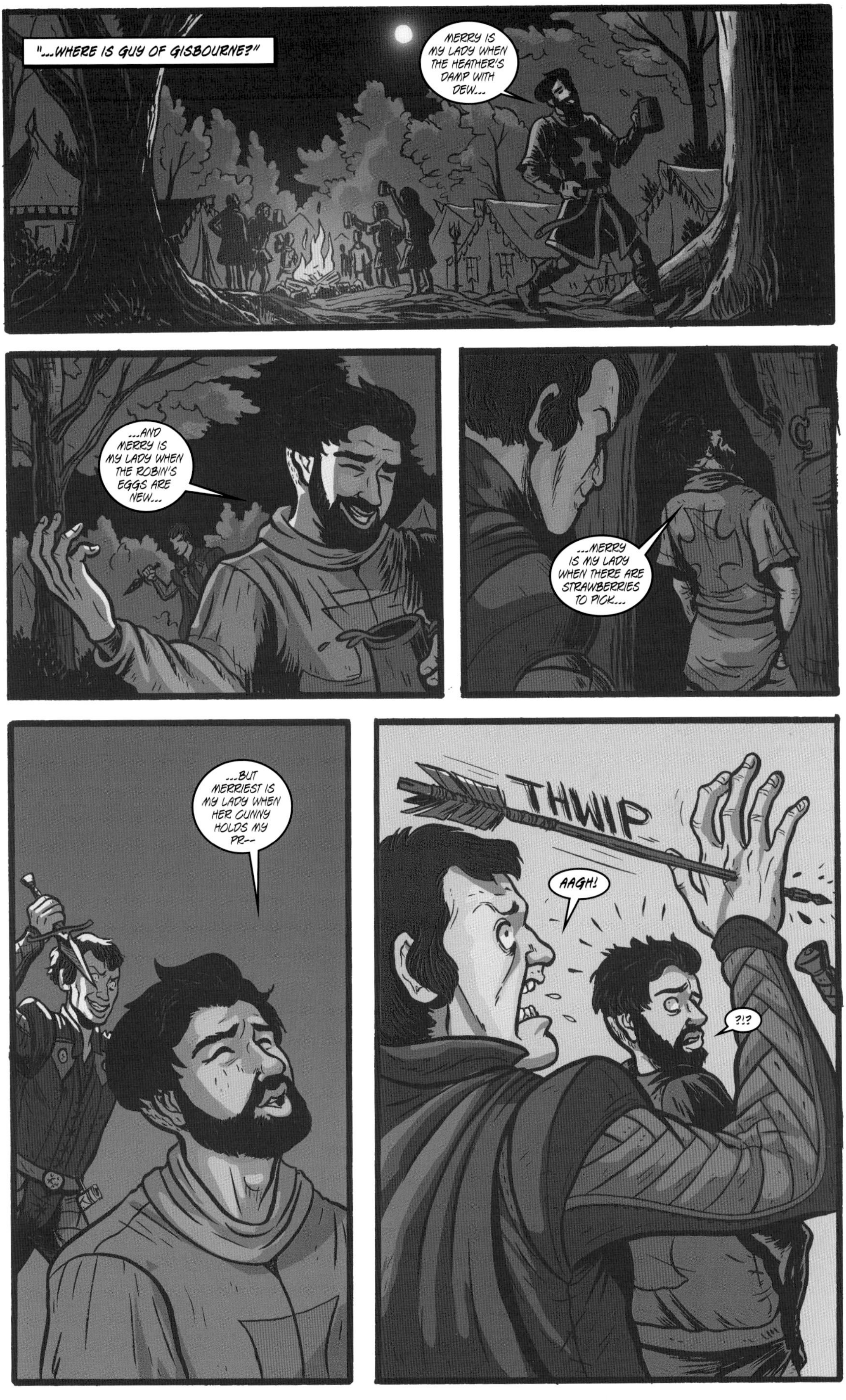
"...WHERE IS GUY OF GISBOURNE?"
MERRY IS MY LADY WHEN THE HEATHER'S DAMP WITH DEW...
...AND MERRY IS MY LADY WHEN THE ROBIN'S EGGS ARE NEW...
...MERRY IS MY LADY WHEN THERE ARE STRAWBERRIES TO PICK...
...BUT MERRIEST IS MY LADY WHEN HER CUNNY HOLDS MY PR--
THWIP
AAGH!
?!?

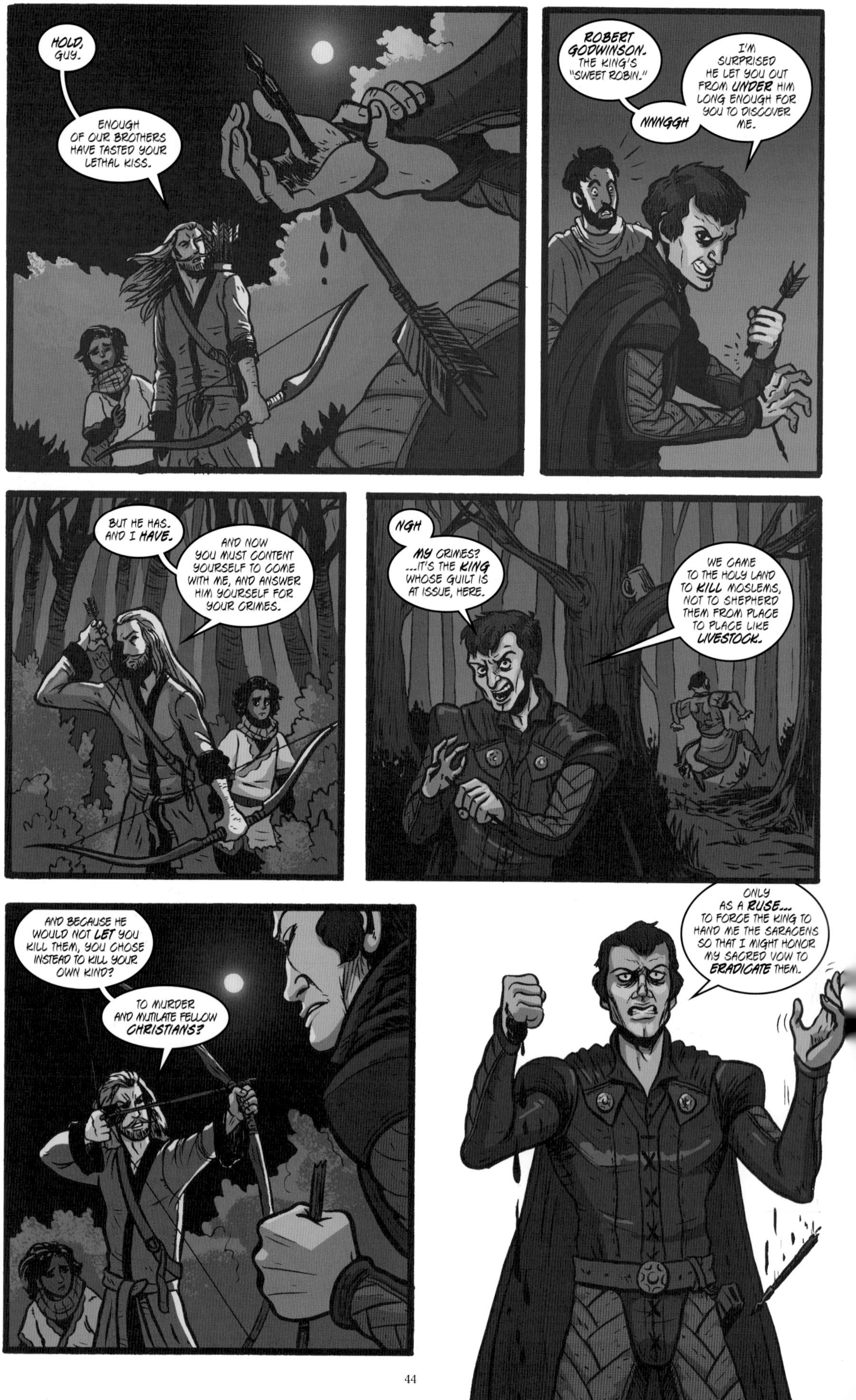
HOLD, GUY.
ENOUGH OF OUR BROTHERS HAVE TASTED YOUR LETHAL KISS.
ROBERT GODWINSON. THE KING'S "SWEET ROBIN."
NNNGGH
I'M SURPRISED HE LET YOU OUT FROM UNDER HIM LONG ENOUGH FOR YOU TO DISCOVER ME.
BUT HE HAS. AND I HAVE.
AND NOW YOU MUST CONTENT YOURSELF TO COME WITH ME, AND ANSWER HIM YOURSELF FOR YOUR CRIMES.
NGH
MY CRIMES? ...IT'S THE KING WHOSE GUILT IS AT ISSUE, HERE.
WE CAME TO THE HOLY LAND TO KILL MOSLEMS, NOT TO SHEPHERD THEM FROM PLACE TO PLACE LIKE LIVESTOCK.
AND BECAUSE HE WOULD NOT LET YOU KILL THEM, YOU CHOSE INSTEAD TO KILL YOUR OWN KIND?
TO MURDER AND MUTILATE FELLOW CHRISTIANS?
ONLY AS A RUSE... TO FORCE THE KING TO HAND ME THE SARACENS SO THAT I MIGHT HONOR MY SACRED VOW TO ERADICATE THEM.

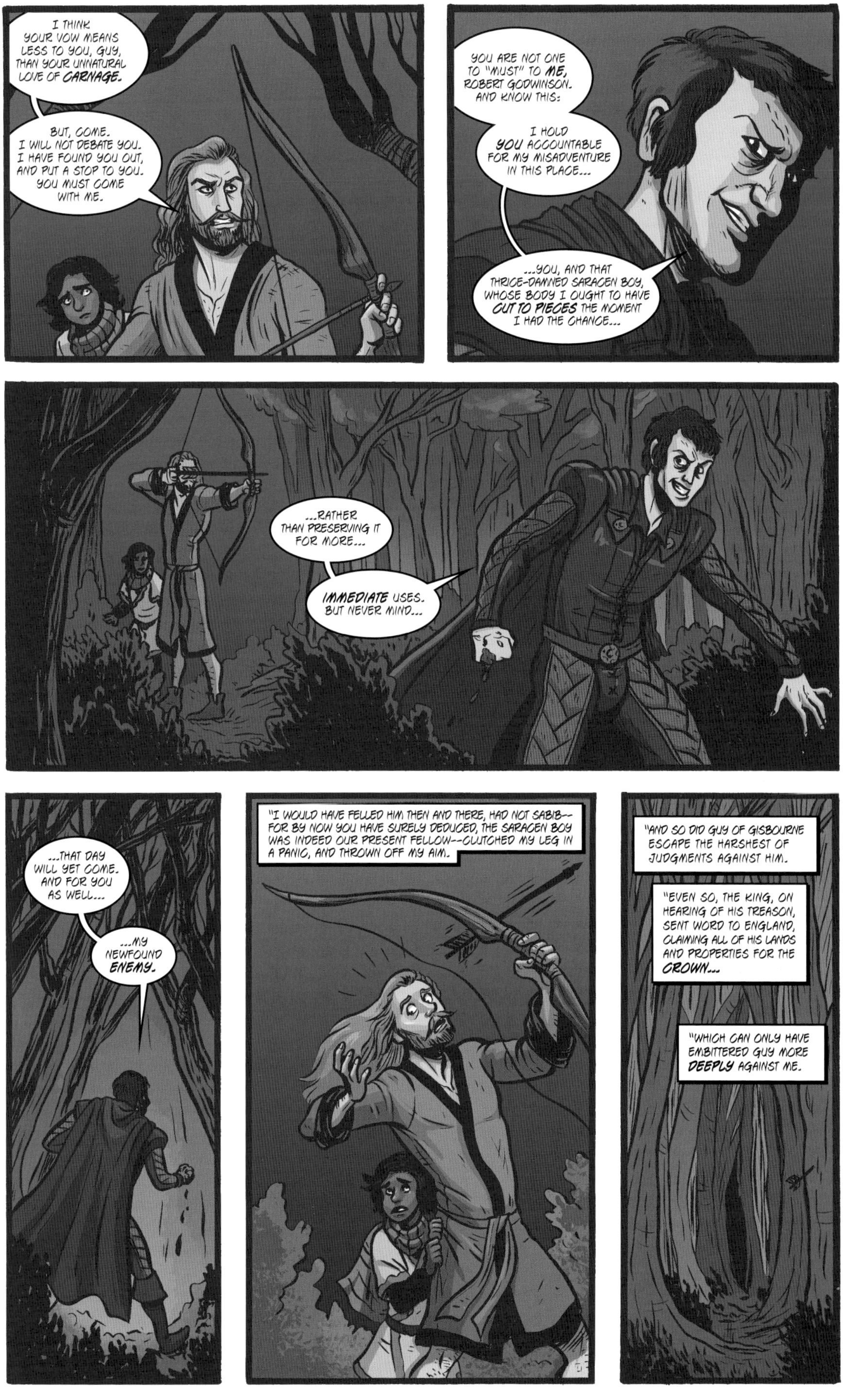
I THINK YOUR VOW MEANS LESS TO YOU, GUY, THAN YOUR UNNATURAL LOVE OF CARNAGE.
BUT, COME. I WILL NOT DEBATE YOU. I HAVE FOUND YOU OUT, AND PUT A STOP TO YOU. YOU MUST COME WITH ME.
YOU ARE NOT ONE TO "MUST" TO ME, ROBERT GODWINSON. AND KNOW THIS:
I HOLD YOU ACCOUNTABLE FOR MY MISADVENTURE IN THIS PLACE...
...YOU, AND THAT THRICE-DAMNED SARACEN BOY, WHOSE BODY I OUGHT TO HAVE CUT TO PIECES THE MOMENT I HAD THE CHANCE...
...RATHER THAN PRESERVING IT FOR MORE...
IMMEDIATE USES. BUT NEVER MIND...
...THAT DAY WILL YET COME. AND FOR YOU AS WELL...
...MY NEWFOUND ENEMY.
"I WOULD HAVE FELLED HIM THEN AND THERE, HAD NOT SABIB--FOR BY NOW YOU HAVE SURELY DEDUCED, THE SARACEN BOY WAS INDEED OUR PRESENT FELLOW--CLUTCHED MY LEG IN A PANIC, AND THROWN OFF MY AIM.
"AND SO DID GUY OF GISBOURNE ESCAPE THE HARSHEST OF JUDGMENTS AGAINST HIM.
"EVEN SO, THE KING, ON HEARING OF HIS TREASON, SENT WORD TO ENGLAND, CLAIMING ALL OF HIS LANDS AND PROPERTIES FOR THE CROWN...
"WHICH CAN ONLY HAVE EMBITTERED GUY MORE DEEPLY AGAINST ME.

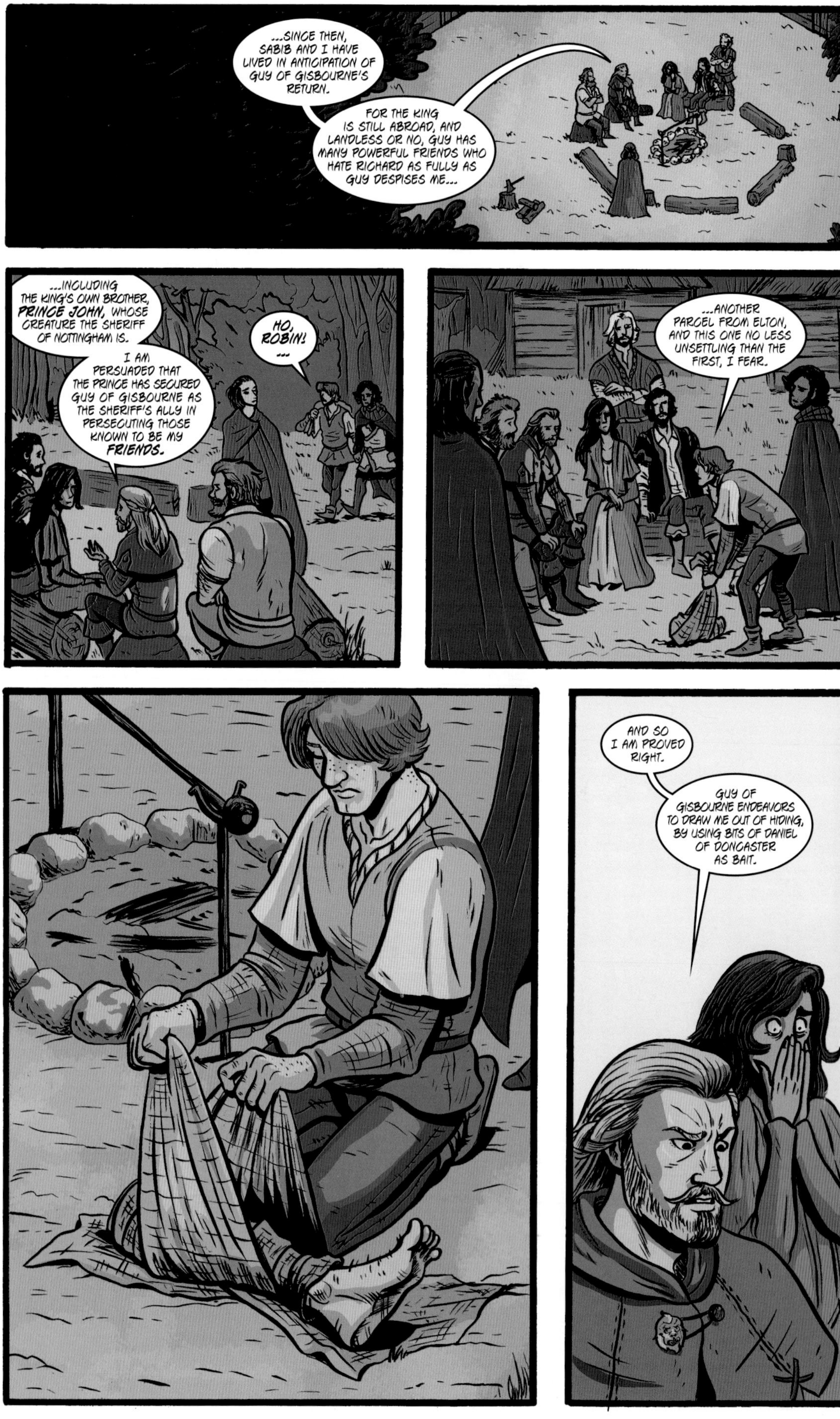
...SINCE THEN, SABIB AND I HAVE LIVED IN ANTICIPATION OF GUY OF GISBOURNE'S RETURN.
FOR THE KING IS STILL ABROAD, AND LANDLESS OR NO, GUY HAS MANY POWERFUL FRIENDS WHO HATE RICHARD AS FULLY AS GUY DESPISES ME...
...INCLUDING THE KING'S OWN BROTHER, PRINCE JOHN, WHOSE CREATURE THE SHERIFF OF NOTTINGHAM IS.
I AM PERSUADED THAT THE PRINCE HAS SECURED GUY OF GISBOURNE AS THE SHERIFF'S ALLY IN PERSECUTING THOSE KNOWN TO BE MY FRIENDS.
HO, ROBIN! ...
...ANOTHER PARCEL FROM ELTON, AND THIS ONE NO LESS UNSETTLING THAN THE FIRST, I FEAR.
AND SO I AM PROVED RIGHT.
GUY OF GISBOURNE ENDEAVORS TO DRAW ME OUT OF HIDING, BY USING BITS OF DANIEL OF DONCASTER AS BAIT.

Chapter
4

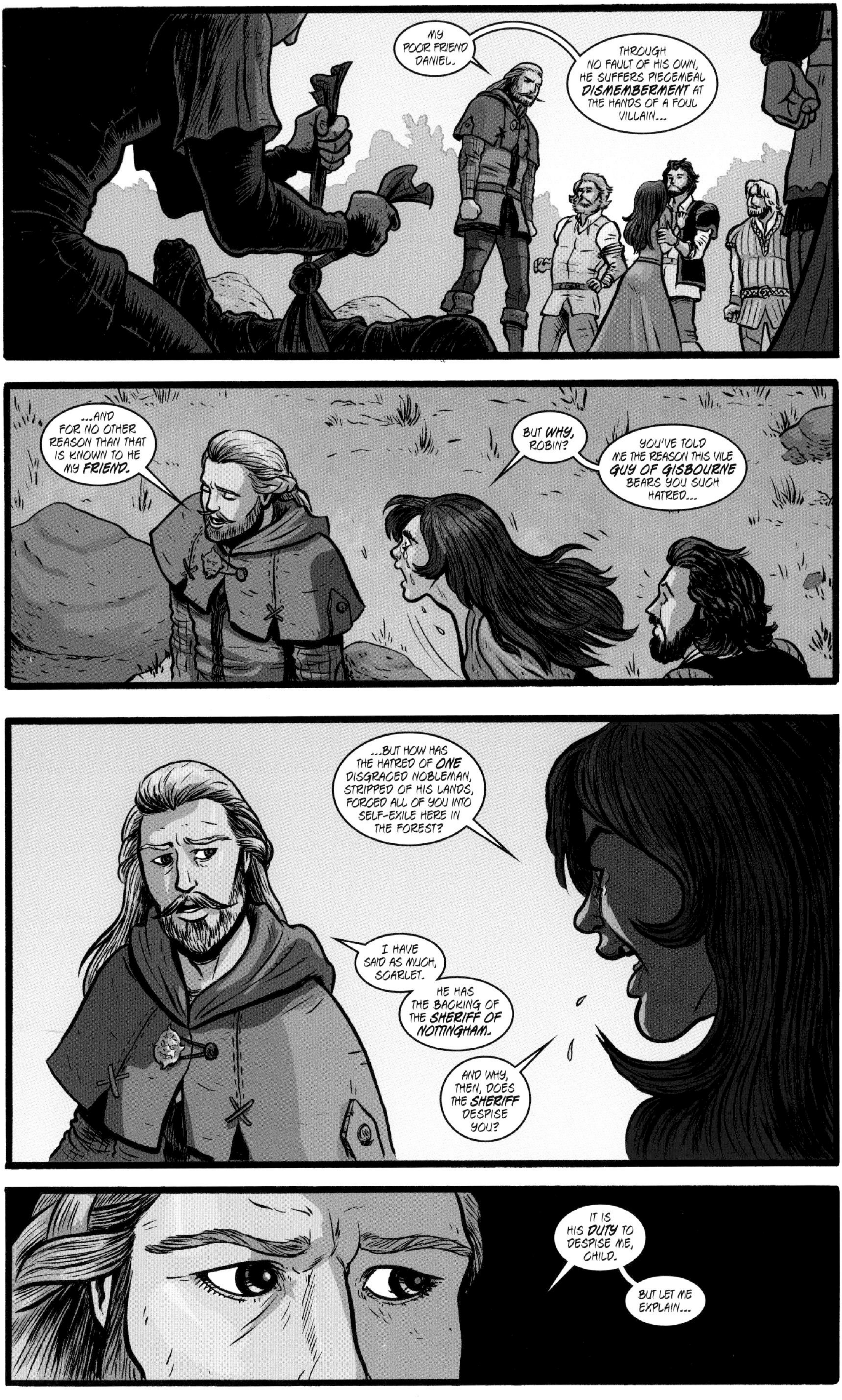
MY POOR FRIEND DANIEL.
THROUGH NO FAULT OF HIS OWN, HE SUFFERS PIECEMEAL DISMEMBERMENT AT THE HANDS OF A FOUL VILLAIN...
...AND FOR NO OTHER REASON THAN THAT IS KNOWN TO BE MY FRIEND.
BUT WHY, ROBIN?
YOU'VE TOLD ME THE REASON THIS VILE GUY OF GISBOURNE BEARS YOU SUCH HATRED...
...BUT HOW HAS THE HATRED OF ONE DISGRACED NOBLEMAN, STRIPPED OF HIS LANDS, FORCED ALL OF YOU INTO SELF-EXILE HERE IN THE FOREST?
I HAVE SAID AS MUCH, SCARLET.
HE HAS THE BACKING OF THE SHERIFF OF NOTTINGHAM.
AND WHY, THEN, DOES THE SHERIFF DESPISE YOU?
IT IS HIS DUTY TO DESPISE ME, CHILD.
BUT LET ME EXPLAIN...

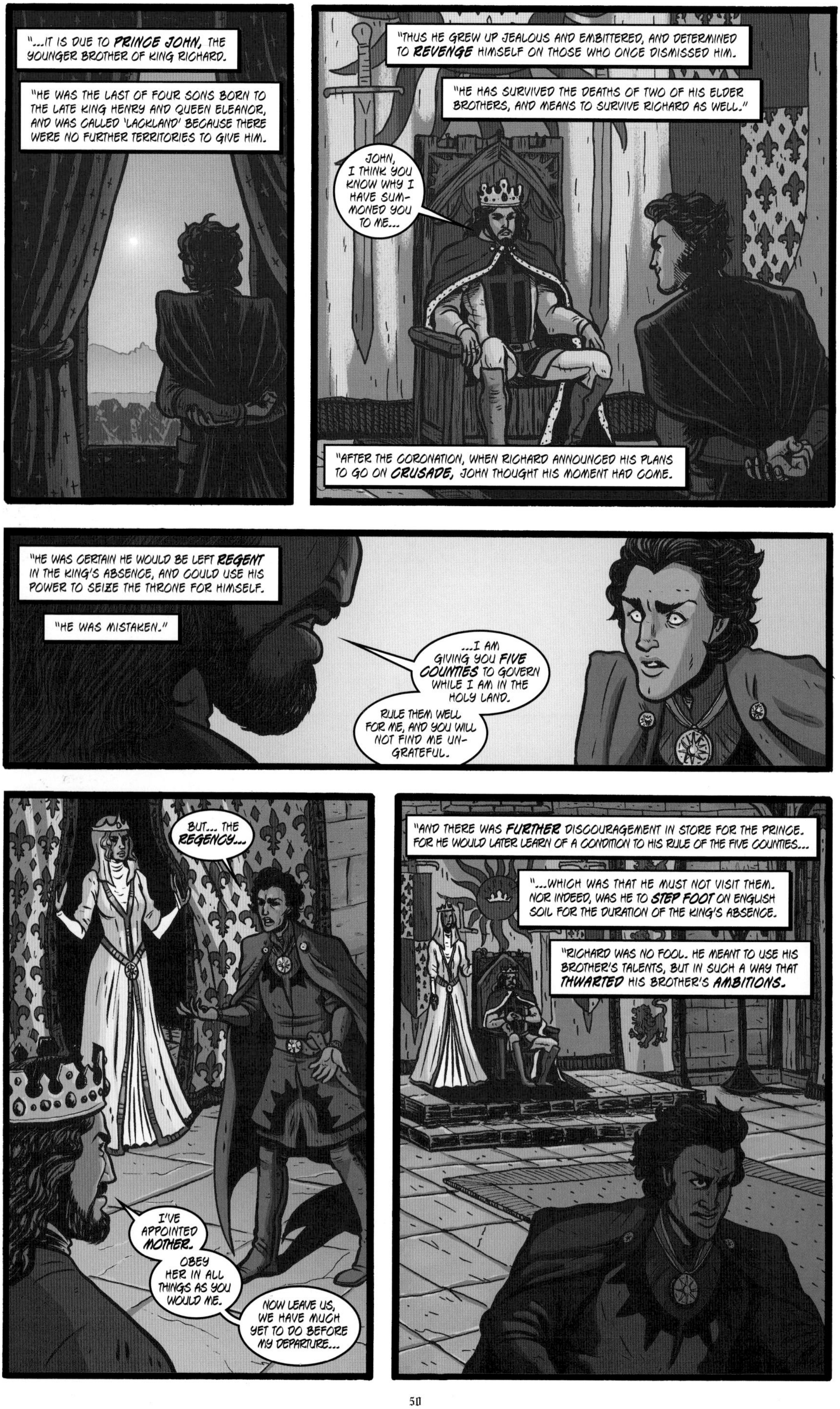

"...IT IS DUE TO PRINCE JOHN, THE YOUNGER BROTHER OF KING RICHARD.
"HE WAS THE LAST OF FOUR SONS BORN TO THE LATE KING HENRY AND QUEEN ELEANOR, AND WAS CALLED 'LACKLAND' BECAUSE THERE WERE NO FURTHER TERRITORIES TO GIVE HIM.
"THUS HE GREW UP JEALOUS AND EMBITTERED, AND DETERMINED TO REVENGE HIMSELF ON THOSE WHO ONCE DISMISSED HIM.
"HE HAS SURVIVED THE DEATHS OF TWO OF HIS ELDER BROTHERS, AND MEANS TO SURVIVE RICHARD AS WELL."
JOHN, I THINK YOU KNOW WHY I HAVE SUMMONED YOU TO ME...
"AFTER THE CORONATION, WHEN RICHARD ANNOUNCED HIS PLANS TO GO ON CRUSADE, JOHN THOUGHT HIS MOMENT HAD COME.
"HE WAS CERTAIN HE WOULD BE LEFT REGENT IN THE KING'S ABSENCE, AND COULD USE HIS POWER TO SEIZE THE THRONE FOR HIMSELF.
"HE WAS MISTAKEN."
...I AM GIVING YOU FIVE COUNTIES TO GOVERN WHILE I AM IN THE HOLY LAND.
RULE THEM WELL FOR ME, AND YOU WILL NOT FIND ME UNGRATEFUL.
BUT... THE REGENCY...
I'VE APPOINTED MOTHER.
OBEY HER IN ALL THINGS AS YOU WOULD ME.
NOW LEAVE US, WE HAVE MUCH YET TO DO BEFORE MY DEPARTURE...
"AND THERE WAS FURTHER DISCOURAGEMENT IN STORE FOR THE PRINCE. FOR HE WOULD LATER LEARN OF A CONDITION TO HIS RULE OF THE FIVE COUNTIES...
"...WHICH WAS THAT HE MUST NOT VISIT THEM. NOR INDEED, WAS HE TO STEP FOOT ON ENGLISH SOIL FOR THE DURATION OF THE KING'S ABSENCE.
"RICHARD WAS NO FOOL. HE MEANT TO USE HIS BROTHER'S TALENTS, BUT IN SUCH A WAY THAT THWARTED HIS BROTHER'S AMBITIONS.

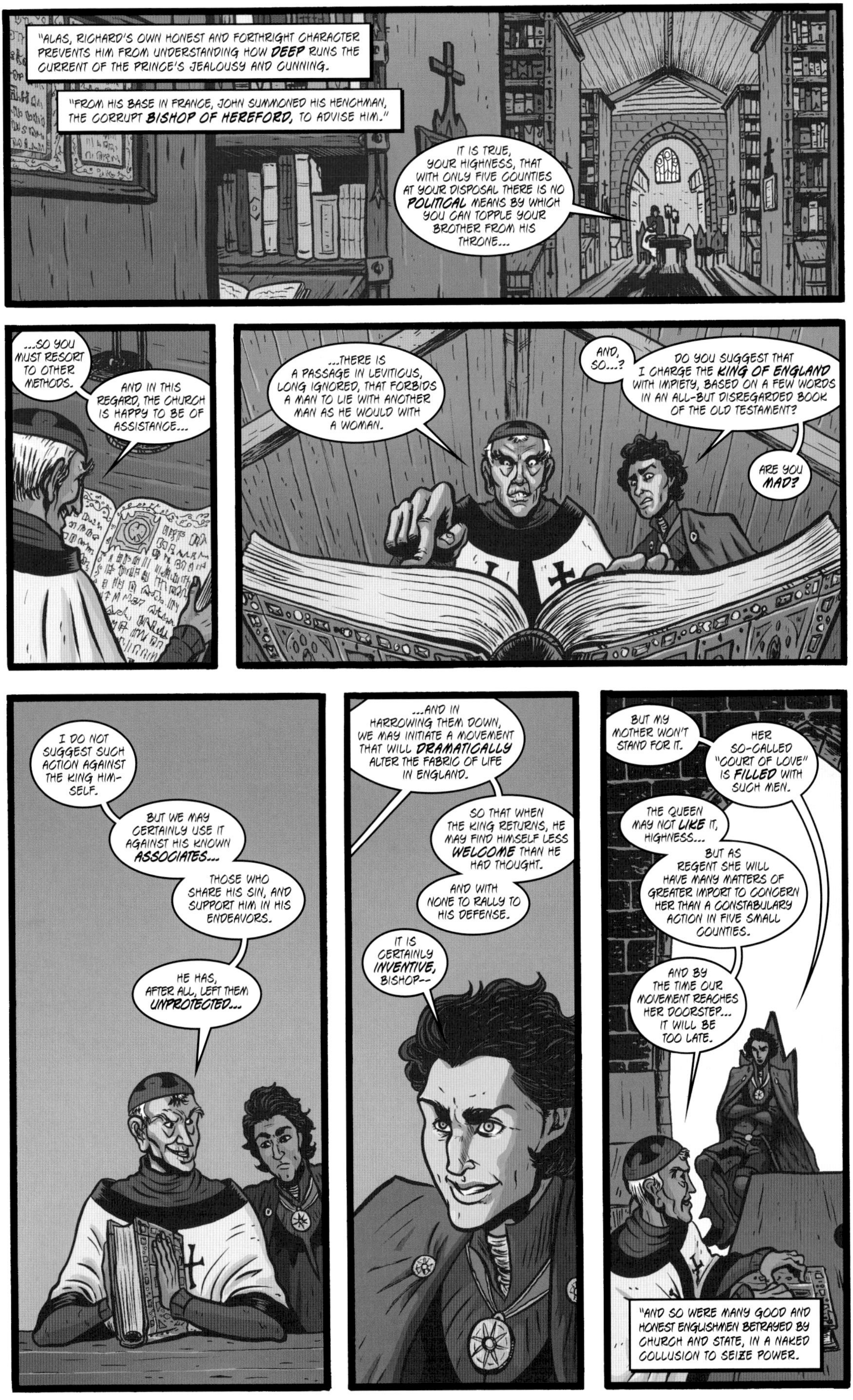

"ALAS, RICHARD'S OWN HONEST AND FORTHRIGHT CHARACTER PREVENTS HIM FROM UNDERSTANDING HOW DEEP RUNS THE CURRENT OF THE PRINCE'S JEALOUSY AND CUNNING.
"FROM HIS BASE IN FRANCE, JOHN SUMMONED HIS HENCHMAN, THE CORRUPT BISHOP OF HEREFORD, TO ADVISE HIM."
IT IS TRUE, YOUR HIGHNESS, THAT WITH ONLY FIVE COUNTIES AT YOUR DISPOSAL THERE IS NO POLITICAL MEANS BY WHICH YOU CAN TOPPLE YOUR BROTHER FROM HIS THRONE...
...SO YOU MUST RESORT TO OTHER METHODS.
AND IN THIS REGARD, THE CHURCH IS HAPPY TO BE OF ASSISTANCE...
...THERE IS A PASSAGE IN LEVITICUS, LONG IGNORED, THAT FORBIDS A MAN TO LIE WITH ANOTHER MAN AS HE WOULD WITH A WOMAN.
AND, SO...?
DO YOU SUGGEST THAT I CHARGE THE KING OF ENGLAND WITH IMPIETY, BASED ON A FEW WORDS IN AN ALL-BUT DISREGARDED BOOK OF THE OLD TESTAMENT?
ARE YOU MAD?
I DO NOT SUGGEST SUCH ACTION AGAINST THE KING HIM-SELF.
BUT WE MAY CERTAINLY USE IT AGAINST HIS KNOWN ASSOCIATES...
THOSE WHO SHARE HIS SIN, AND SUPPORT HIM IN HIS ENDEAVORS.
HE HAS, AFTER ALL, LEFT THEM UNPROTECTED...
...AND IN HARROWING THEM DOWN, WE MAY INITIATE A MOVEMENT THAT WILL DRAMATICALLY ALTER THE FABRIC OF LIFE IN ENGLAND.
SO THAT WHEN THE KING RETURNS, HE MAY FIND HIMSELF LESS WELCOME THAN HE HAD THOUGHT.
AND WITH NONE TO RALLY TO HIS DEFENSE.
IT IS CERTAINLY INVENTIVE, BISHOP--
BUT MY MOTHER WON'T STAND FOR IT.
HER SO-CALLED "COURT OF LOVE" IS FILLED WITH SUCH MEN.
THE QUEEN MAY NOT LIKE IT, HIGHNESS...
BUT AS REGENT SHE WILL HAVE MANY MATTERS OF GREATER IMPORT TO CONCERN HER THAN A CONSTABULARY ACTION IN FIVE SMALL COUNTIES.
AND BY THE TIME OUR MOVEMENT REACHES HER DOORSTEP... IT WILL BE TOO LATE.
"AND SO WERE MANY GOOD AND HONEST ENGLISHMEN BETRAYED BY CHURCH AND STATE, IN A NAKED COLLUSION TO SEIZE POWER.

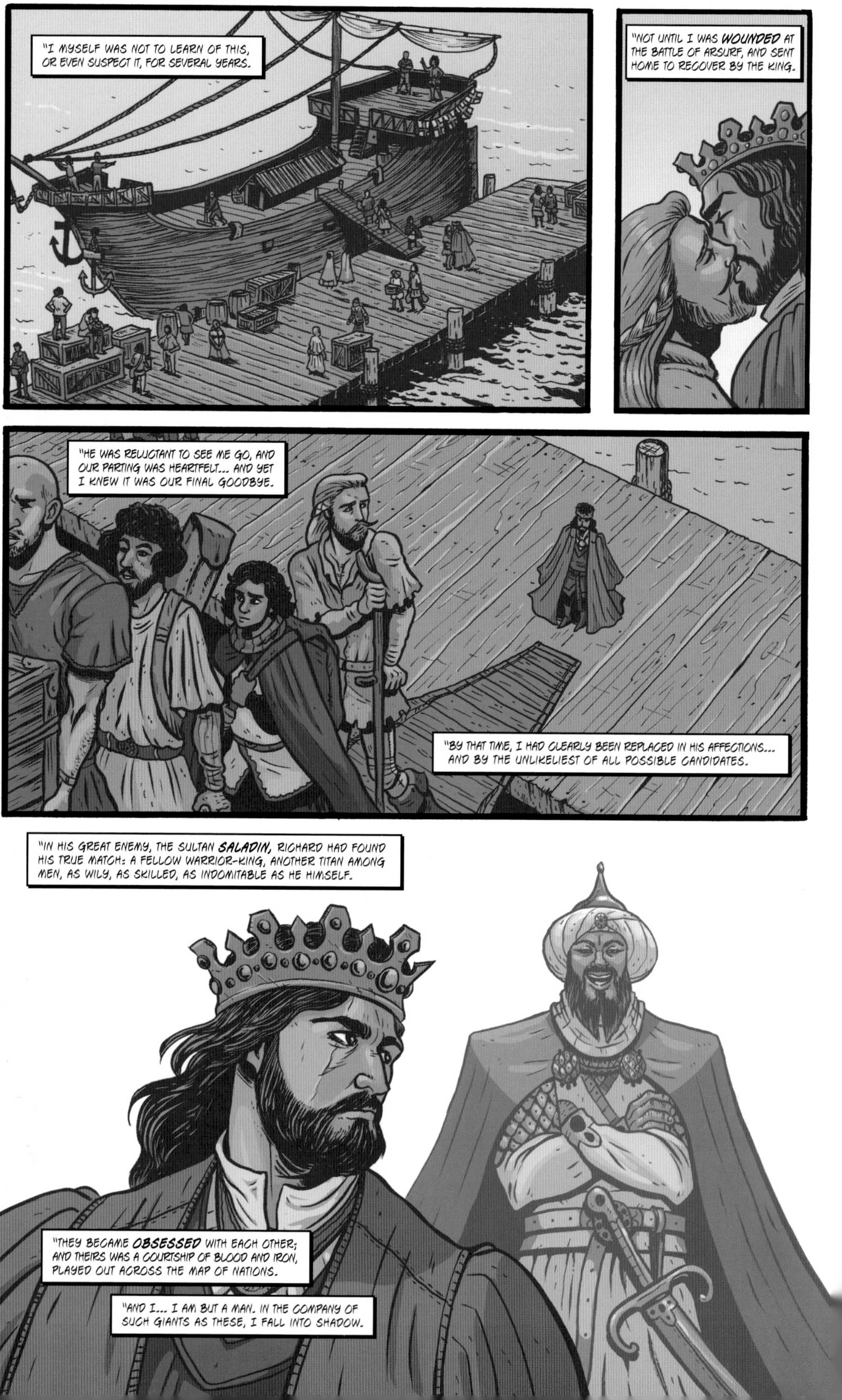
"I MYSELF WAS NOT TO LEARN OF THIS, OR EVEN SUSPECT IT, FOR SEVERAL YEARS.
"NOT UNTIL I WAS WOUNDED AT THE BATTLE OF ARSURF, AND SENT HOME TO RECOVER BY THE KING.
"HE WAS RELUCTANT TO SEE ME GO, AND OUR PARTING WAS HEARTFELT... AND YET I KNEW IT WAS OUR FINAL GOODBYE.
"BY THAT TIME, I HAD CLEARLY BEEN REPLACED IN HIS AFFECTIONS... AND BY THE UNLIKELIEST OF ALL POSSIBLE CANDIDATES.
"IN HIS GREAT ENEMY, THE SULTAN SALADIN, RICHARD HAD FOUND HIS TRUE MATCH: A FELLOW WARRIOR-KING, ANOTHER TITAN AMONG MEN, AS WILY, AS SKILLED, AS INDOMITABLE AS HE HIMSELF.
"THEY BECAME OBSESSED WITH EACH OTHER; AND THEIRS WAS A COURTSHIP OF BLOOD AND IRON, PLAYED OUT ACROSS THE MAP OF NATIONS.
"AND I... I AM BUT A MAN. IN THE COMPANY OF SUCH GIANTS AS THESE, I FALL INTO SHADOW.

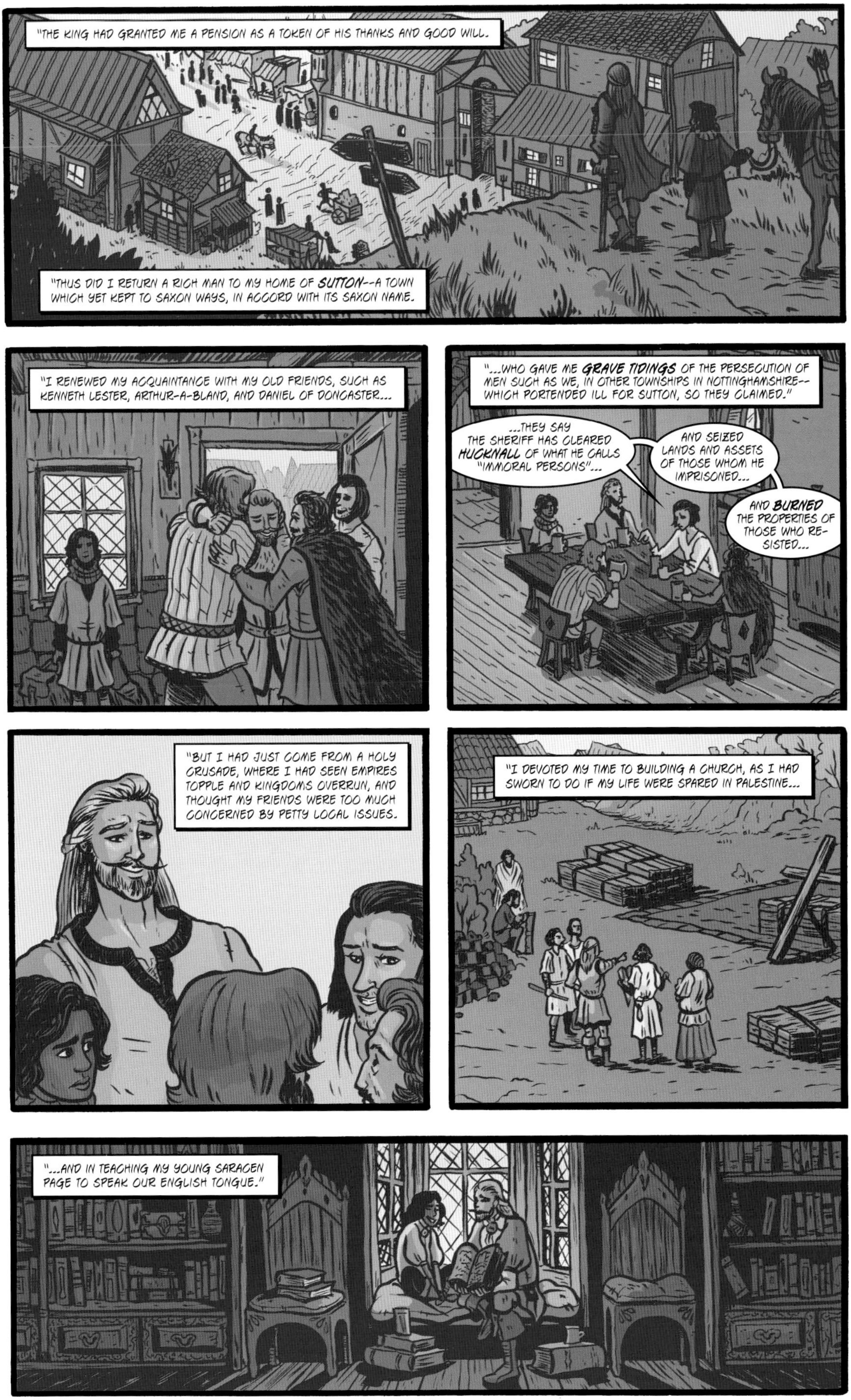
"THE KING HAD GRANTED ME A PENSION AS A TOKEN OF HIS THANKS AND GOOD WILL.
"THUS DID I RETURN A RICH MAN TO MY HOME OF SUTTON--A TOWN WHICH YET KEPT TO SAXON WAYS, IN ACCORD WITH ITS SAXON NAME.
"I RENEWED MY ACQUAINTANCE WITH MY OLD FRIENDS, SUCH AS KENNETH LESTER, ARTHUR-A-BLAND, AND DANIEL OF DONCASTER...
"...WHO GAVE ME GRAVE TIDINGS OF THE PERSECUTION OF MEN SUCH AS WE, IN OTHER TOWNSHIPS IN NOTTINGHAMSHIRE--WHICH PORTENDED ILL FOR SUTTON, SO THEY CLAIMED."
...THEY SAY THE SHERIFF HAS CLEARED HUCKNALL OF WHAT HE CALLS "IMMORAL PERSONS"...
AND SEIZED LANDS AND ASSETS OF THOSE WHOM HE IMPRISONED...
AND BURNED THE PROPERTIES OF THOSE WHO RE-SISTED...
"BUT I HAD JUST COME FROM A HOLY CRUSADE, WHERE I HAD SEEN EMPIRES TOPPLE AND KINGDOMS OVERRUN, AND THOUGHT MY FRIENDS WERE TOO MUCH CONCERNED BY PETTY LOCAL ISSUES.
"I DEVOTED MY TIME TO BUILDING A CHURCH, AS I HAD SWORN TO DO IF MY LIFE WERE SPARED IN PALESTINE...
"...AND IN TEACHING MY YOUNG SARACEN PAGE TO SPEAK OUR ENGLISH TONGUE."

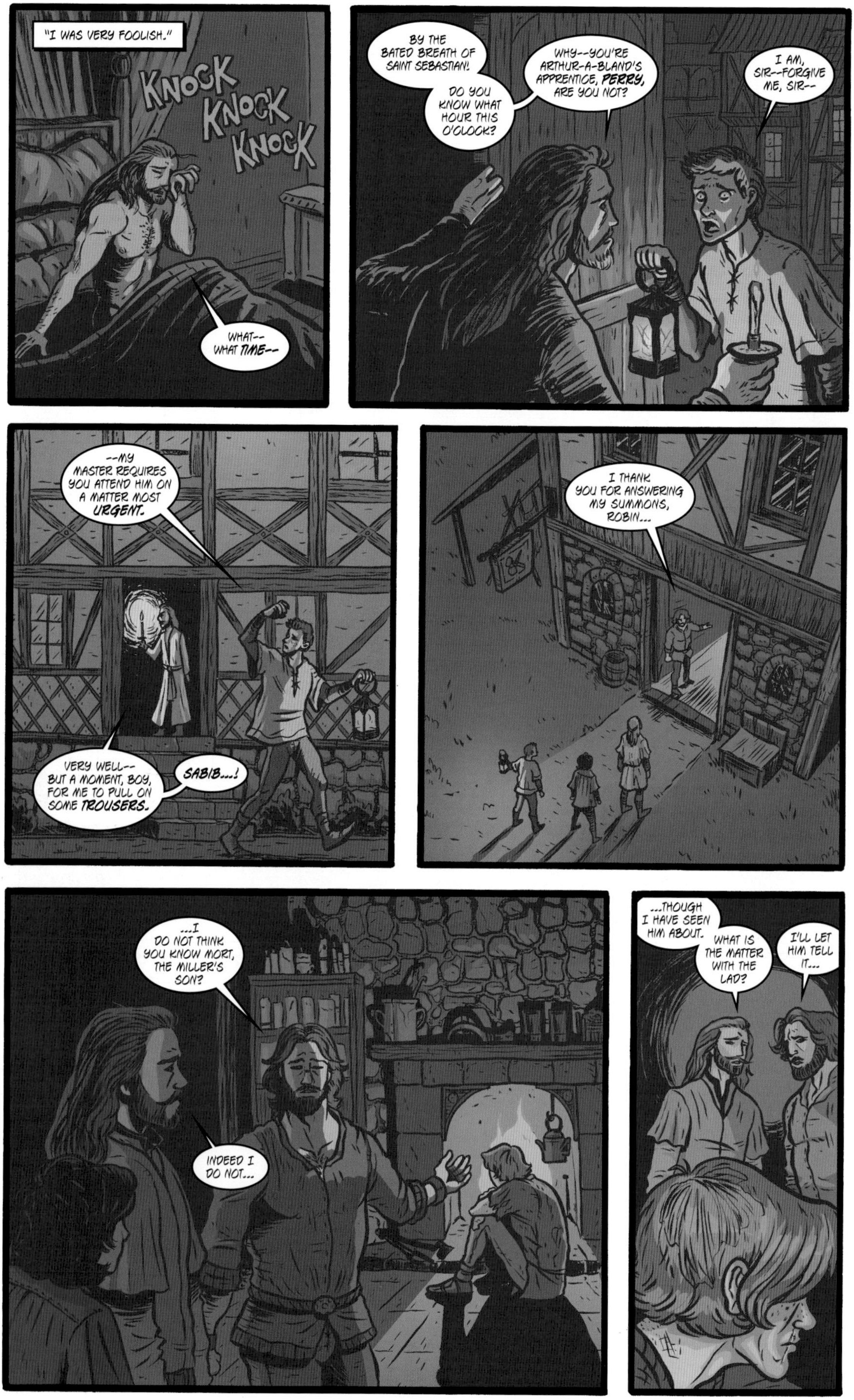
"I WAS VERY FOOLISH."
KNOCK KNOCK KNOCK
WHAT-- WHAT TIME--
BY THE BATED BREATH OF SAINT SEBASTIAN!
DO YOU KNOW WHAT HOUR THIS O'CLOCK?
WHY--YOU'RE ARTHUR-A-BLAND'S APPRENTICE, PERRY, ARE YOU NOT?
I AM, SIR--FORGIVE ME, SIR--
--MY MASTER REQUIRES YOU ATTEND HIM ON A MATTER MOST URGENT.
VERY WELL-- BUT A MOMENT, BOY, FOR ME TO PULL ON SOME TROUSERS.
SABIB...!
I THANK YOU FOR ANSWERING MY SUMMONS, ROBIN...
...I DO NOT THINK YOU KNOW MORT, THE MILLER'S SON?
INDEED I DO NOT...
...THOUGH I HAVE SEEN HIM ABOUT.
WHAT IS THE MATTER WITH THE LAD?
I'LL LET HIM TELL IT...

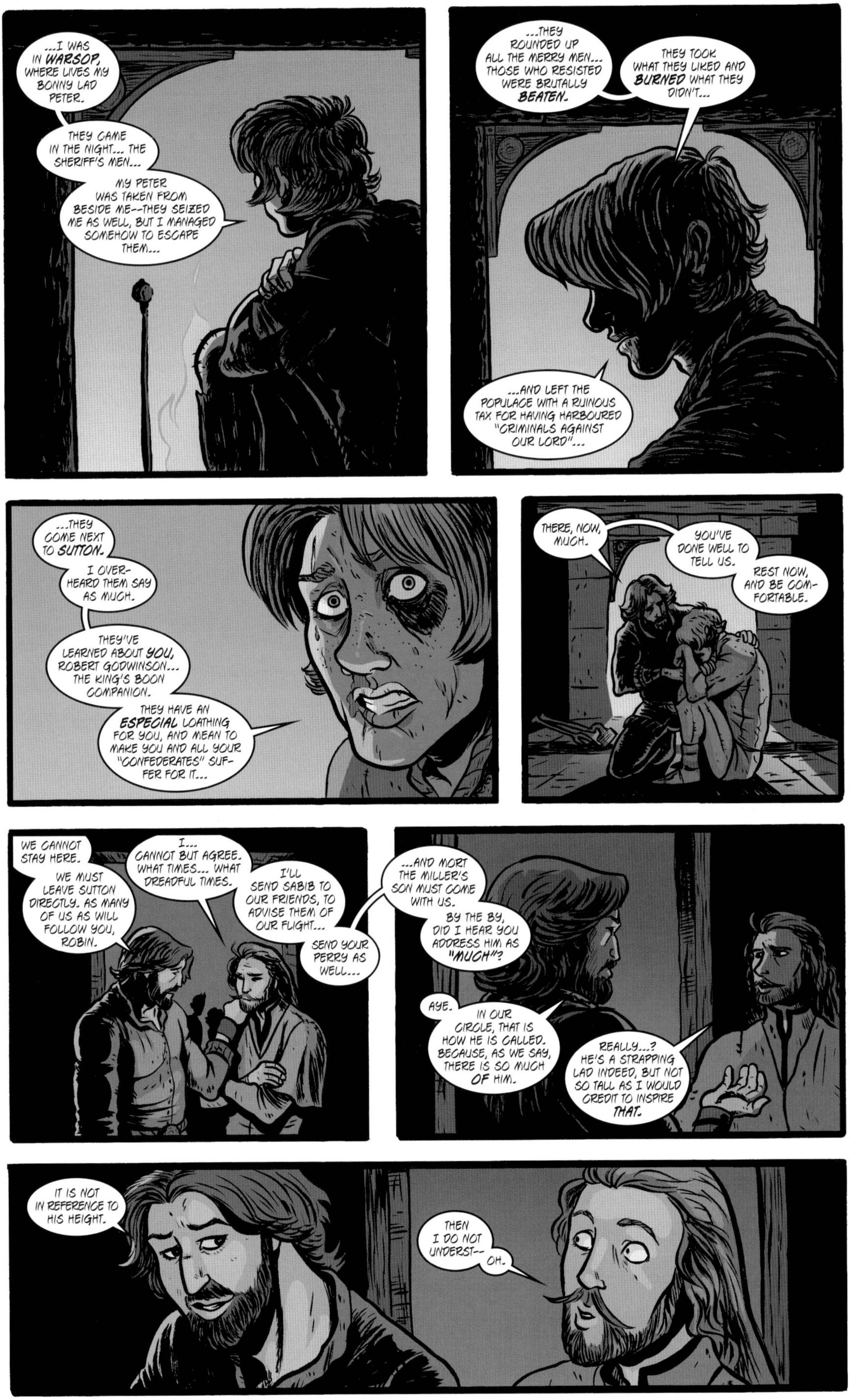

...I WAS IN WARSOP, WHERE LIVES MY BONNY LAD PETER.
THEY CAME IN THE NIGHT... THE SHERIFF'S MEN...
MY PETER WAS TAKEN FROM BESIDE ME--THEY SEIZED ME AS WELL, BUT I MANAGED SOMEHOW TO ESCAPE THEM...
...THEY ROUNDED UP ALL THE MERRY MEN... THOSE WHO RESISTED WERE BRUTALLY BEATEN.
THEY TOOK WHAT THEY LIKED AND BURNED WHAT THEY DIDN'T...
...AND LEFT THE POPULACE WITH A RUINOUS TAX FOR HAVING HARBOURED "CRIMINALS AGAINST OUR LORD"...
...THEY COME NEXT TO SUTTON.
I OVERHEARD THEM SAY AS MUCH.
THEY'VE LEARNED ABOUT YOU, ROBERT GODWINSON... THE KING'S BOON COMPANION.
THEY HAVE AN ESPECIAL LOATHING FOR YOU, AND MEAN TO MAKE YOU AND ALL YOUR "CONFEDERATES" SUFFER FOR IT...
THERE, NOW, MUCH.
YOU'VE DONE WELL TO TELL US.
REST NOW, AND BE COMFORTABLE.
WE CANNOT STAY HERE.
WE MUST LEAVE SUTTON DIRECTLY. AS MANY OF US AS WILL FOLLOW YOU, ROBIN.
I... CANNOT BUT AGREE. WHAT TIMES... WHAT DREADFUL TIMES.
I'LL SEND SABIB TO OUR FRIENDS, TO ADVISE THEM OF OUR FLIGHT...
SEND YOUR PERRY AS WELL...
...AND MORT THE MILLER'S SON MUST COME WITH US.
BY THE BY, DID I HEAR YOU ADDRESS HIM AS "MUCH"?
AYE.
IN OUR CIRCLE, THAT IS HOW HE IS CALLED. BECAUSE, AS WE SAY, THERE IS SO MUCH OF HIM.
REALLY...? HE'S A STRAPPING LAD INDEED, BUT NOT SO TALL AS I WOULD CREDIT TO INSPIRE THAT.
IT IS NOT IN REFERENCE TO HIS HEIGHT.
THEN I DO NOT UNDERST-- OH.

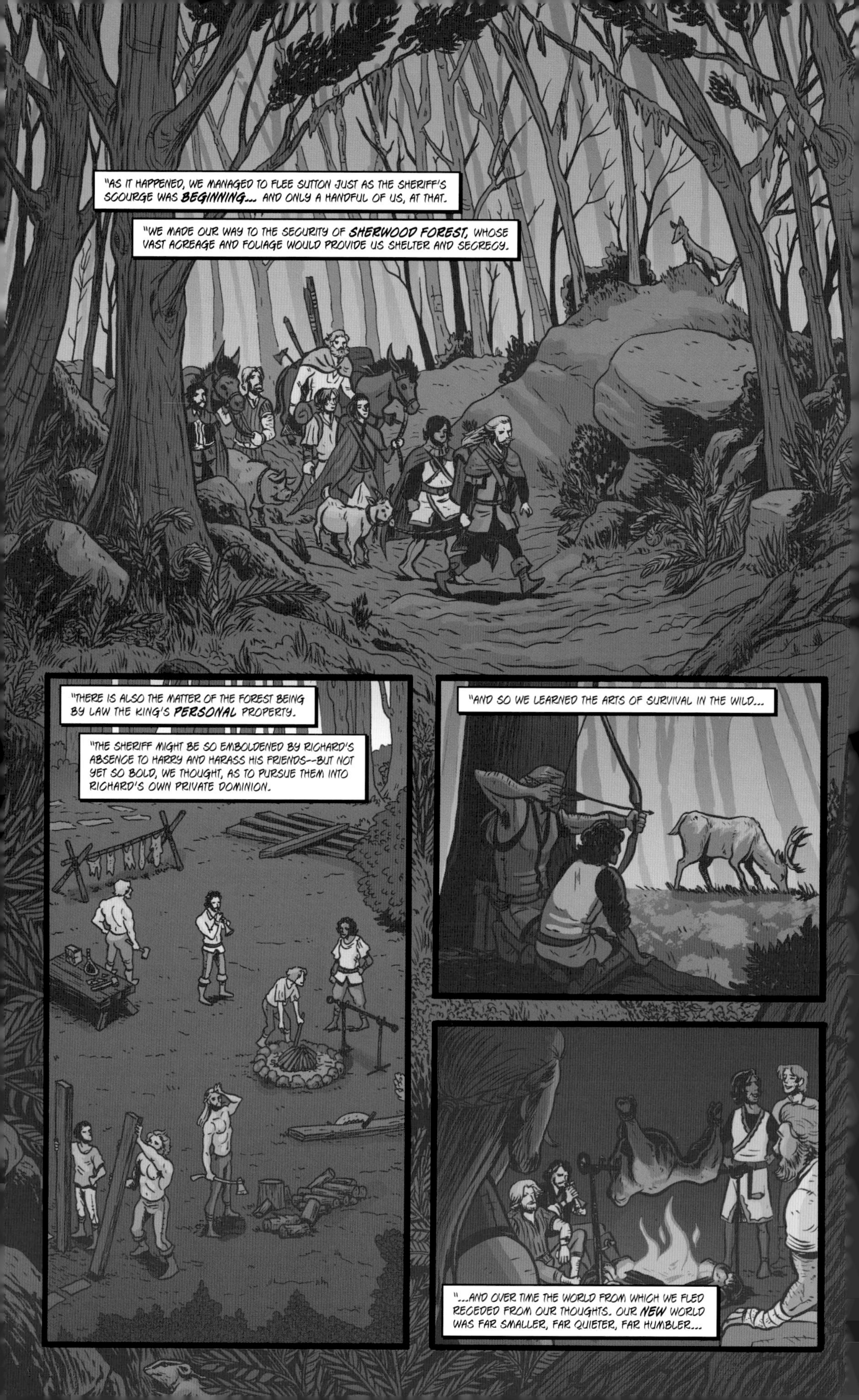
"AS IT HAPPENED, WE MANAGED TO FLEE SUTTON JUST AS THE SHERIFF'S SCOURGE WAS BEGINNING... AND ONLY A HANDFUL OF US, AT THAT.
"WE MADE OUR WAY TO THE SECURITY OF SHERWOOD FOREST, WHOSE VAST ACREAGE AND FOLIAGE WOULD PROVIDE US SHELTER AND SECRECY.
"THERE IS ALSO THE MATTER OF THE FOREST BEING BY LAW THE KING'S PERSONAL PROPERTY.
"THE SHERIFF MIGHT BE SO EMBOLDENED BY RICHARD'S ABSENCE TO HARRY AND HARASS HIS FRIENDS--BUT NOT YET SO BOLD, WE THOUGHT, AS TO PURSUE THEM INTO RICHARD'S OWN PRIVATE DOMINION.
"AND SO WE LEARNED THE ARTS OF SURVIVAL IN THE WILD...
"...AND OVER TIME THE WORLD FROM WHICH WE FLED RECEDED FROM OUR THOUGHTS. OUR NEW WORLD WAS FAR SMALLER, FAR QUIETER, FAR HUMBLER...

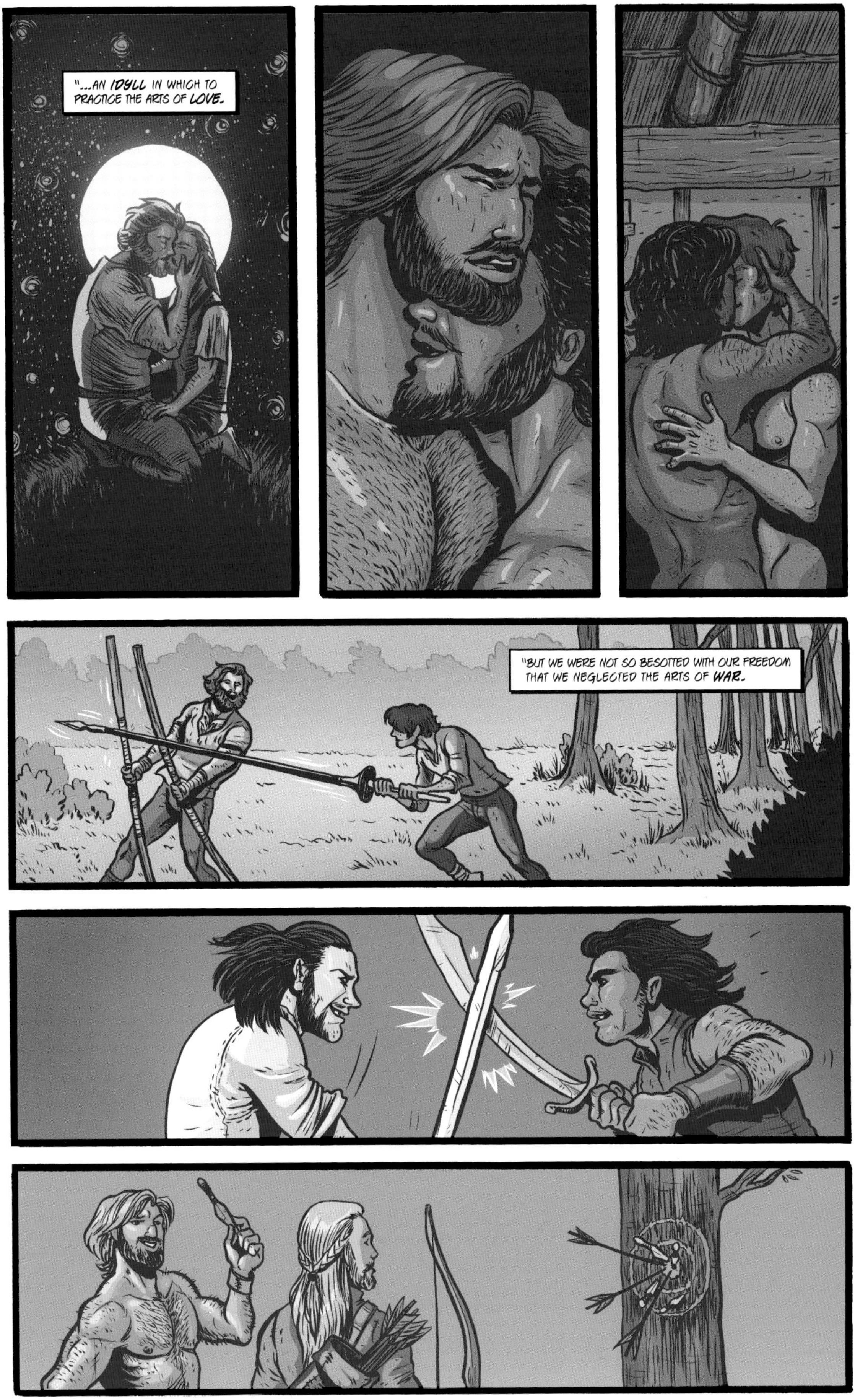
"...AN IDYLL IN WHICH TO PRACTICE THE ARTS OF LOVE.
"BUT WE WERE NOT SO BESOTTED WITH OUR FREEDOM THAT WE NEGLECTED THE ARTS OF WAR.

"AND SO WE HAVE REMAINED UNTIL THIS PRESENT TIME.

"WHY OUR FORTUNES HAVE NOW CHANGED, I CANNOT BE CERTAIN... BUT I CAN GUESS."

PRINCE JOHN IS IN A *RAGE*, SHERIFF...

...OF ALL HIS BROTHER'S FRIENDS AND ASSOCIATES, IT IS *ROBERT GODWINSON* WHO HE CHIEFLY WISHES APPREHENDED.

IF WE DO NOT SOON SECURE HIM, THE PRINCE WILL HAVE OUR *HEADS* FOR IT.

BUT GODWINSON AND HIS DAMNABLE ALLIES HAVE FLED INTO *SHERWOOD*, I AM TOLD...

...I HAVE NOT THE MANPOWER, NOR THE HOURS, TO POLICE AN ENTIRE *FOREST*.

THERE MAY BE NO NEED OF THAT, MY FRIEND...

...FOR IF WE CANNOT FIND OUR WAY TO *HIM*, WE CAN MAKE HIM COME TO *US*.

GODWINSON IS SAID TO BE A MAN OF THE *PEOPLE*. HE WILL NOT SIT IDLY BY WHILE INNOCENTS ARE MADE TO SUFFER.

TIGHTEN YOUR *IRON GRIP* OVER NOTTINGHAMSHIRE, SHERIFF.

PERSECUTE THOSE WHO OPPOSE YOU AND TERRORIZE THOSE WHO DO NOT.

WE WILL FORCE GODWINSON'S HAND.

WE WILL *MAKE* HIM COME TO THEIR RESCUE.

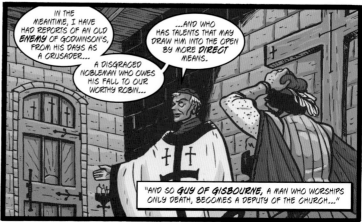

IN THE MEANTIME, I HAVE HAD REPORTS OF AN OLD *ENEMY* OF GODWINSON'S, FROM HIS DAYS AS A CRUSADER...

A DISGRACED NOBLEMAN WHO OWES HIS FALL TO OUR WORTHY ROBIN...

...AND WHO HAS TALENTS THAT MAY DRAW HIM INTO THE OPEN BY MORE *DIRECT* MEANS.

"AND SO *GUY OF GISBOURNE*, A MAN WHO WORSHIPS ONLY DEATH, BECOMES A DEPUTY OF THE CHURCH..."

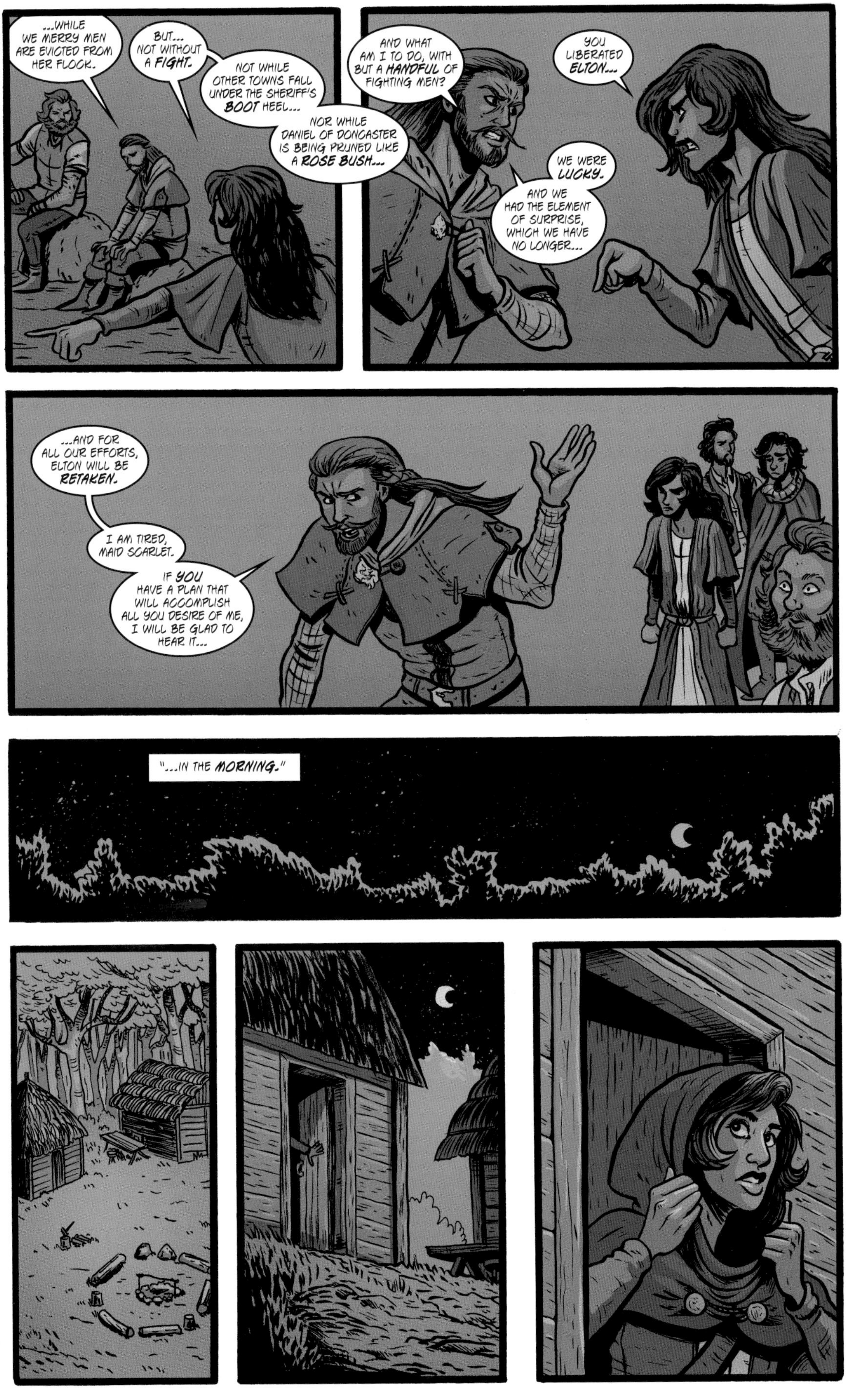
...WHILE WE MERRY MEN ARE EVICTED FROM HER FLOCK.
BUT... NOT WITHOUT A FIGHT.
NOT WHILE OTHER TOWNS FALL UNDER THE SHERIFF'S BOOT HEEL...
NOR WHILE DANIEL OF DONCASTER IS BEING PRUNED LIKE A ROSE BUSH...
AND WHAT AM I TO DO, WITH BUT A HANDFUL OF FIGHTING MEN?
YOU LIBERATED ELTON...
WE WERE LUCKY.
AND WE HAD THE ELEMENT OF SURPRISE, WHICH WE HAVE NO LONGER...
...AND FOR ALL OUR EFFORTS, ELTON WILL BE RETAKEN.
I AM TIRED, MAID SCARLET.
IF YOU HAVE A PLAN THAT WILL ACCOMPLISH ALL YOU DESIRE OF ME, I WILL BE GLAD TO HEAR IT...
"...IN THE MORNING."

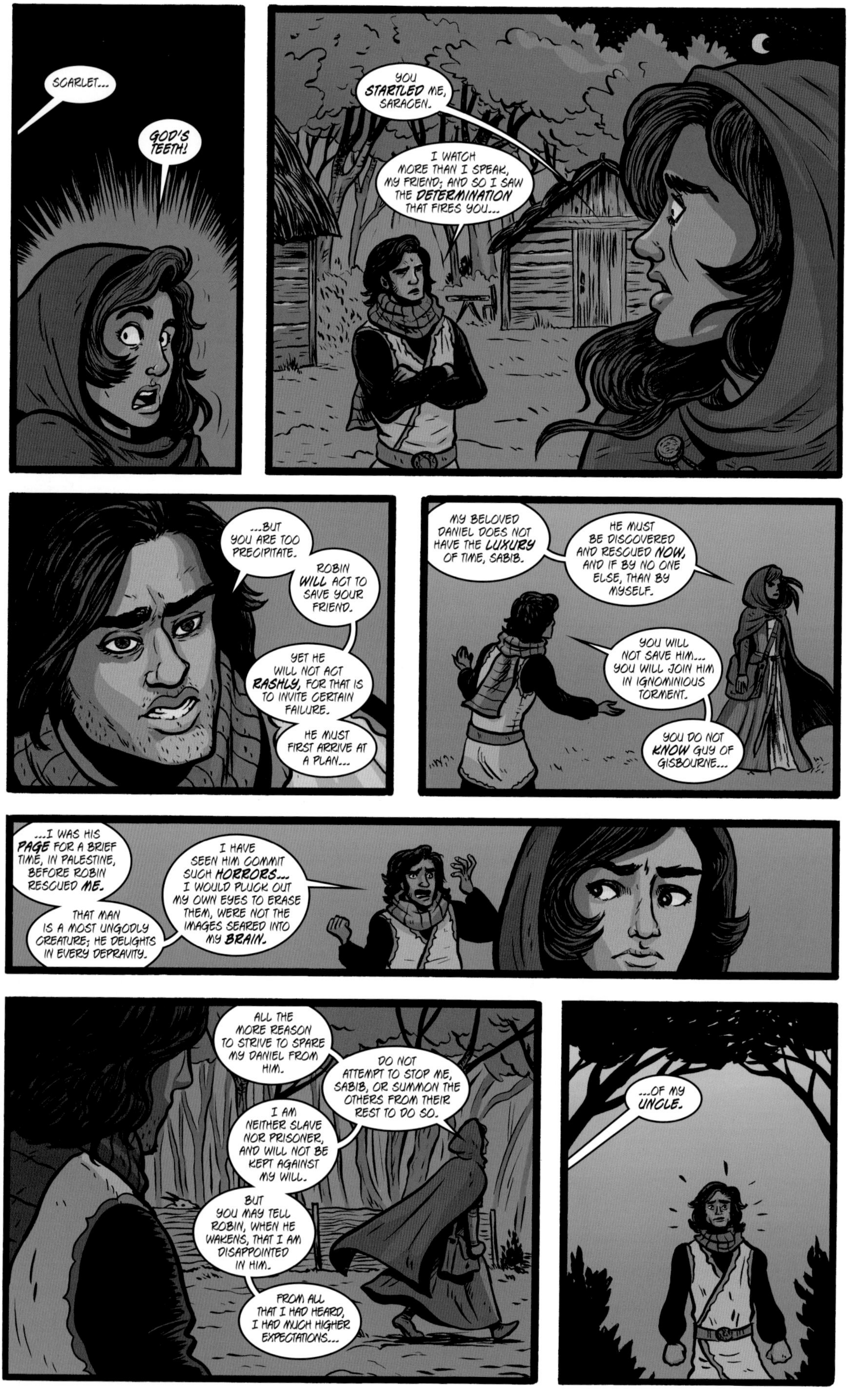
SCARLET...
GOD'S TEETH!
YOU STARTLED ME, SARACEN.
I WATCH MORE THAN I SPEAK, MY FRIEND; AND SO I SAW THE DETERMINATION THAT FIRES YOU...
...BUT YOU ARE TOO PRECIPITATE.
ROBIN WILL ACT TO SAVE YOUR FRIEND.
YET HE WILL NOT ACT RASHLY, FOR THAT IS TO INVITE CERTAIN FAILURE.
HE MUST FIRST ARRIVE AT A PLAN...
MY BELOVED DANIEL DOES NOT HAVE THE LUXURY OF TIME, SABIB.
HE MUST BE DISCOVERED AND RESCUED NOW, AND IF BY NO ONE ELSE, THAN BY MYSELF.
YOU WILL NOT SAVE HIM... YOU WILL JOIN HIM IN IGNOMINIOUS TORMENT.
YOU DO NOT KNOW GUY OF GISBOURNE...
...I WAS HIS PAGE FOR A BRIEF TIME, IN PALESTINE, BEFORE ROBIN RESCUED ME.
THAT MAN IS A MOST UNGODLY CREATURE; HE DELIGHTS IN EVERY DEPRAVITY.
I HAVE SEEN HIM COMMIT SUCH HORRORS... I WOULD PLUCK OUT MY OWN EYES TO ERASE THEM, WERE NOT THE IMAGES SEARED INTO MY BRAIN.
ALL THE MORE REASON TO STRIVE TO SPARE MY DANIEL FROM HIM.
DO NOT ATTEMPT TO STOP ME, SABIB, OR SUMMON THE OTHERS FROM THEIR REST TO DO SO.
I AM NEITHER SLAVE NOR PRISONER, AND WILL NOT BE KEPT AGAINST MY WILL.
BUT YOU MAY TELL ROBIN, WHEN HE WAKENS, THAT I AM DISAPPOINTED IN HIM.
FROM ALL THAT I HAD HEARD, I HAD MUCH HIGHER EXPECTATIONS...
...OF MY UNCLE.

Chapter

5

...MY *WHAT?*

AND YOU WAITED UNTIL NOW TO *TELL* ME THIS, SABIB?

I WAITED UNTIL SHE HAD GONE, ROBIN...

...AT *HER* REQUEST. SHE DID NOT WISH TO REMAIN, AND NO ONE HERE HAS SUFFICIENT CLAIM ON HER TO PREVENT HER.

"SUFFICIENT CLAIM"...?

YOU'VE JUST SAID I'M HER *UNCLE,* BOY!

WHAT-- WHAT'S THAT? *SCARLET* IS GONE, YOU SAY?

AYE, SHE'S GONE, AND SHE'S ALSO MY KIN, IT SEEMS.

MY SISTER EMMA'S CHILD, APPARENTLY RUN AWAY FROM HOME IN *BARNSDALE.*

I NEVER KNEW.

SHE DID NOT "RUN AWAY."

SHE IS OF AN AGE TO GO WHERE SHE CHOOSES.

AND OF AN AGE TO GET HERSELF KILLED, AS WELL.

NEVER MIND, IT FALLS TO *ME* TO FETCH THE FOOL BACK. BRING ME MY BOW AND QUIVER.

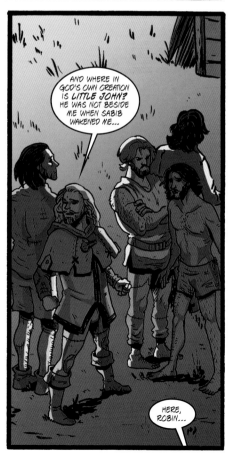

AND WHERE IN GOD'S OWN CREATION IS *LITTLE JOHN?* HE WAS NOT BESIDE ME WHEN SABIB WAKENED ME...

HERE, ROBIN...

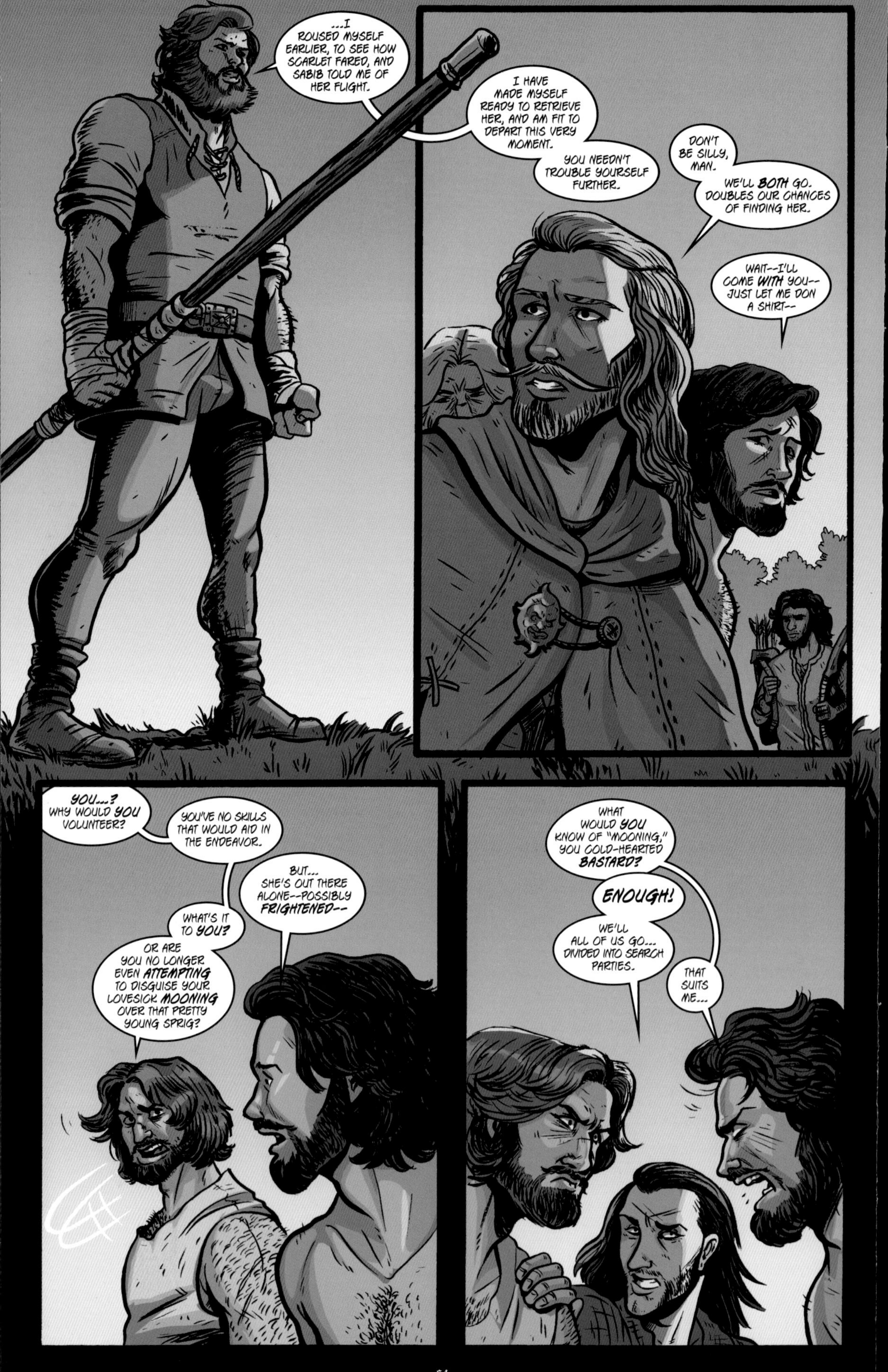
...I ROUSED MYSELF EARLIER, TO SEE HOW SCARLET FARED, AND SABIB TOLD ME OF HER FLIGHT.
I HAVE MADE MYSELF READY TO RETRIEVE HER, AND AM FIT TO DEPART THIS VERY MOMENT.
YOU NEEDN'T TROUBLE YOURSELF FURTHER.
DON'T BE SILLY, MAN.
WE'LL BOTH GO. DOUBLES OUR CHANCES OF FINDING HER.
WAIT--I'LL COME WITH YOU--JUST LET ME DON A SHIRT--
YOU...? WHY WOULD YOU VOLUNTEER?
YOU'VE NO SKILLS THAT WOULD AID IN THE ENDEAVOR.
BUT... SHE'S OUT THERE ALONE--POSSIBLY FRIGHTENED--
WHAT'S IT TO YOU?
OR ARE YOU NO LONGER EVEN ATTEMPTING TO DISGUISE YOUR LOVESICK MOONING OVER THAT PRETTY YOUNG SPRIG?
WHAT WOULD YOU KNOW OF "MOONING," YOU COLD-HEARTED BASTARD?
ENOUGH!
WE'LL ALL OF US GO... DIVIDED INTO SEARCH PARTIES.
THAT SUITS ME...

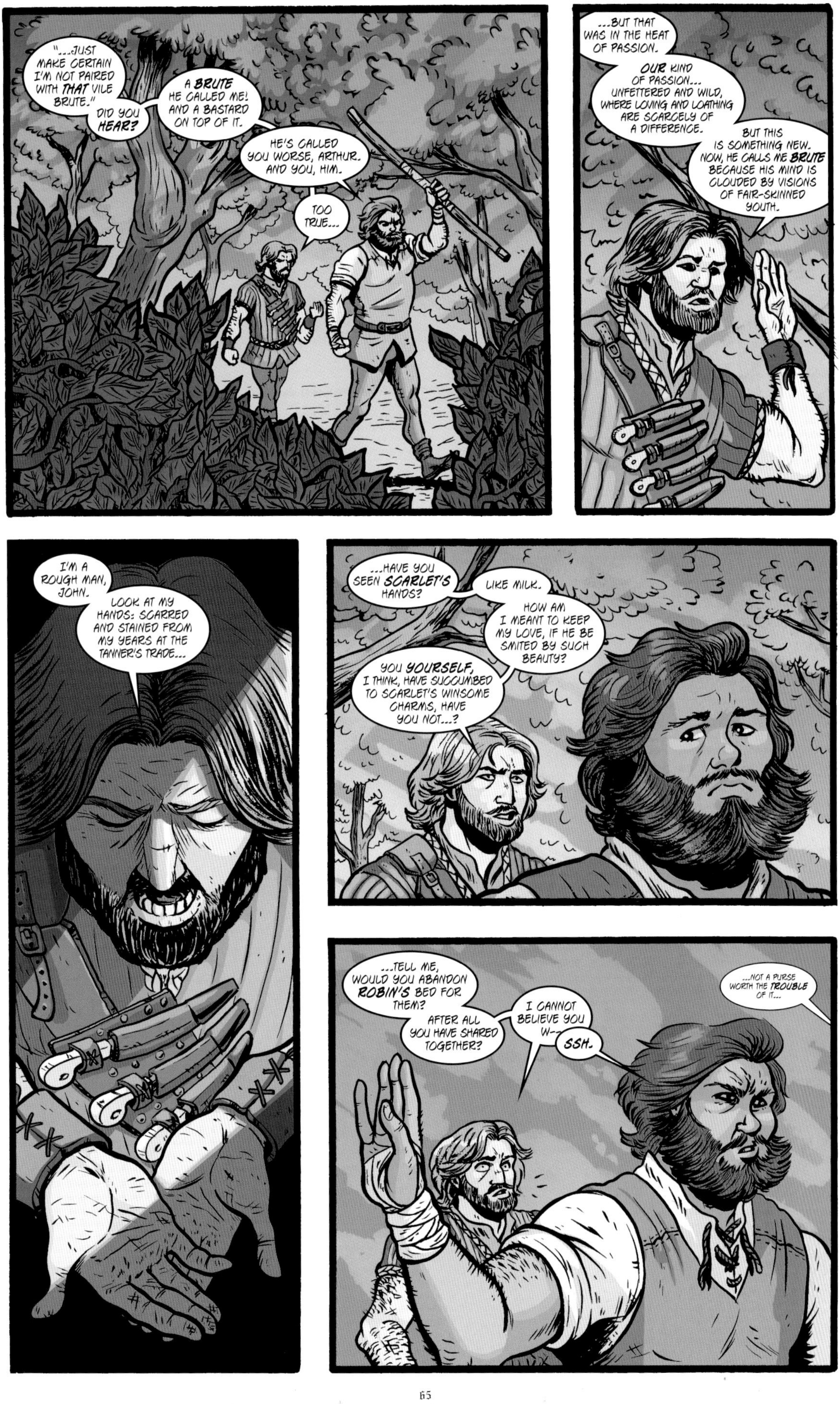
"...JUST MAKE CERTAIN I'M NOT PAIRED WITH THAT VILE BRUTE."
DID YOU HEAR?
A BRUTE HE CALLED ME! AND A BASTARD ON TOP OF IT.
HE'S CALLED YOU WORSE, ARTHUR. AND YOU, HIM.
TOO TRUE...
...BUT THAT WAS IN THE HEAT OF PASSION.
OUR KIND OF PASSION... UNFETTERED AND WILD, WHERE LOVING AND LOATHING ARE SCARCELY OF A DIFFERENCE.
BUT THIS IS SOMETHING NEW. NOW, HE CALLS ME BRUTE BECAUSE HIS MIND IS CLOUDED BY VISIONS OF FAIR-SKINNED YOUTH.
I'M A ROUGH MAN, JOHN.
LOOK AT MY HANDS: SCARRED AND STAINED FROM MY YEARS AT THE TANNER'S TRADE...
...HAVE YOU SEEN SCARLET'S HANDS?
LIKE MILK.
HOW AM I MEANT TO KEEP MY LOVE, IF HE BE SMITED BY SUCH BEAUTY?
YOU YOURSELF, I THINK, HAVE SUCCUMBED TO SCARLET'S WINSOME CHARMS, HAVE YOU NOT...?
...TELL ME, WOULD YOU ABANDON ROBIN'S BED FOR THEM?
AFTER ALL YOU HAVE SHARED TOGETHER?
I CANNOT BELIEVE YOU W--
SSH.
...NOT A PURSE WORTH THE TROUBLE OF IT...

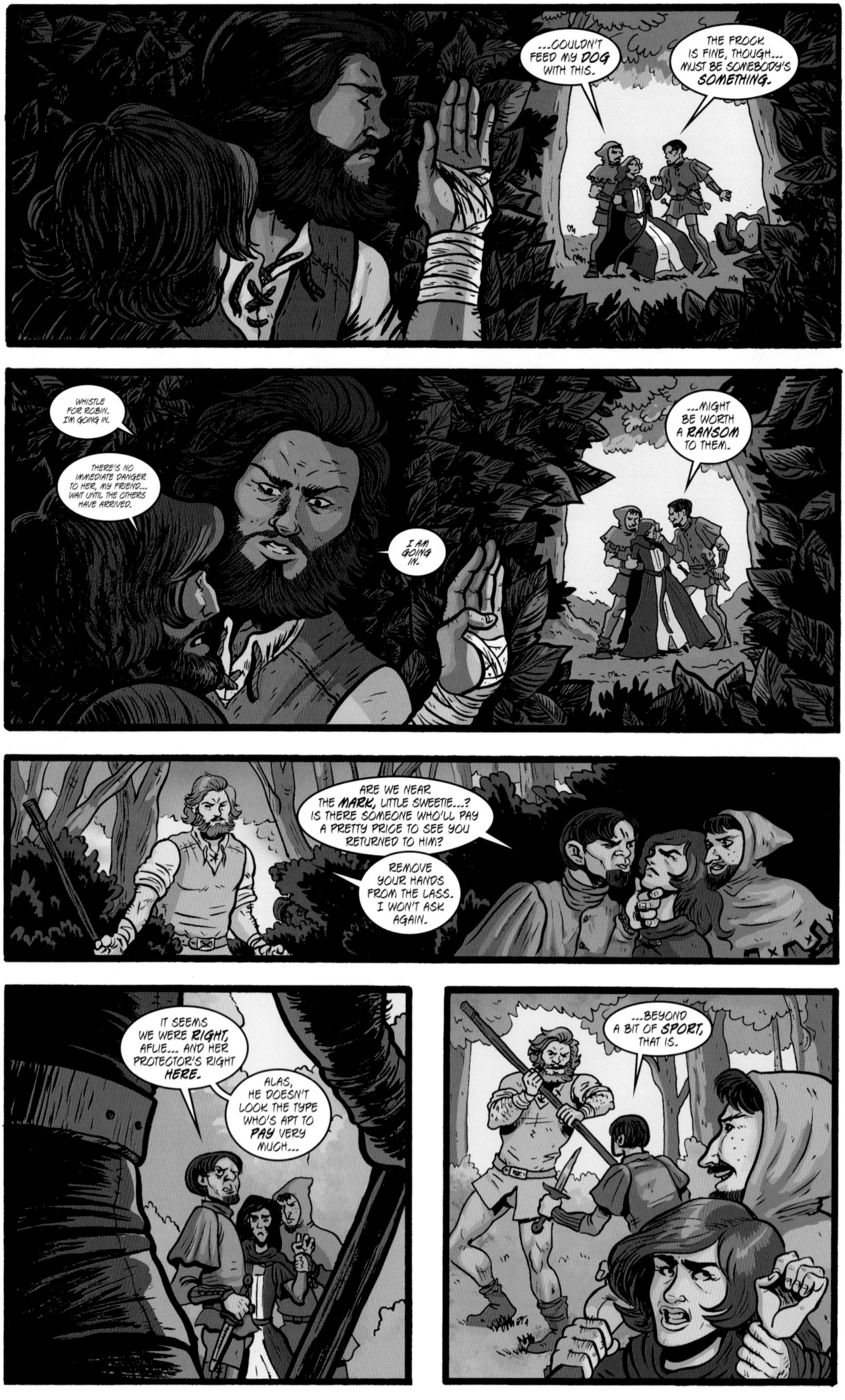
...COULDN'T FEED MY DOG WITH THIS.
THE FROCK IS FINE, THOUGH... MUST BE SOMEBODY'S SOMETHING.
WHISTLE FOR ROBIN. I'M GOING IN.
THERE'S NO IMMEDIATE DANGER TO HER, MY FRIEND... WAIT UNTIL THE OTHERS HAVE ARRIVED.
I AM GOING IN.
...MIGHT BE WORTH A RANSOM TO THEM.
ARE WE NEAR THE MARK, LITTLE SWEETIE...? IS THERE SOMEONE WHO'LL PAY A PRETTY PRICE TO SEE YOU RETURNED TO HIM?
REMOVE YOUR HANDS FROM THE LASS. I WON'T ASK AGAIN.
IT SEEMS WE WERE RIGHT, AFLIE... AND HER PROTECTOR'S RIGHT HERE.
ALAS, HE DOESN'T LOOK THE TYPE WHO'S APT TO PAY VERY MUCH...
...BEYOND A BIT OF SPORT, THAT IS.

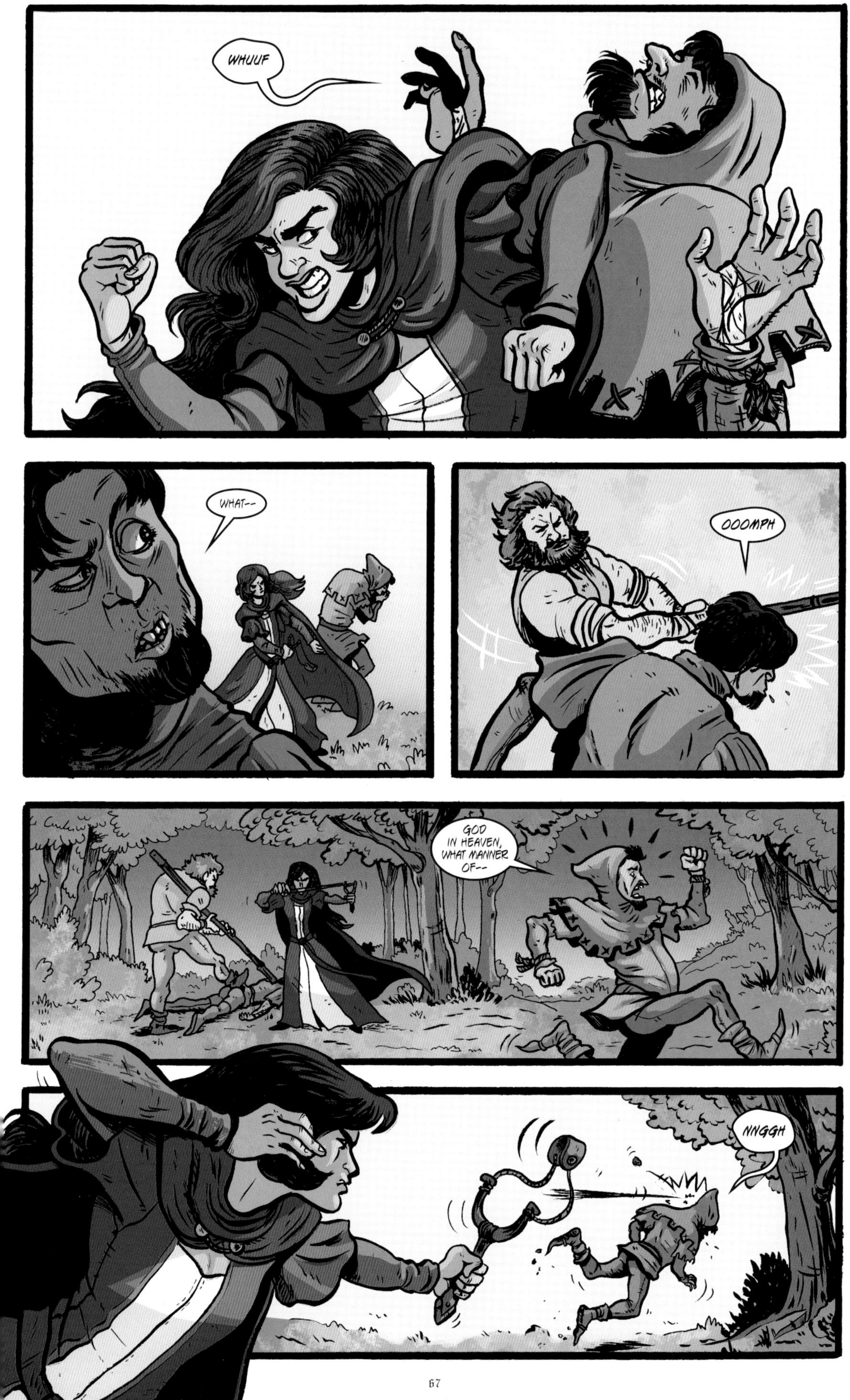
WHUUF
WHAT--
OOOMPH
GOD IN HEAVEN, WHAT MANNER OF--
NNGGH

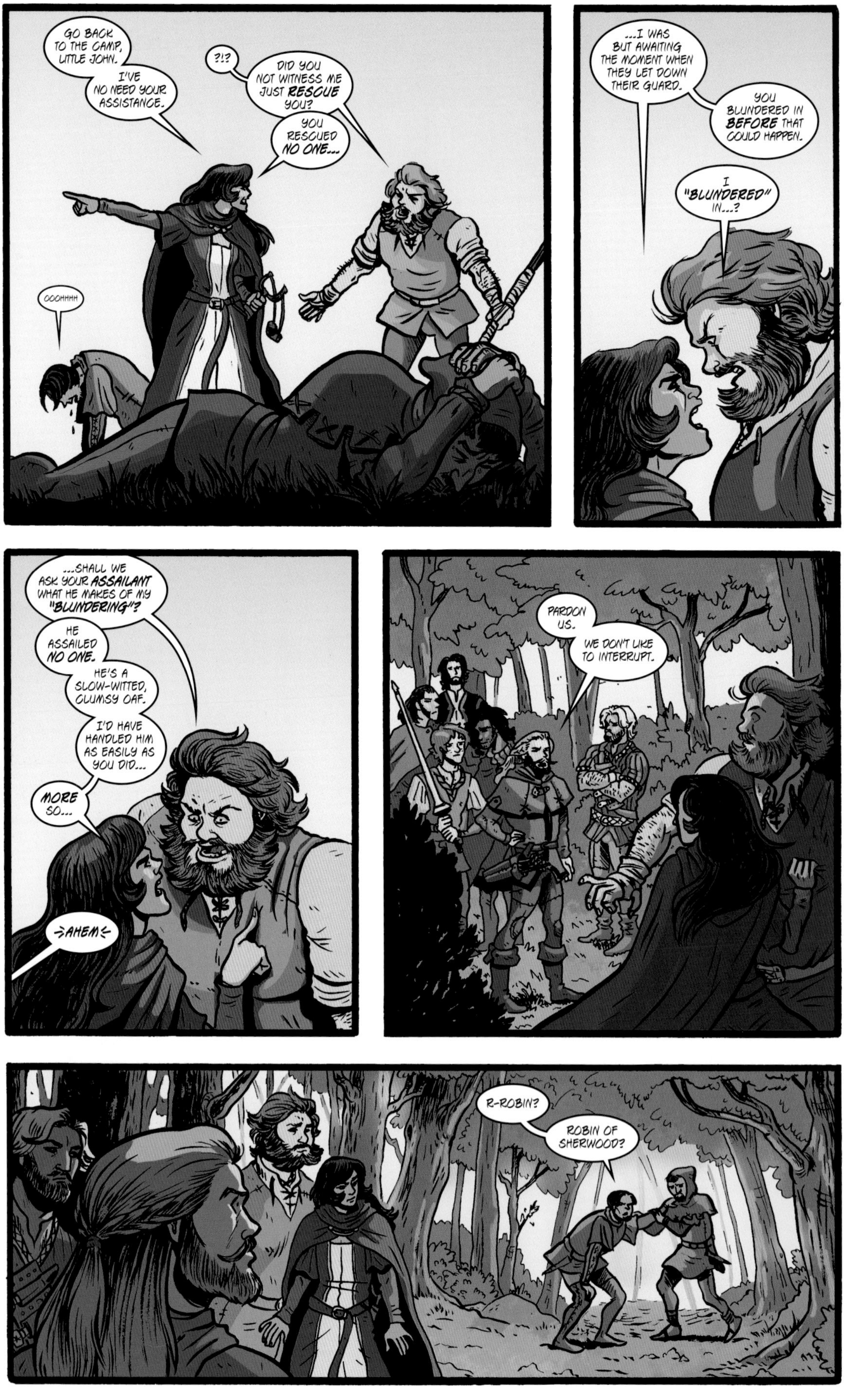
GO BACK TO THE CAMP, LITTLE JOHN.
I'VE NO NEED YOUR ASSISTANCE.
?!?
DID YOU NOT WITNESS ME JUST RESCUE YOU?
YOU RESCUED NO ONE...
OOOHHHH
...I WAS BUT AWAITING THE MOMENT WHEN THEY LET DOWN THEIR GUARD.
YOU BLUNDERED IN BEFORE THAT COULD HAPPEN.
I "BLUNDERED" IN...?
...SHALL WE ASK YOUR ASSAILANT WHAT HE MAKES OF MY "BLUNDERING"?
HE ASSAILED NO ONE.
HE'S A SLOW-WITTED, CLUMSY OAF.
I'D HAVE HANDLED HIM AS EASILY AS YOU DID...
MORE SO...
AHEM
PARDON US.
WE DON'T LIKE TO INTERRUPT.
R-ROBIN?
ROBIN OF SHERWOOD?

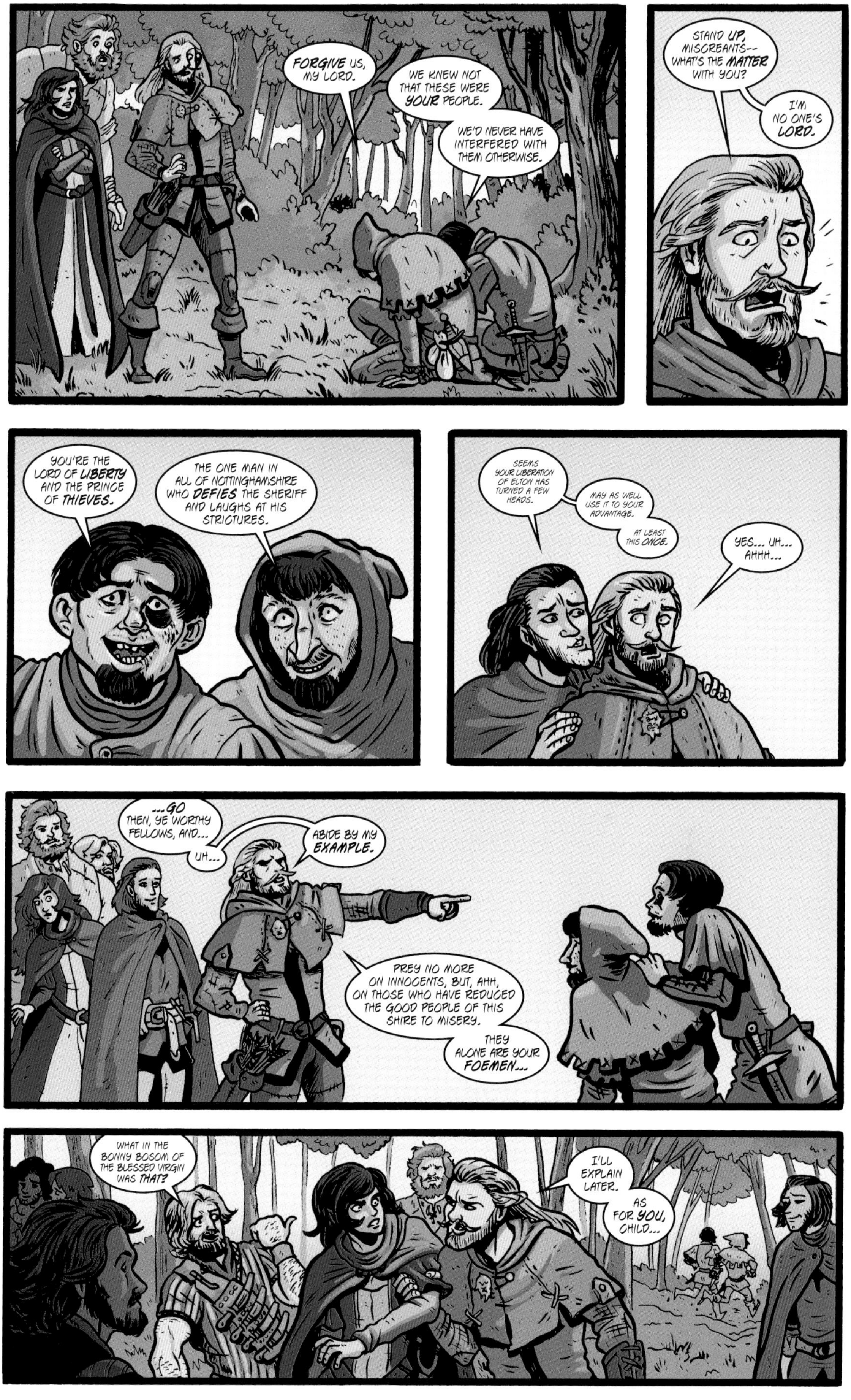
FORGIVE US, MY LORD.
WE KNEW NOT THAT THESE WERE YOUR PEOPLE.
WE'D NEVER HAVE INTERFERED WITH THEM OTHERWISE.
STAND UP, MISCREANTS-- WHAT'S THE MATTER WITH YOU?
I'M NO ONE'S LORD.
YOU'RE THE LORD OF LIBERTY AND THE PRINCE OF THIEVES.
THE ONE MAN IN ALL OF NOTTINGHAMSHIRE WHO DEFIES THE SHERIFF AND LAUGHS AT HIS STRICTURES.
SEEMS YOUR LIBERATION OF ELTON HAS TURNED A FEW HEADS.
MAY AS WELL USE IT TO YOUR ADVANTAGE.
AT LEAST THIS ONCE.
YES... UH... AHHH...
...GO THEN, YE WORTHY FELLOWS, AND...
UH...
ABIDE BY MY EXAMPLE.
PREY NO MORE ON INNOCENTS, BUT, AHH, ON THOSE WHO HAVE REDUCED THE GOOD PEOPLE OF THIS SHIRE TO MISERY.
THEY ALONE ARE YOUR FOEMEN...
WHAT IN THE BONNY BOSOM OF THE BLESSED VIRGIN WAS THAT?
I'LL EXPLAIN LATER.
AS FOR YOU, CHILD...

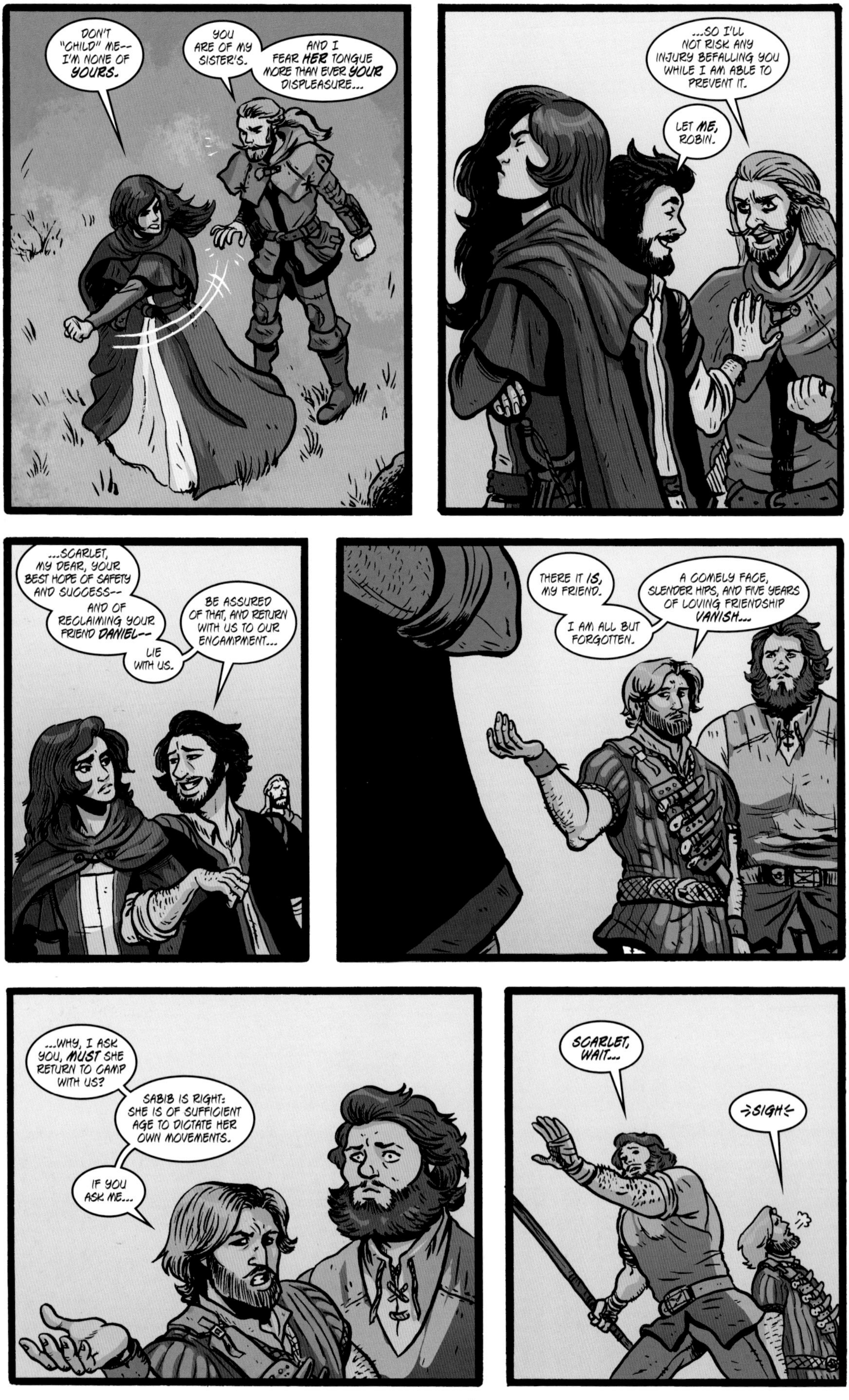
DON'T "CHILD" ME-- I'M NONE OF YOURS.
YOU ARE OF MY SISTER'S.
AND I FEAR HER TONGUE MORE THAN EVER YOUR DISPLEASURE...
...SO I'LL NOT RISK ANY INJURY BEFALLING YOU WHILE I AM ABLE TO PREVENT IT.
LET ME, ROBIN.
...SCARLET, MY DEAR, YOUR BEST HOPE OF SAFETY AND SUCCESS--
AND OF RECLAIMING YOUR FRIEND DANIEL--
LIE WITH US.
BE ASSURED OF THAT, AND RETURN WITH US TO OUR ENCAMPMENT...
THERE IT IS, MY FRIEND.
I AM ALL BUT FORGOTTEN.
A COMELY FACE, SLENDER HIPS, AND FIVE YEARS OF LOVING FRIENDSHIP VANISH...
...WHY, I ASK YOU, MUST SHE RETURN TO CAMP WITH US?
SABIB IS RIGHT: SHE IS OF SUFFICIENT AGE TO DICTATE HER OWN MOVEMENTS.
IF YOU ASK ME...
SCARLET, WAIT...
>SIGH<

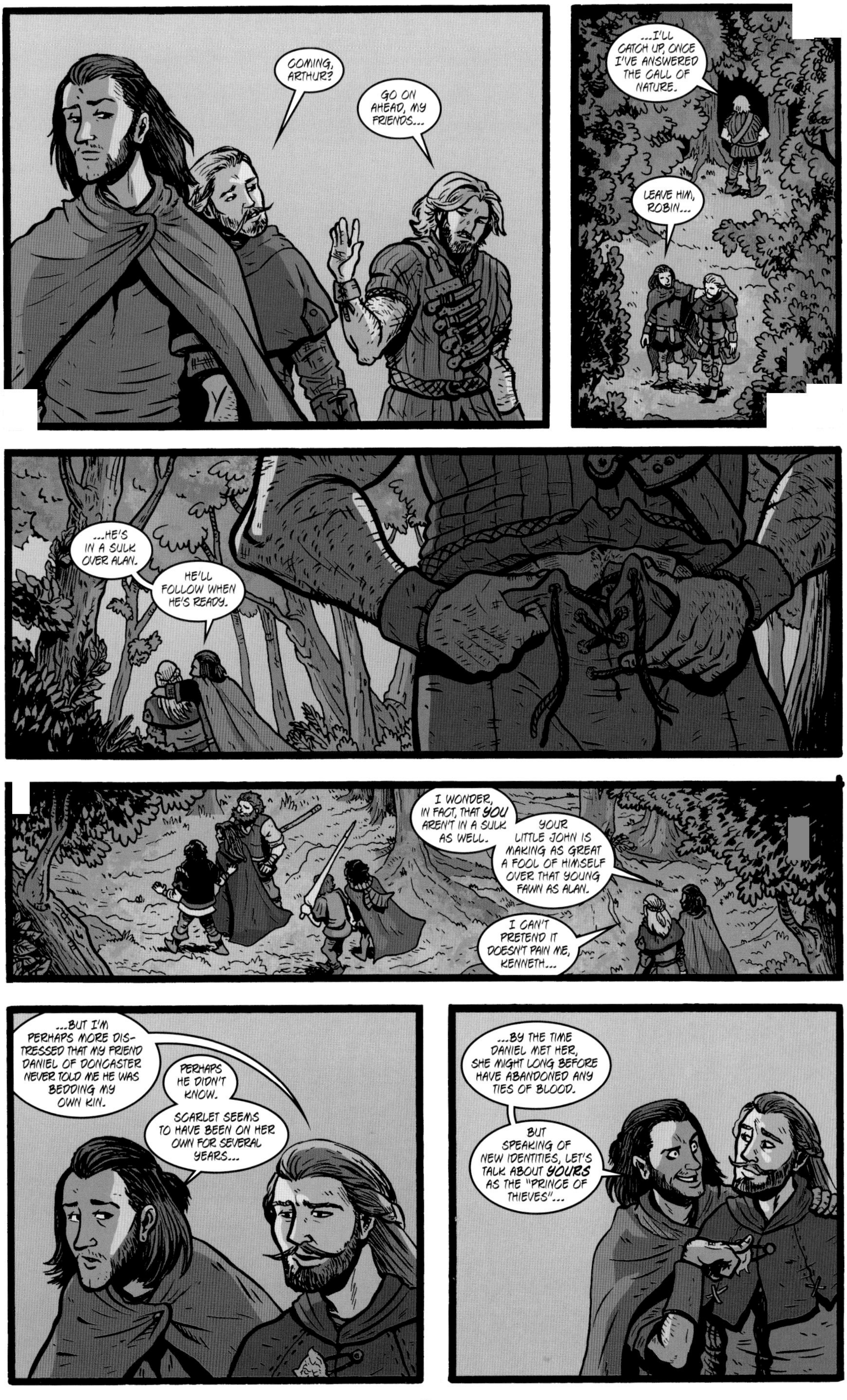
COMING, ARTHUR?
GO ON AHEAD, MY FRIENDS...
...I'LL CATCH UP, ONCE I'VE ANSWERED THE CALL OF NATURE.
LEAVE HIM, ROBIN...
...HE'S IN A SULK OVER ALAN.
HE'LL FOLLOW WHEN HE'S READY.
I WONDER, IN FACT, THAT YOU AREN'T IN A SULK AS WELL.
YOUR LITTLE JOHN IS MAKING AS GREAT A FOOL OF HIMSELF OVER THAT YOUNG FAWN AS ALAN.
I CAN'T PRETEND IT DOESN'T PAIN ME, KENNETH...
...BUT I'M PERHAPS MORE DIS-TRESSED THAT MY FRIEND DANIEL OF DONCASTER NEVER TOLD ME HE WAS BEDDING MY OWN KIN.
PERHAPS HE DIDN'T KNOW.
SCARLET SEEMS TO HAVE BEEN ON HER OWN FOR SEVERAL YEARS...
...BY THE TIME DANIEL MET HER, SHE MIGHT LONG BEFORE HAVE ABANDONED ANY TIES OF BLOOD.
BUT SPEAKING OF NEW IDENTITIES, LET'S TALK ABOUT YOURS AS THE "PRINCE OF THIEVES"...

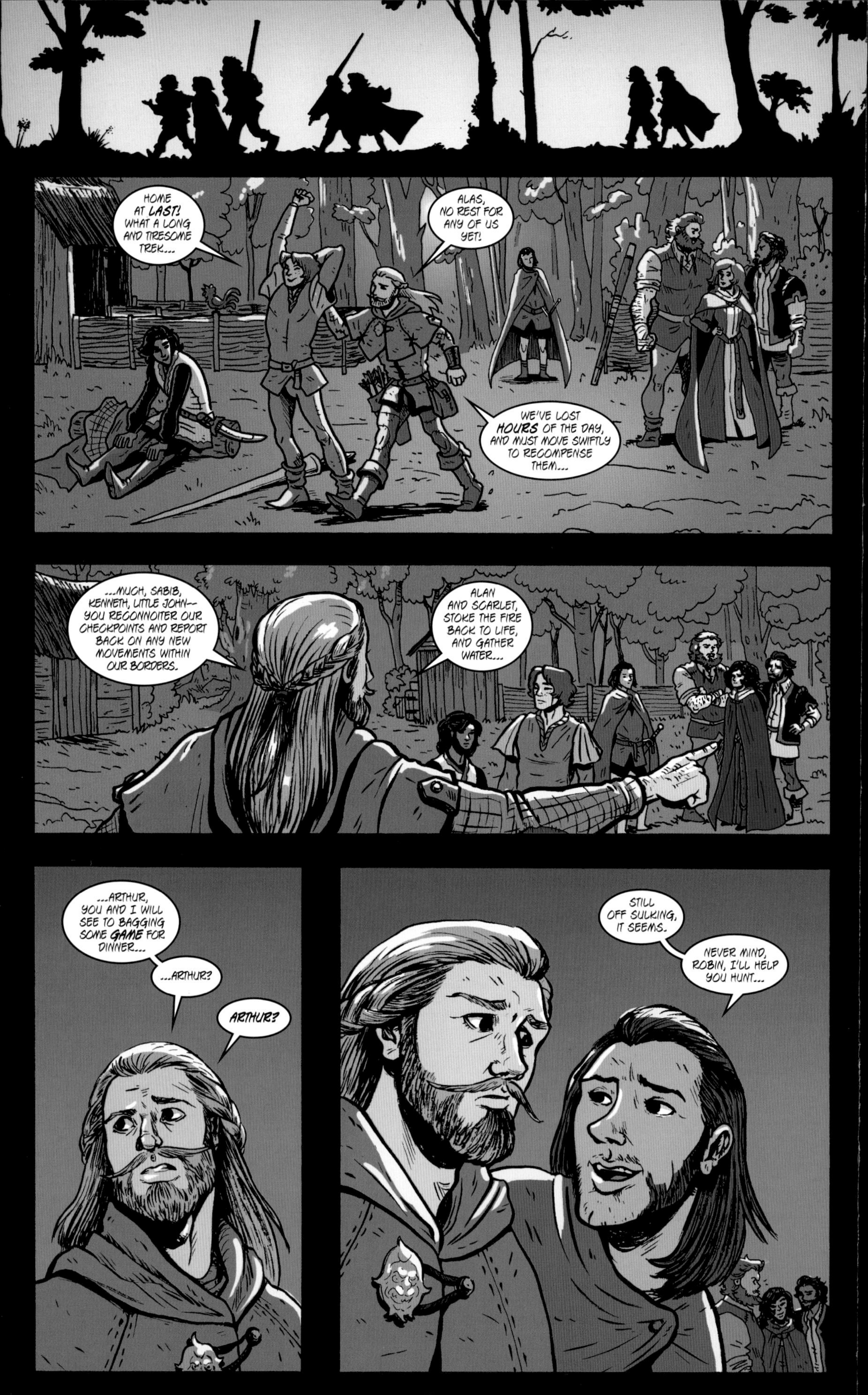
HOME AT LAST! WHAT A LONG AND TIRESOME TREK...
ALAS, NO REST FOR ANY OF US YET!
WE'VE LOST HOURS OF THE DAY, AND MUST MOVE SWIFTLY TO RECOMPENSE THEM...
...MUCH, SABIB, KENNETH, LITTLE JOHN-- YOU RECONNOITER OUR CHECKPOINTS AND REPORT BACK ON ANY NEW MOVEMENTS WITHIN OUR BORDERS.
ALAN AND SCARLET, STOKE THE FIRE BACK TO LIFE, AND GATHER WATER...
...ARTHUR, YOU AND I WILL SEE TO BAGGING SOME GAME FOR DINNER...
...ARTHUR?
ARTHUR?
STILL OFF SULKING, IT SEEMS.
NEVER MIND, ROBIN, I'LL HELP YOU HUNT...

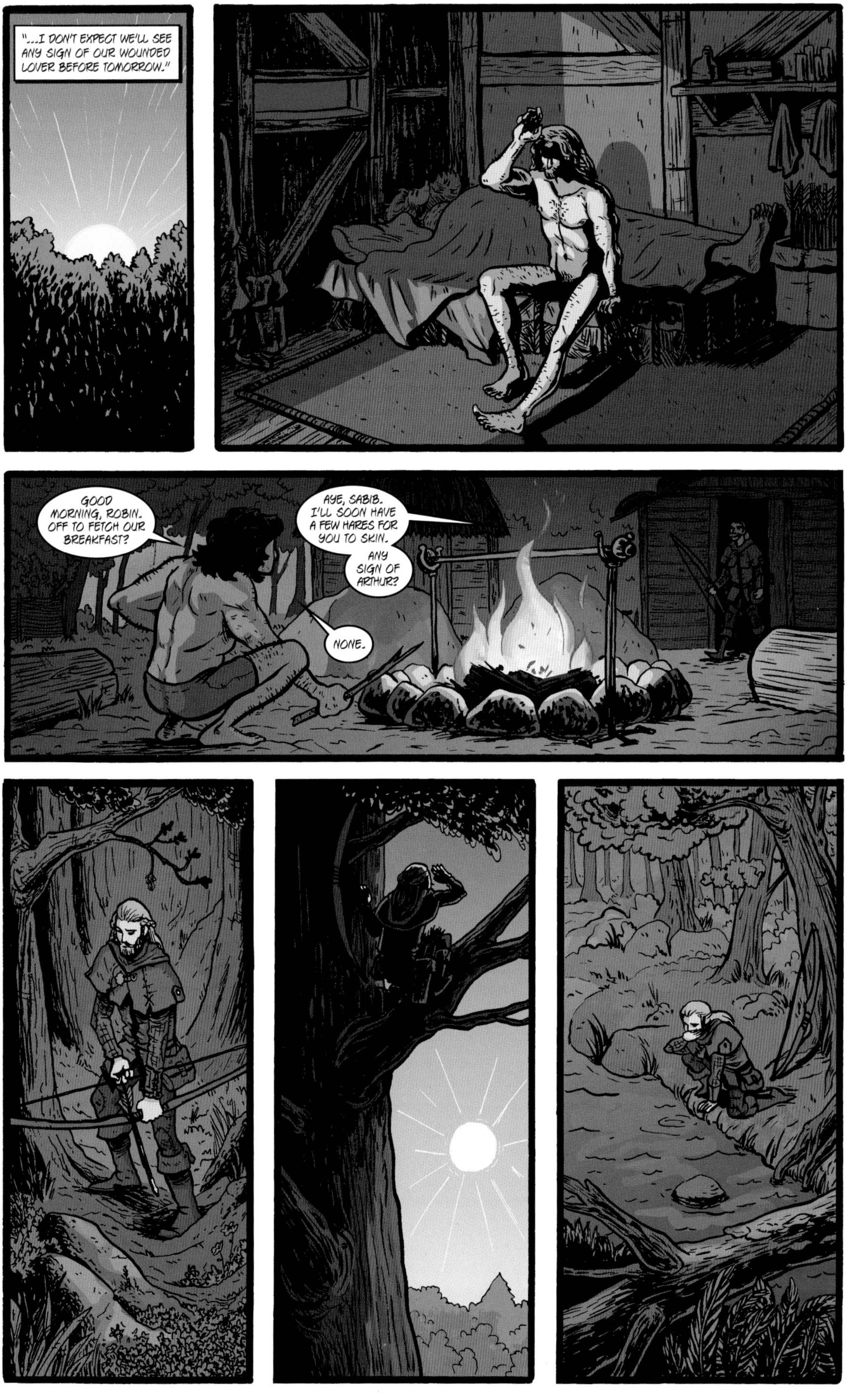
"...I DON'T EXPECT WE'LL SEE ANY SIGN OF OUR WOUNDED LOVER BEFORE TOMORROW."
GOOD MORNING, ROBIN. OFF TO FETCH OUR BREAKFAST?
AYE, SABIB. I'LL SOON HAVE A FEW HARES FOR YOU TO SKIN.
ANY SIGN OF ARTHUR?
NONE.

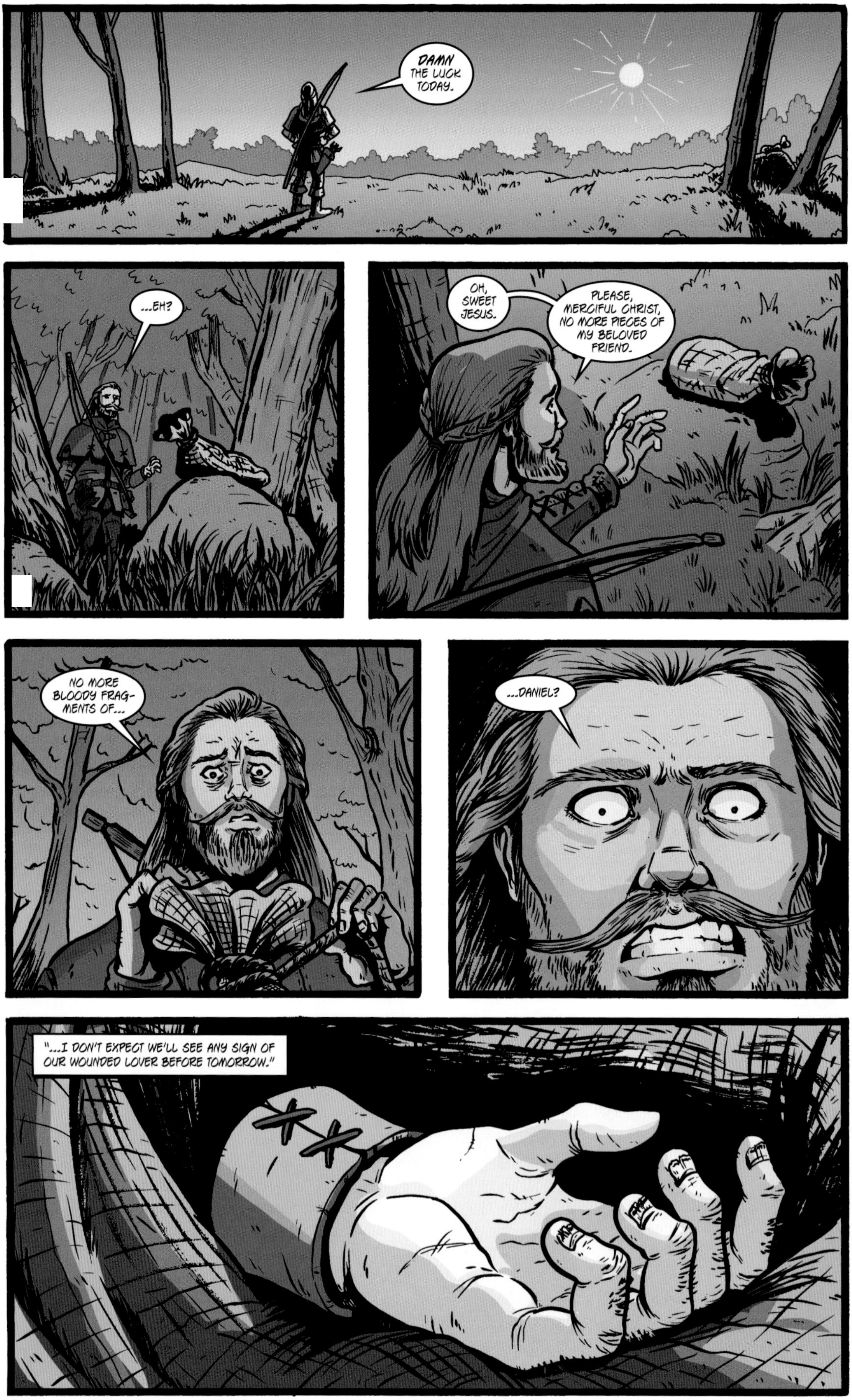
DAMN THE LUCK TODAY.
...EH?
OH, SWEET JESUS.
PLEASE, MERCIFUL CHRIST, NO MORE PIECES OF MY BELOVED FRIEND.
NO MORE BLOODY FRAGMENTS OF...
...DANIEL?
"...I DON'T EXPECT WE'LL SEE ANY SIGN OF OUR WOUNDED LOVER BEFORE TOMORROW."

Chapter

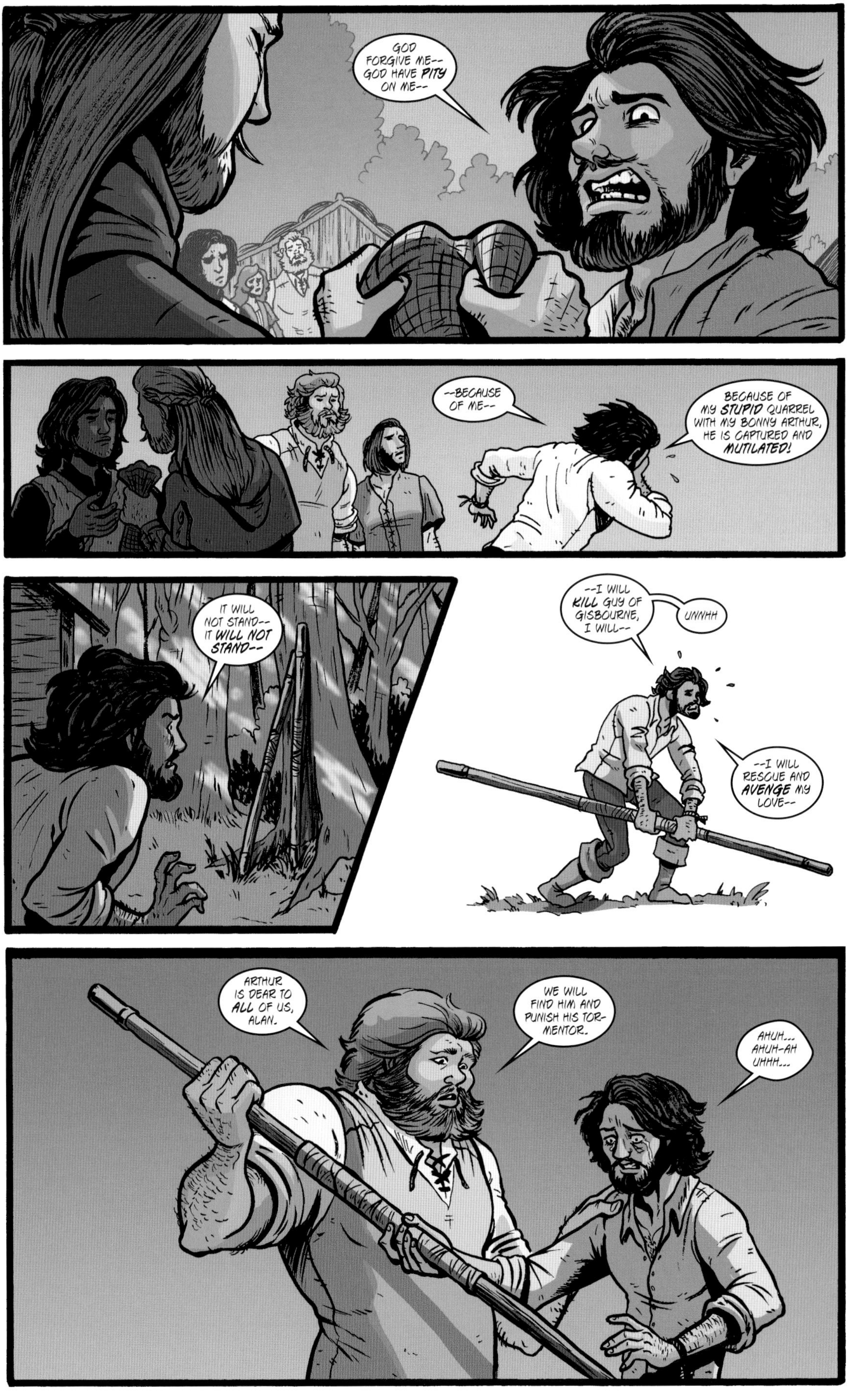
GOD FORGIVE ME-- GOD HAVE PITY ON ME--
--BECAUSE OF ME--
BECAUSE OF MY STUPID QUARREL WITH MY BONNY ARTHUR, HE IS CAPTURED AND MUTILATED!
IT WILL NOT STAND-- IT WILL NOT STAND--
--I WILL KILL GUY OF GISBOURNE, I WILL--
UNNHH
--I WILL RESCUE AND AVENGE MY LOVE--
ARTHUR IS DEAR TO ALL OF US, ALAN.
WE WILL FIND HIM AND PUNISH HIS TOR-MENTOR.
AHUH... AHUH-AH UHHH...

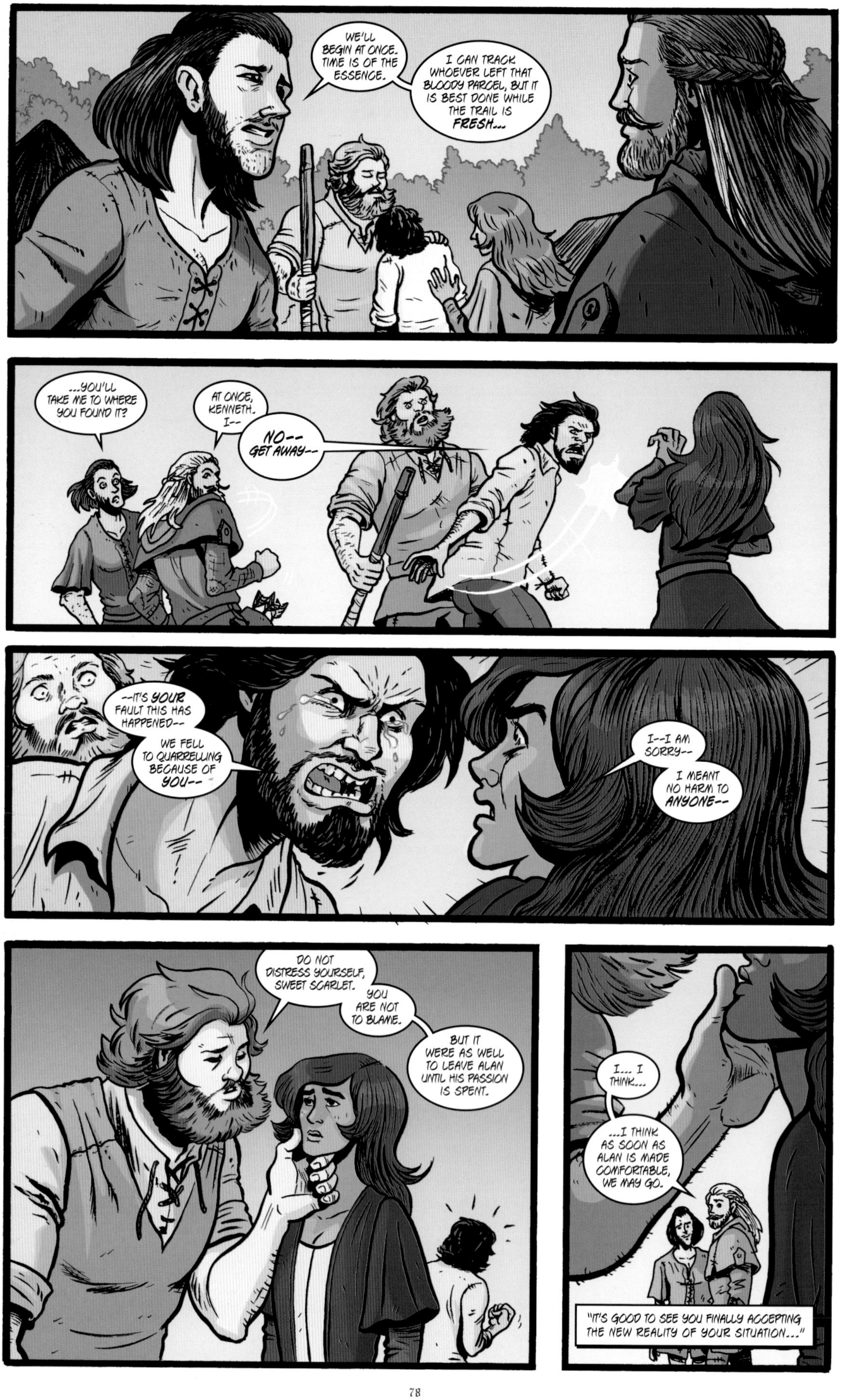

WE'LL BEGIN AT ONCE. TIME IS OF THE ESSENCE.
I CAN TRACK WHOEVER LEFT THAT BLOODY PARCEL, BUT IT IS BEST DONE WHILE THE TRAIL IS FRESH...
...YOU'LL TAKE ME TO WHERE YOU FOUND IT?
AT ONCE, KENNETH. I--
NO-- GET AWAY--
--IT'S YOUR FAULT THIS HAS HAPPENED--
WE FELL TO QUARRELLING BECAUSE OF YOU--
I--I AM SORRY--
I MEANT NO HARM TO ANYONE--
DO NOT DISTRESS YOURSELF, SWEET SCARLET.
YOU ARE NOT TO BLAME.
BUT IT WERE AS WELL TO LEAVE ALAN UNTIL HIS PASSION IS SPENT.
I... I THINK...
...I THINK AS SOON AS ALAN IS MADE COMFORTABLE, WE MAY GO.
"IT'S GOOD TO SEE YOU FINALLY ACCEPTING THE NEW REALITY OF YOUR SITUATION..."

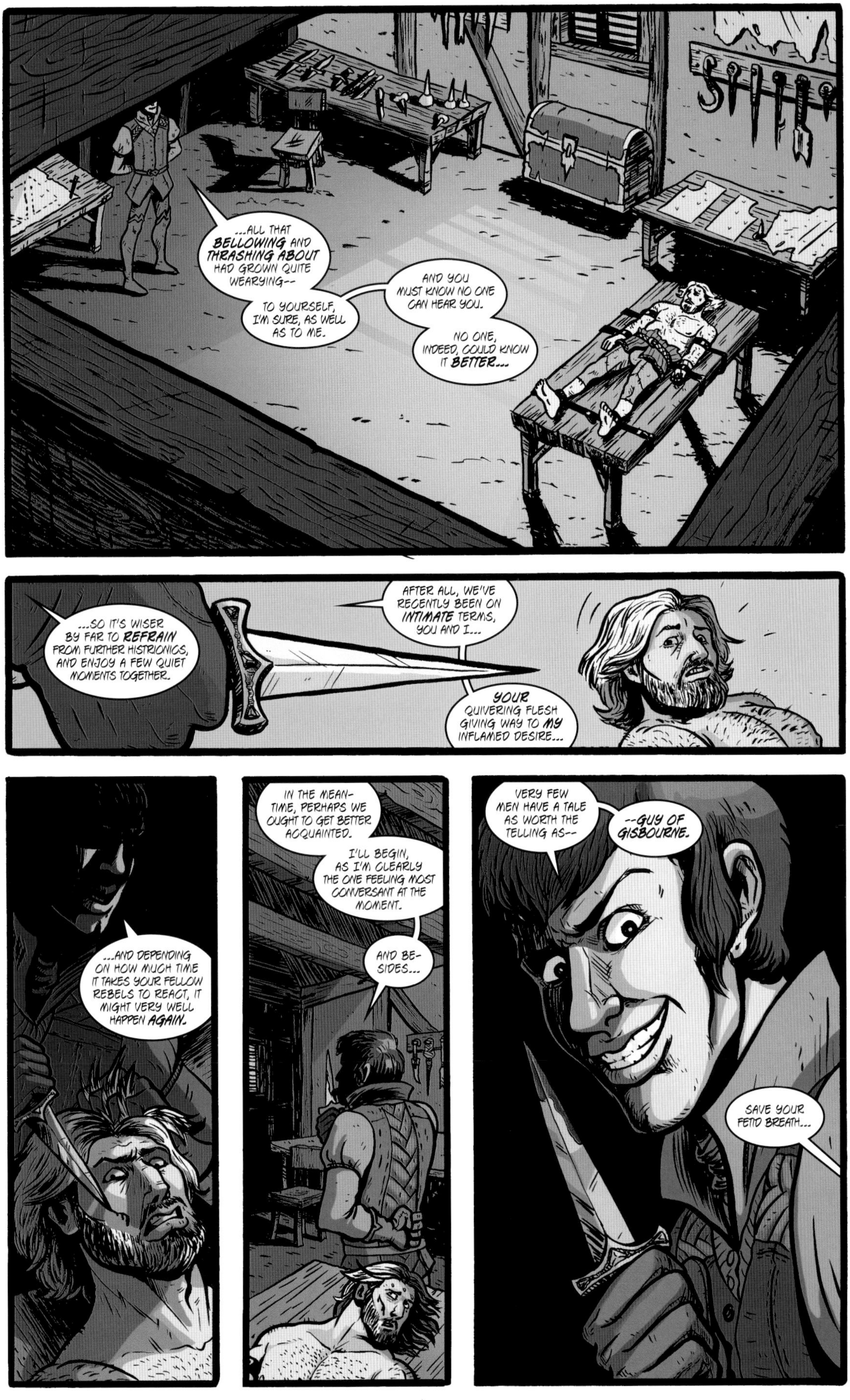
...ALL THAT BELLOWING AND THRASHING ABOUT HAD GROWN QUITE WEARYING--
TO YOURSELF, I'M SURE, AS WELL AS TO ME.
AND YOU MUST KNOW NO ONE CAN HEAR YOU.
NO ONE, INDEED, COULD KNOW IT BETTER...
...SO IT'S WISER BY FAR TO REFRAIN FROM FURTHER HISTRIONICS, AND ENJOY A FEW QUIET MOMENTS TOGETHER.
AFTER ALL, WE'VE RECENTLY BEEN ON INTIMATE TERMS, YOU AND I...
YOUR QUIVERING FLESH GIVING WAY TO MY INFLAMED DESIRE...
...AND DEPENDING ON HOW MUCH TIME IT TAKES YOUR FELLOW REBELS TO REACT, IT MIGHT VERY WELL HAPPEN AGAIN.
IN THE MEAN-TIME, PERHAPS WE OUGHT TO GET BETTER ACQUAINTED.
I'LL BEGIN, AS I'M CLEARLY THE ONE FEELING MOST CONVERSANT AT THE MOMENT.
AND BE-SIDES...
VERY FEW MEN HAVE A TALE AS WORTH THE TELLING AS--
--GUY OF GISBOURNE.
SAVE YOUR FETID BREATH...

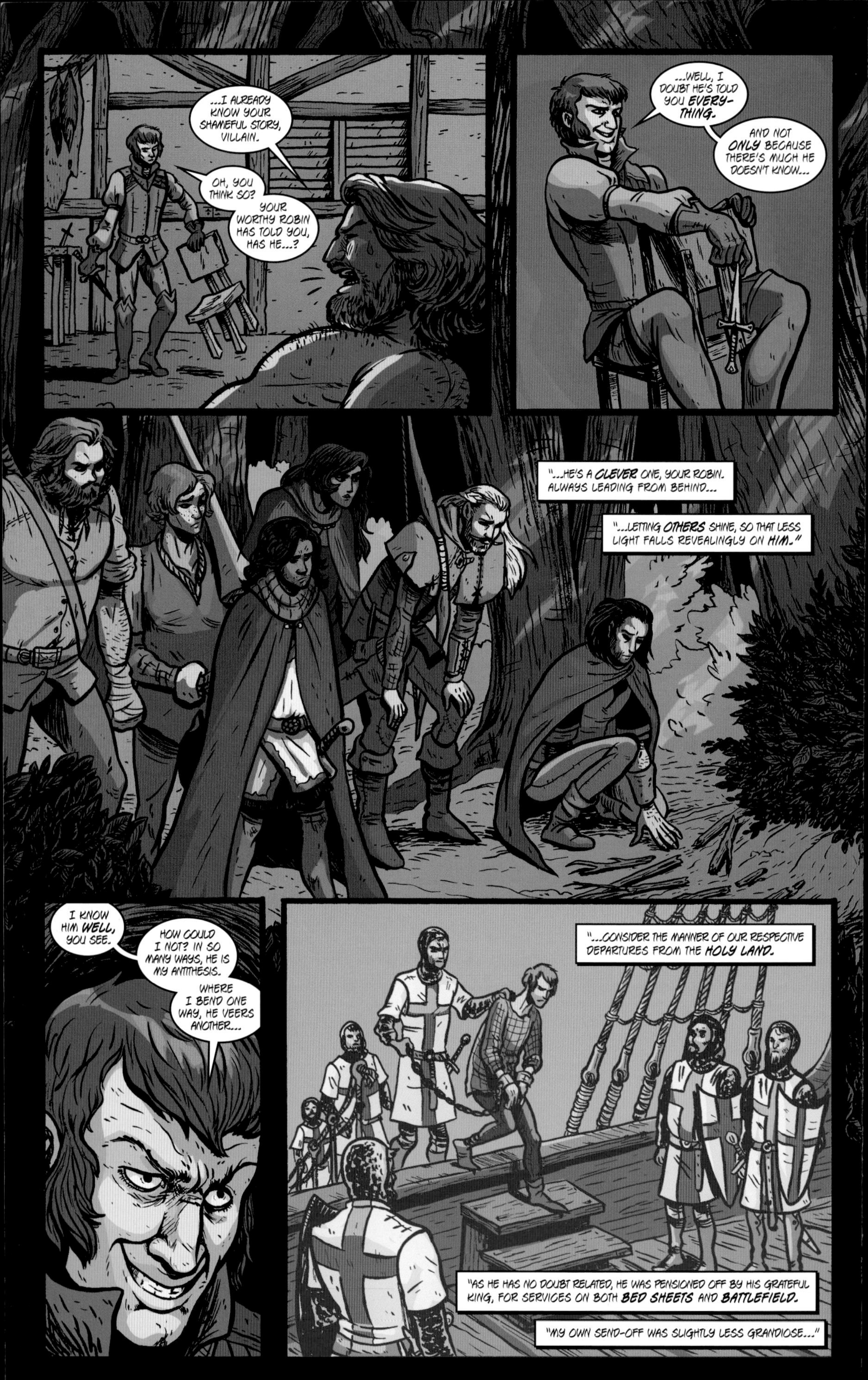

...I ALREADY KNOW YOUR SHAMEFUL STORY, VILLAIN.
OH, YOU THINK SO?
YOUR WORTHY ROBIN HAS TOLD YOU, HAS HE...?
...WELL, I DOUBT HE'S TOLD YOU EVERY-THING.
AND NOT ONLY BECAUSE THERE'S MUCH HE DOESN'T KNOW...
"...HE'S A CLEVER ONE, YOUR ROBIN. ALWAYS LEADING FROM BEHIND...
"...LETTING OTHERS SHINE, SO THAT LESS LIGHT FALLS REVEALINGLY ON HIM."
I KNOW HIM WELL, YOU SEE.
HOW COULD I NOT? IN SO MANY WAYS, HE IS MY ANTITHESIS.
WHERE I BEND ONE WAY, HE VEERS ANOTHER...
"...CONSIDER THE MANNER OF OUR RESPECTIVE DEPARTURES FROM THE HOLY LAND.
"AS HE HAS NO DOUBT RELATED, HE WAS PENSIONED OFF BY HIS GRATEFUL KING, FOR SERVICES ON BOTH BED SHEETS AND BATTLEFIELD.
"MY OWN SEND-OFF WAS SLIGHTLY LESS GRANDIOSE..."

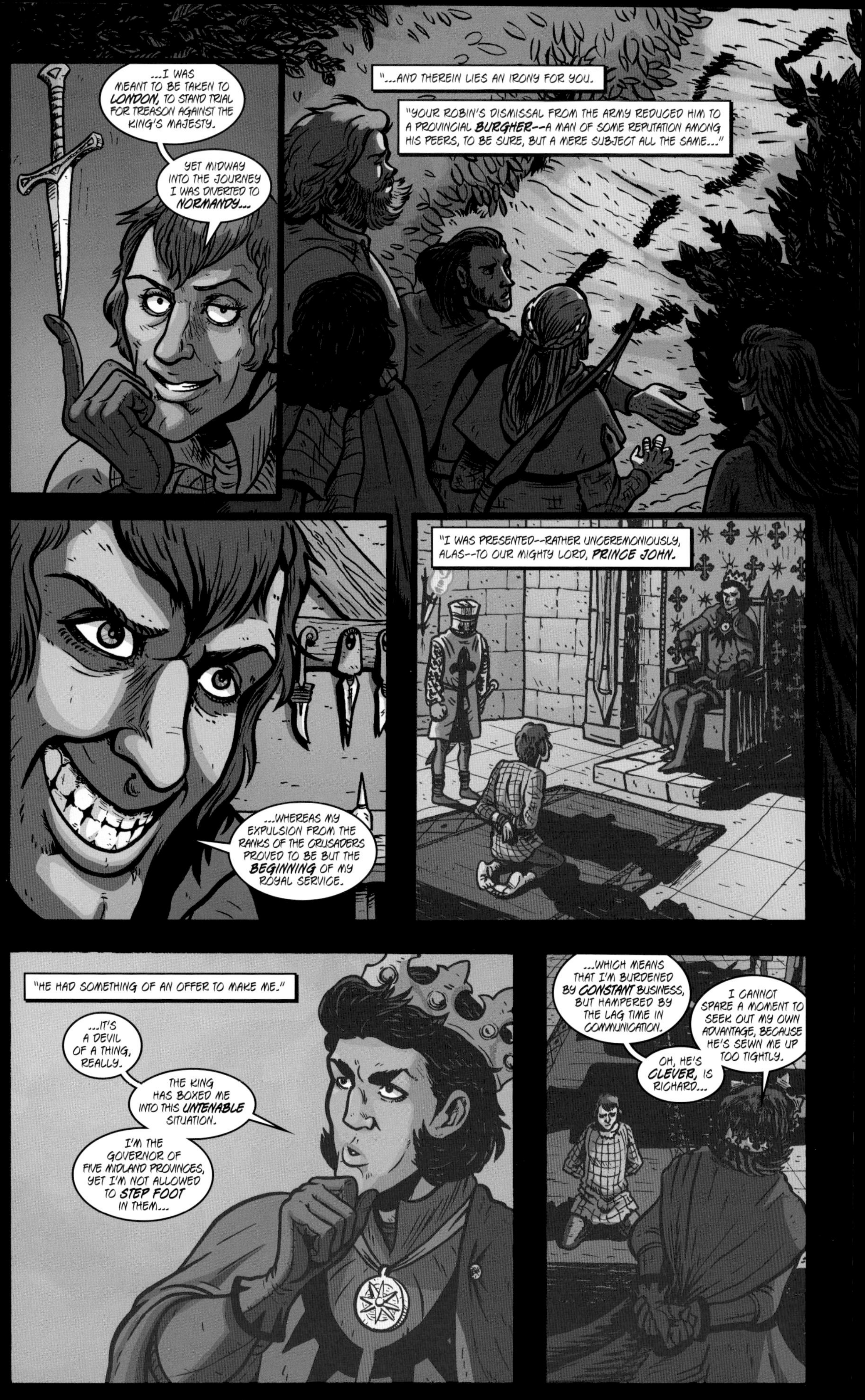
...I WAS MEANT TO BE TAKEN TO LONDON, TO STAND TRIAL FOR TREASON AGAINST THE KING'S MAJESTY.
YET MIDWAY INTO THE JOURNEY I WAS DIVERTED TO NORMANDY...
"...AND THEREIN LIES AN IRONY FOR YOU.
"YOUR ROBIN'S DISMISSAL FROM THE ARMY REDUCED HIM TO A PROVINCIAL BURGHER--A MAN OF SOME REPUTATION AMONG HIS PEERS, TO BE SURE, BUT A MERE SUBJECT ALL THE SAME..."
...WHEREAS MY EXPULSION FROM THE RANKS OF THE CRUSADERS PROVED TO BE BUT THE BEGINNING OF MY ROYAL SERVICE.
"I WAS PRESENTED--RATHER UNCEREMONIOUSLY, ALAS--TO OUR MIGHTY LORD, PRINCE JOHN.
"HE HAD SOMETHING OF AN OFFER TO MAKE ME."
...IT'S A DEVIL OF A THING, REALLY.
THE KING HAS BOXED ME INTO THIS UNTENABLE SITUATION.
I'M THE GOVERNOR OF FIVE MIDLAND PROVINCES, YET I'M NOT ALLOWED TO STEP FOOT IN THEM...
...WHICH MEANS THAT I'M BURDENED BY CONSTANT BUSINESS, BUT HAMPERED BY THE LAG TIME IN COMMUNICATION.
OH, HE'S CLEVER, IS RICHARD...
I CANNOT SPARE A MOMENT TO SEEK OUT MY OWN ADVANTAGE, BECAUSE HE'S SEWN ME UP TOO TIGHTLY.

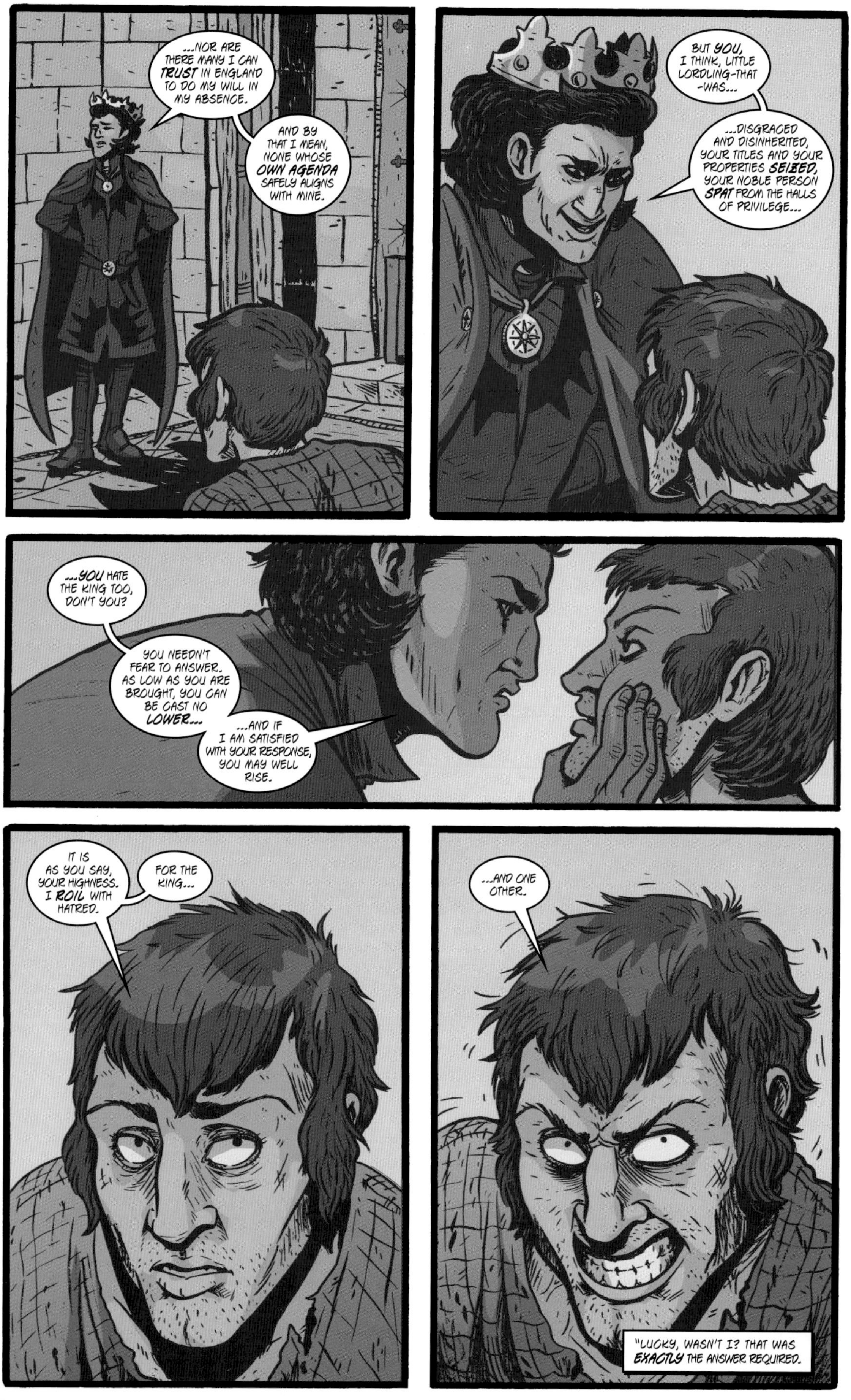
...NOR ARE THERE MANY I CAN TRUST IN ENGLAND TO DO MY WILL IN MY ABSENCE.
AND BY THAT I MEAN, NONE WHOSE OWN AGENDA SAFELY ALIGNS WITH MINE.
BUT YOU, I THINK, LITTLE LORDLING-THAT-WAS...
...DISGRACED AND DISINHERITED, YOUR TITLES AND YOUR PROPERTIES SEIZED, YOUR NOBLE PERSON SPAT FROM THE HALLS OF PRIVILEGE...
...YOU HATE THE KING TOO, DON'T YOU?
YOU NEEDN'T FEAR TO ANSWER. AS LOW AS YOU ARE BROUGHT, YOU CAN BE CAST NO LOWER...
...AND IF I AM SATISFIED WITH YOUR RESPONSE, YOU MAY WELL RISE.
IT IS AS YOU SAY, YOUR HIGHNESS. I ROIL WITH HATRED.
FOR THE KING...
...AND ONE OTHER.
"LUCKY, WASN'T I? THAT WAS EXACTLY THE ANSWER REQUIRED.

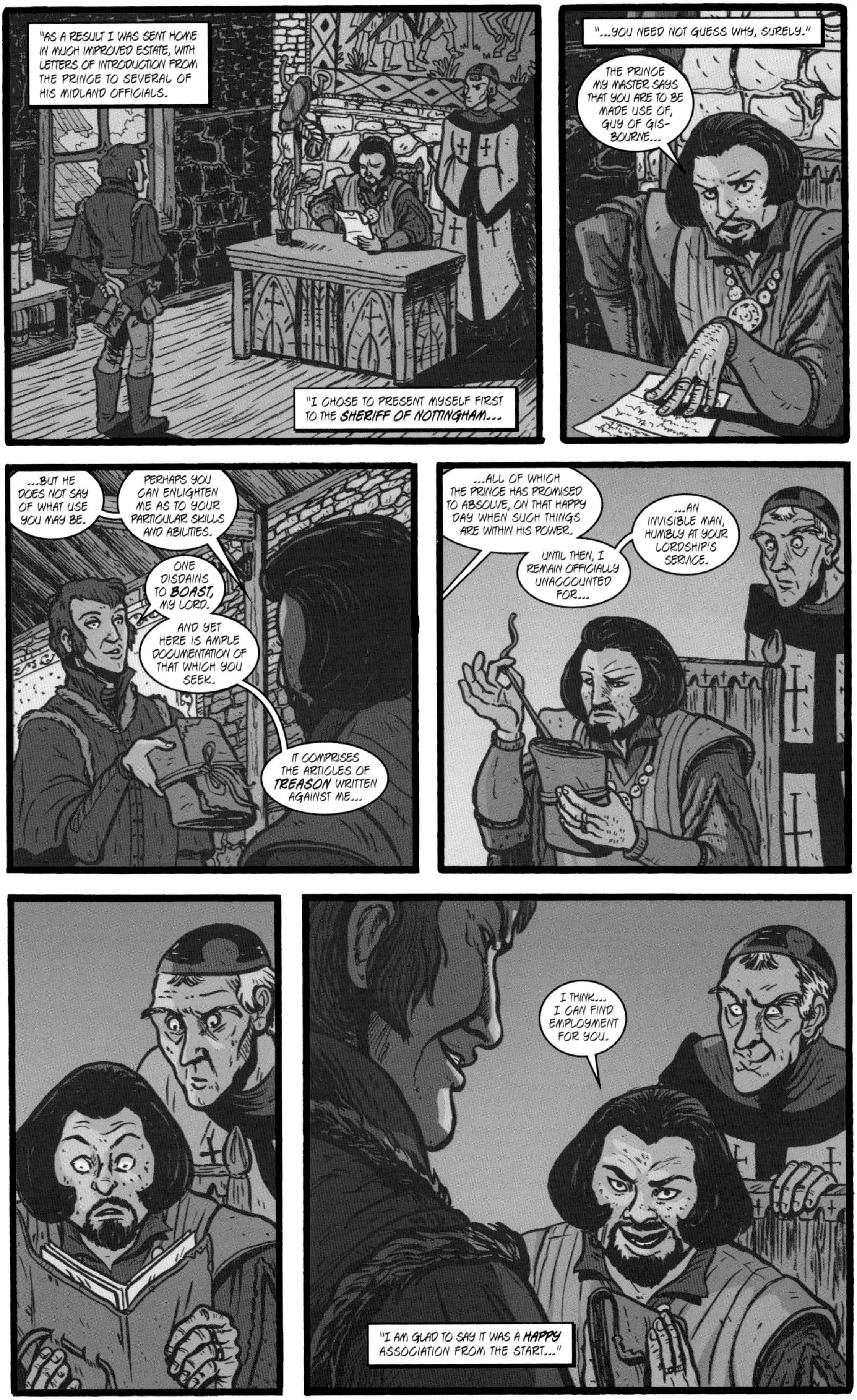
"AS A RESULT I WAS SENT HOME IN MUCH IMPROVED ESTATE, WITH LETTERS OF INTRODUCTION FROM THE PRINCE TO SEVERAL OF HIS MIDLAND OFFICIALS.
"I CHOSE TO PRESENT MYSELF FIRST TO THE SHERIFF OF NOTTINGHAM...
"...YOU NEED NOT GUESS WHY, SURELY."
THE PRINCE MY MASTER SAYS THAT YOU ARE TO BE MADE USE OF, GUY OF GIS-BOURNE...
...BUT HE DOES NOT SAY OF WHAT USE YOU MAY BE.
PERHAPS YOU CAN ENLIGHTEN ME AS TO YOUR PARTICULAR SKILLS AND ABILITIES.
ONE DISDAINS TO BOAST, MY LORD.
AND YET HERE IS AMPLE DOCUMENTATION OF THAT WHICH YOU SEEK.
IT COMPRISES THE ARTICLES OF TREASON WRITTEN AGAINST ME...
...ALL OF WHICH THE PRINCE HAS PROMISED TO ABSOLVE, ON THAT HAPPY DAY WHEN SUCH THINGS ARE WITHIN HIS POWER.
UNTIL THEN, I REMAIN OFFICIALLY UNACCOUNTED FOR...
...AN INVISIBLE MAN, HUMBLY AT YOUR LORDSHIP'S SERVICE.
I THINK... I CAN FIND EMPLOYMENT FOR YOU.
"I AM GLAD TO SAY IT WAS A HAPPY ASSOCIATION FROM THE START..."

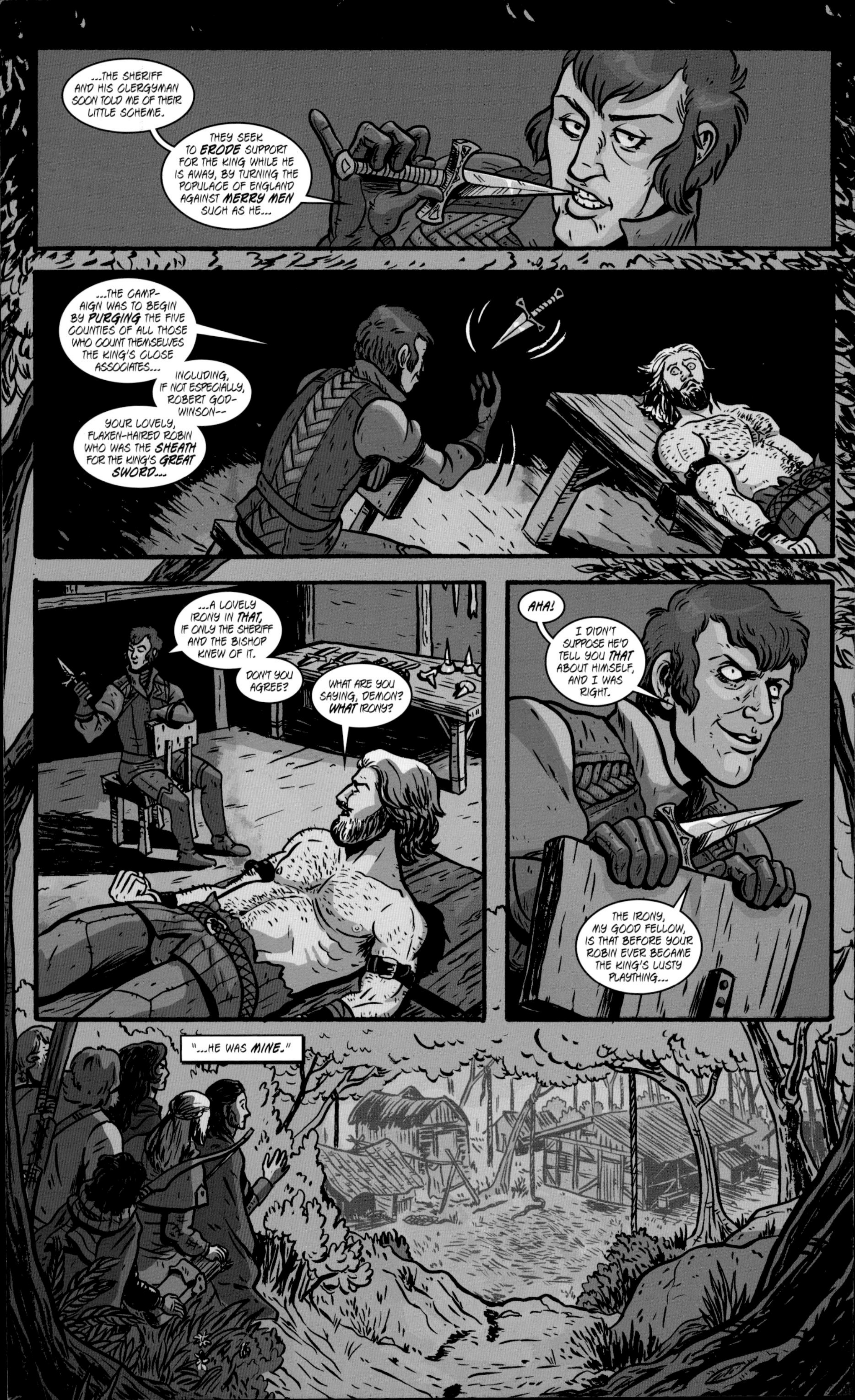
...THE SHERIFF AND HIS CLERGYMAN SOON TOLD ME OF THEIR LITTLE SCHEME.
THEY SEEK TO ERODE SUPPORT FOR THE KING WHILE HE IS AWAY, BY TURNING THE POPULACE OF ENGLAND AGAINST MERRY MEN SUCH AS HE...
...THE CAMP-AIGN WAS TO BEGIN BY PURGING THE FIVE COUNTIES OF ALL THOSE WHO COUNT THEMSELVES THE KING'S CLOSE ASSOCIATES...
INCLUDING, IF NOT ESPECIALLY, ROBERT GOD-WINSON--
YOUR LOVELY, FLAXEN-HAIRED ROBIN WHO WAS THE SHEATH FOR THE KING'S GREAT SWORD...
...A LOVELY IRONY IN THAT, IF ONLY THE SHERIFF AND THE BISHOP KNEW OF IT.
DON'T YOU AGREE?
WHAT ARE YOU SAYING, DEMON? WHAT IRONY?
AHA!
I DIDN'T SUPPOSE HE'D TELL YOU THAT ABOUT HIMSELF, AND I WAS RIGHT.
THE IRONY, MY GOOD FELLOW, IS THAT BEFORE YOUR ROBIN EVER BECAME THE KING'S LUSTY PLAYTHING...
"...HE WAS MINE."

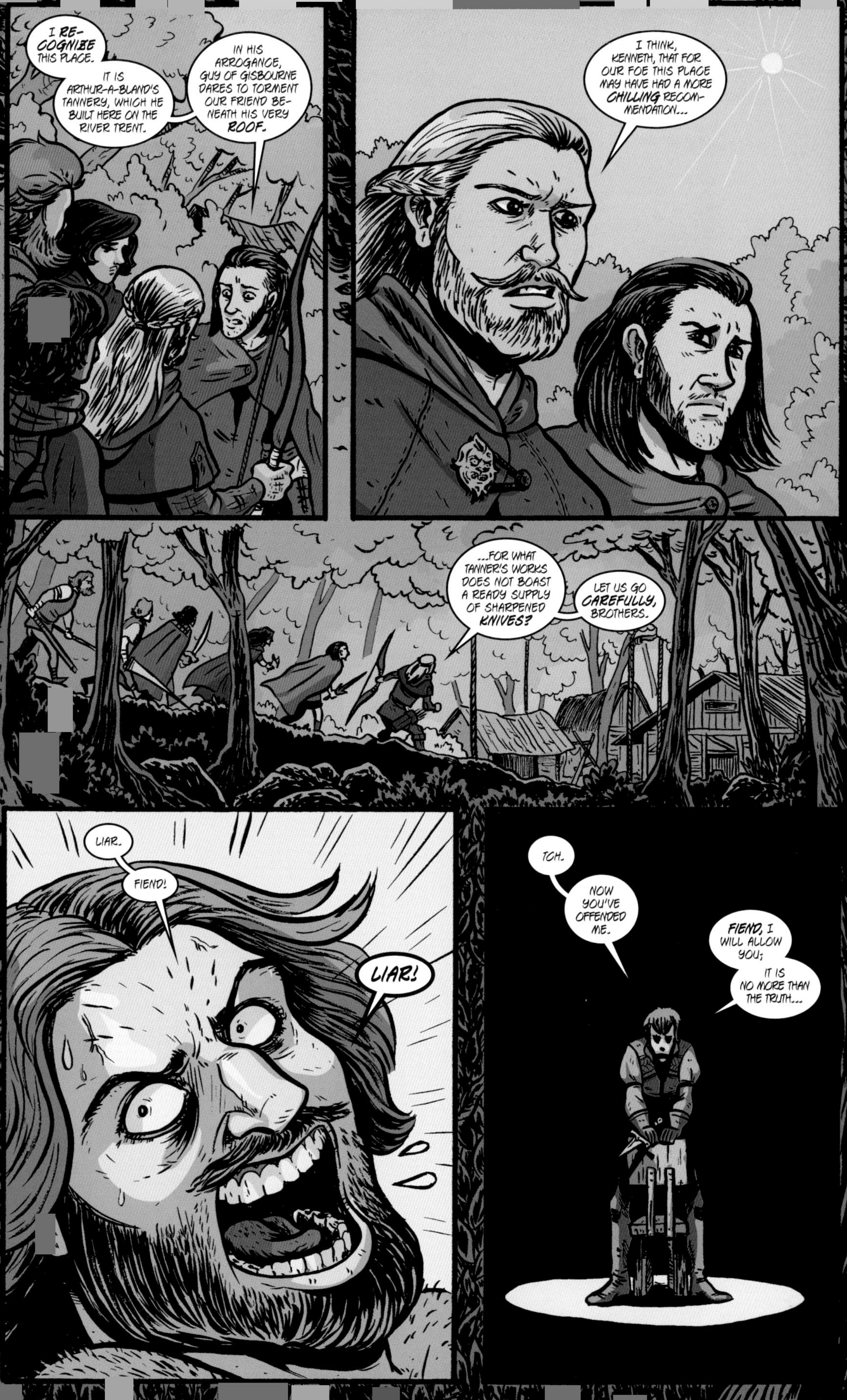

I RE-COGNIZE THIS PLACE.
IT IS ARTHUR-A-BLAND'S TANNERY, WHICH HE BUILT HERE ON THE RIVER TRENT.
IN HIS ARROGANCE, GUY OF GISBOURNE DARES TO TORMENT OUR FRIEND BE-NEATH HIS VERY ROOF.
I THINK, KENNETH, THAT FOR OUR FOE THIS PLACE MAY HAVE HAD A MORE CHILLING RECOM-MENDATION...
...FOR WHAT TANNER'S WORKS DOES NOT BOAST A READY SUPPLY OF SHARPENED KNIVES?
LET US GO CAREFULLY, BROTHERS.
LIAR.
FIEND!
LIAR!
TCH.
NOW YOU'VE OFFENDED ME.
FIEND, I WILL ALLOW YOU;
IT IS NO MORE THAN THE TRUTH...

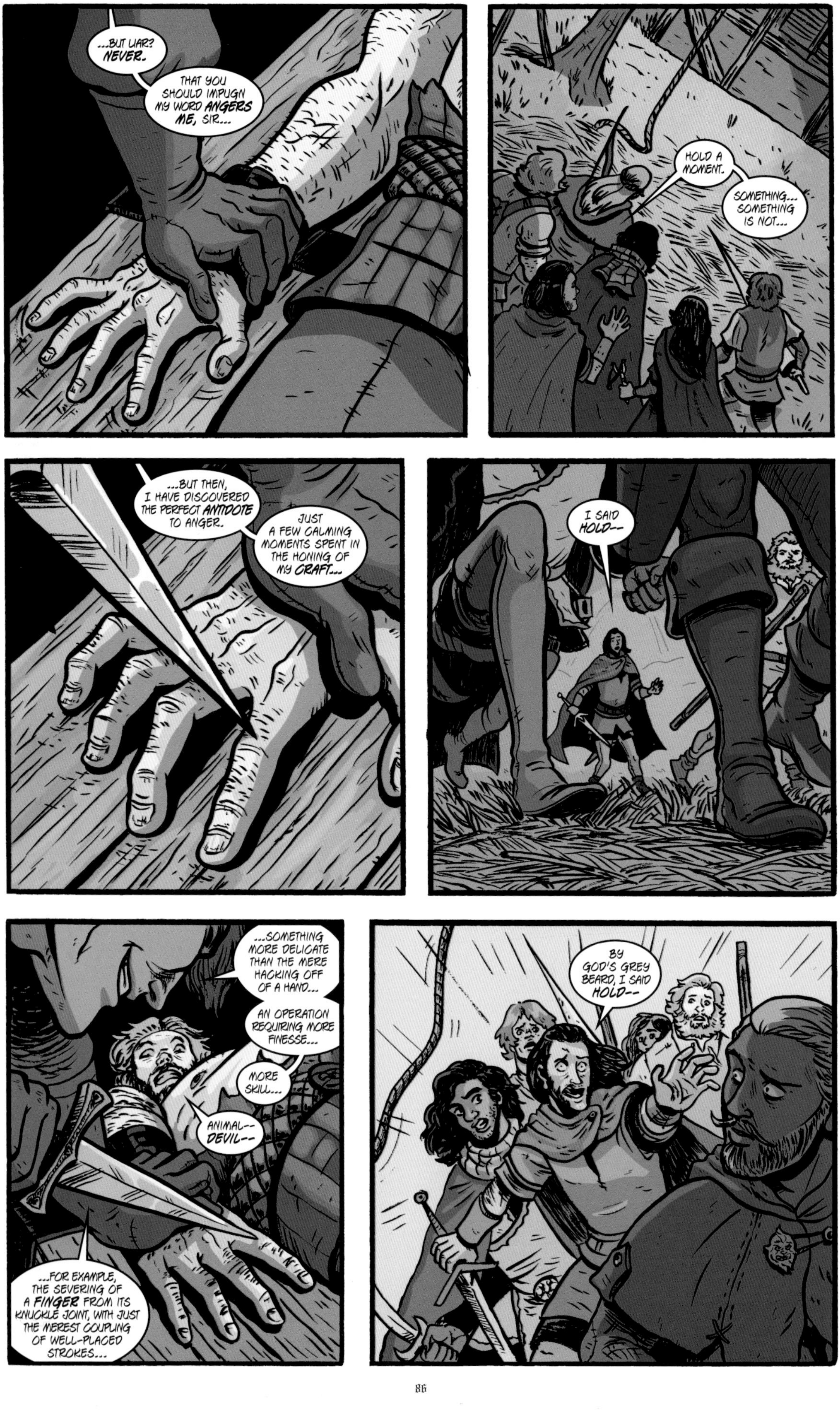
...BUT LIAR? NEVER.
THAT YOU SHOULD IMPUGN MY WORD ANGERS ME, SIR...
HOLD A MOMENT.
SOMETHING... SOMETHING IS NOT...
...BUT THEN, I HAVE DISCOVERED THE PERFECT ANTIDOTE TO ANGER.
JUST A FEW CALMING MOMENTS SPENT IN THE HONING OF MY CRAFT...
I SAID HOLD--
...SOMETHING MORE DELICATE THAN THE MERE HACKING OFF OF A HAND...
AN OPERATION REQUIRING MORE FINESSE...
MORE SKILL...
ANIMAL-- DEVIL--
...FOR EXAMPLE, THE SEVERING OF A FINGER FROM ITS KNUCKLE JOINT, WITH JUST THE MEREST COUPLING OF WELL-PLACED STROKES...
BY GOD'S GREY BEARD, I SAID HOLD--

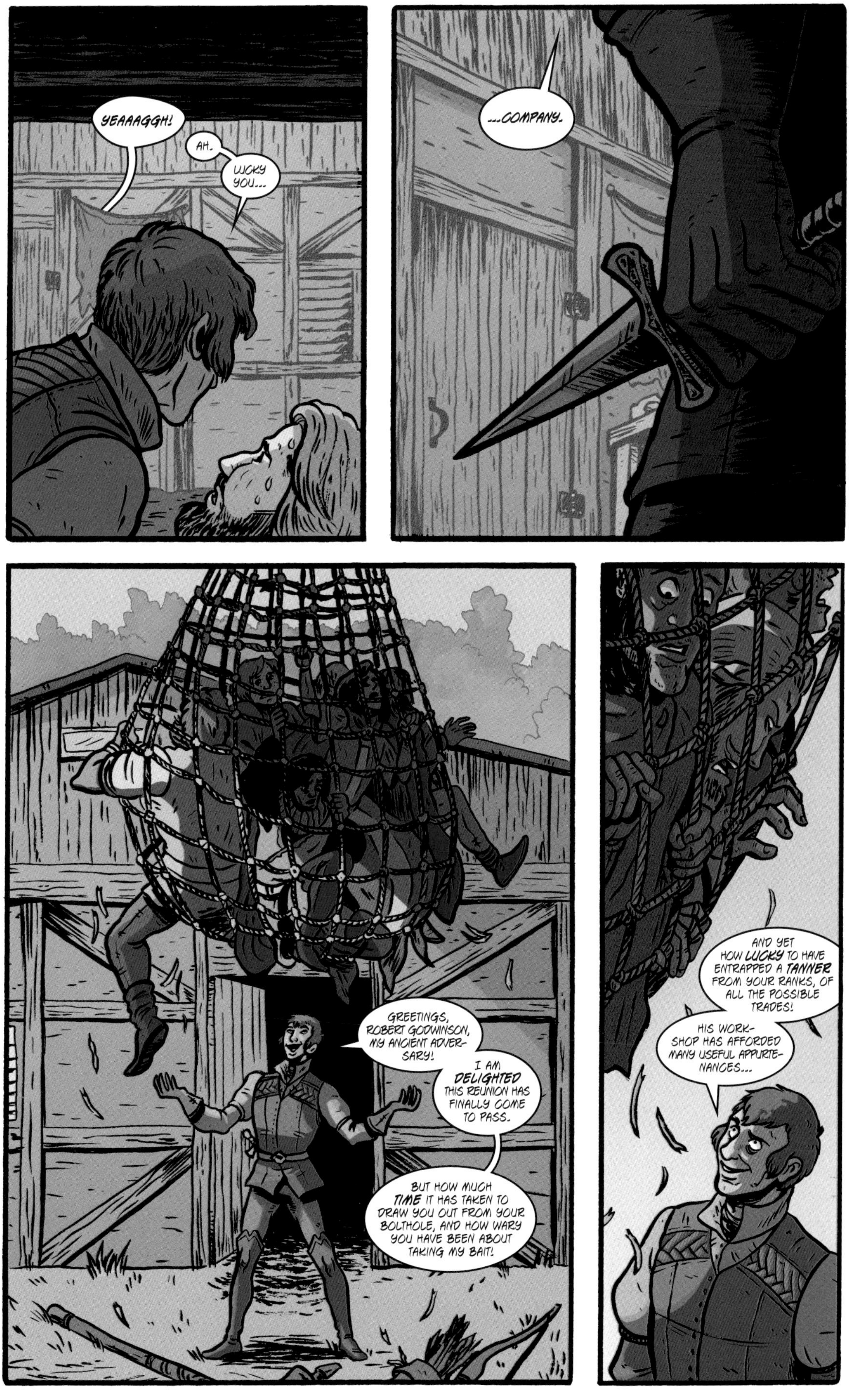
YEAAAGGH!
AH.
LUCKY YOU...
...COMPANY.
GREETINGS, ROBERT GODWINSON, MY ANCIENT ADVERSARY!
I AM DELIGHTED THIS REUNION HAS FINALLY COME TO PASS.
BUT HOW MUCH TIME IT HAS TAKEN TO DRAW YOU OUT FROM YOUR BOLTHOLE, AND HOW WARY YOU HAVE BEEN ABOUT TAKING MY BAIT!
AND YET HOW LUCKY TO HAVE ENTRAPPED A TANNER FROM YOUR RANKS, OF ALL THE POSSIBLE TRADES!
HIS WORKSHOP HAS AFFORDED MANY USEFUL APPURTENANCES...

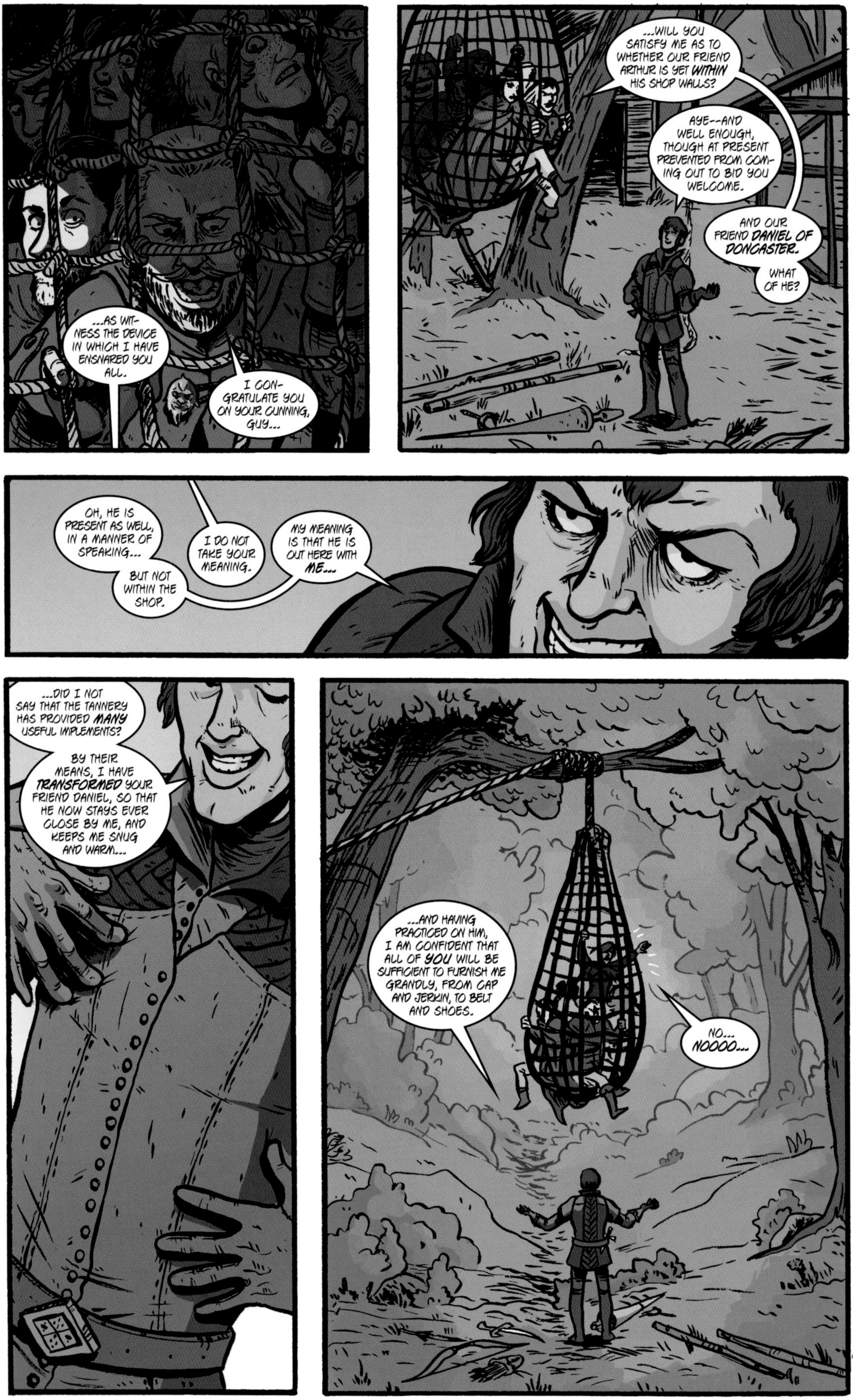
...AS WIT-NESS THE DEVICE IN WHICH I HAVE ENSNARED YOU ALL.
I CON-GRATULATE YOU ON YOUR CUNNING, GUY...
...WILL YOU SATISFY ME AS TO WHETHER OUR FRIEND ARTHUR IS YET WITHIN HIS SHOP WALLS?
AYE--AND WELL ENOUGH, THOUGH AT PRESENT PREVENTED FROM COM-ING OUT TO BID YOU WELCOME.
AND OUR FRIEND DANIEL OF DONCASTER.
WHAT OF HE?
OH, HE IS PRESENT AS WELL, IN A MANNER OF SPEAKING...
BUT NOT WITHIN THE SHOP.
I DO NOT TAKE YOUR MEANING.
MY MEANING IS THAT HE IS OUT HERE WITH ME...
...DID I NOT SAY THAT THE TANNERY HAS PROVIDED MANY USEFUL IMPLEMENTS?
BY THEIR MEANS, I HAVE TRANSFORMED YOUR FRIEND DANIEL, SO THAT HE NOW STAYS EVER CLOSE BY ME, AND KEEPS ME SNUG AND WARM...
...AND HAVING PRACTICED ON HIM, I AM CONFIDENT THAT ALL OF YOU WILL BE SUFFICIENT TO FURNISH ME GRANDLY, FROM CAP AND JERKIN, TO BELT AND SHOES.
NO... NOOOO...

Chapter
7

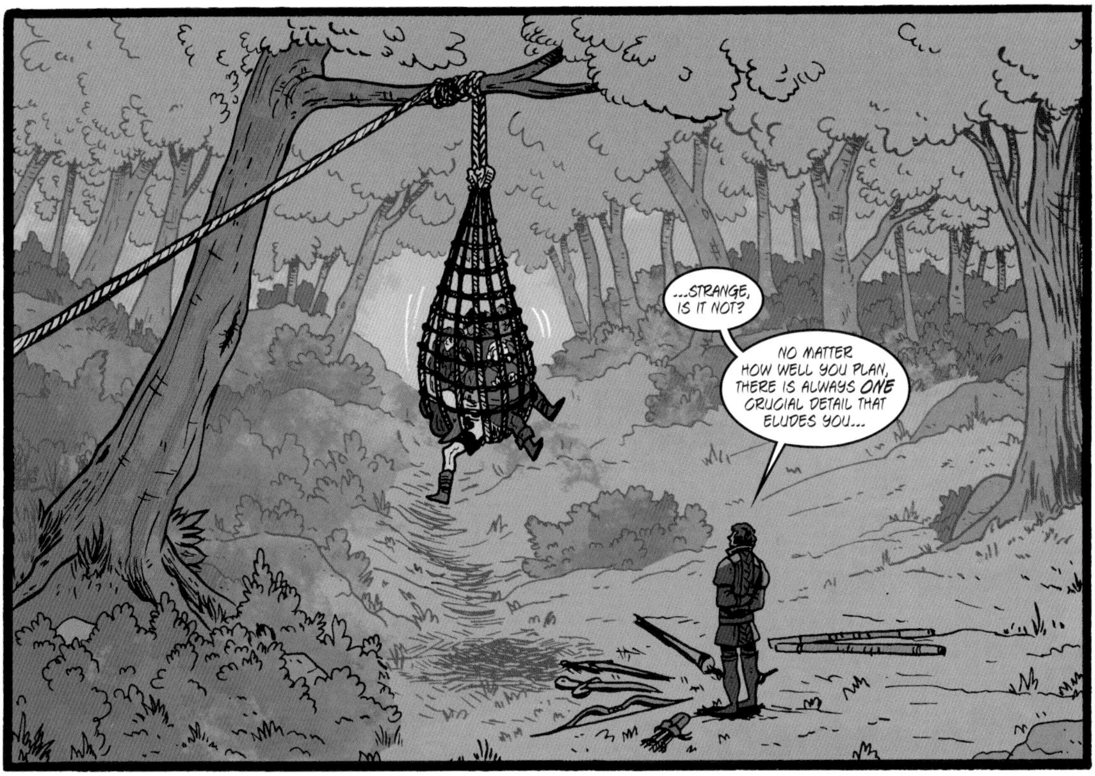
...STRANGE, IS IT NOT?
NO MATTER HOW WELL YOU PLAN, THERE IS ALWAYS ONE CRUCIAL DETAIL THAT ELUDES YOU...

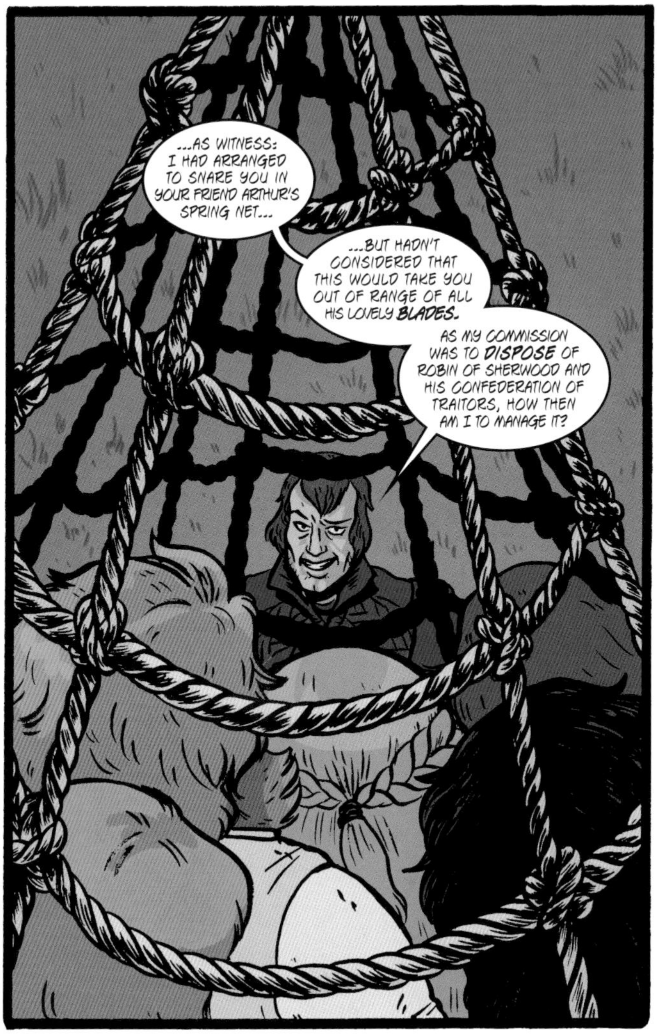
...AS WITNESS: I HAD ARRANGED TO SNARE YOU IN YOUR FRIEND ARTHUR'S SPRING NET...
...BUT HADN'T CONSIDERED THAT THIS WOULD TAKE YOU OUT OF RANGE OF ALL HIS LOVELY BLADES.
AS MY COMMISSION WAS TO DISPOSE OF ROBIN OF SHERWOOD AND HIS CONFEDERATION OF TRAITORS, HOW THEN AM I TO MANAGE IT?

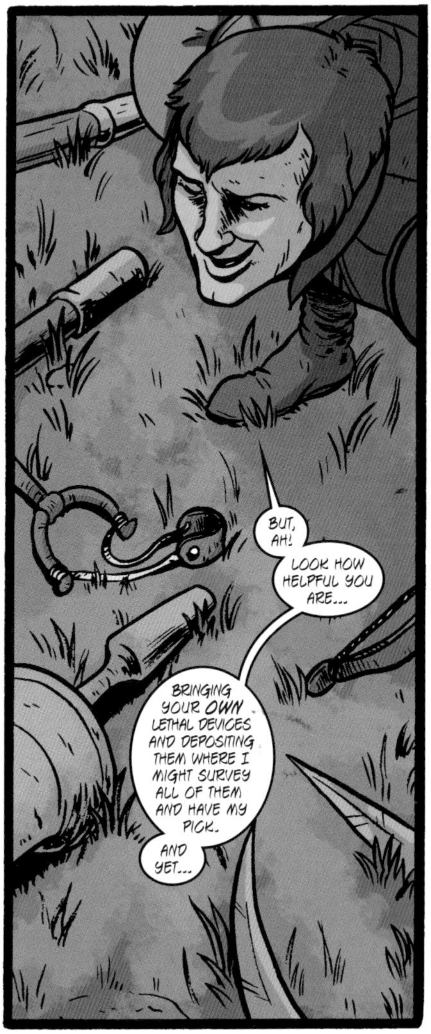
BUT, AH!
LOOK HOW HELPFUL YOU ARE...
BRINGING YOUR OWN LETHAL DEVICES AND DEPOSITING THEM WHERE I MIGHT SURVEY ALL OF THEM AND HAVE MY PICK.
AND YET...

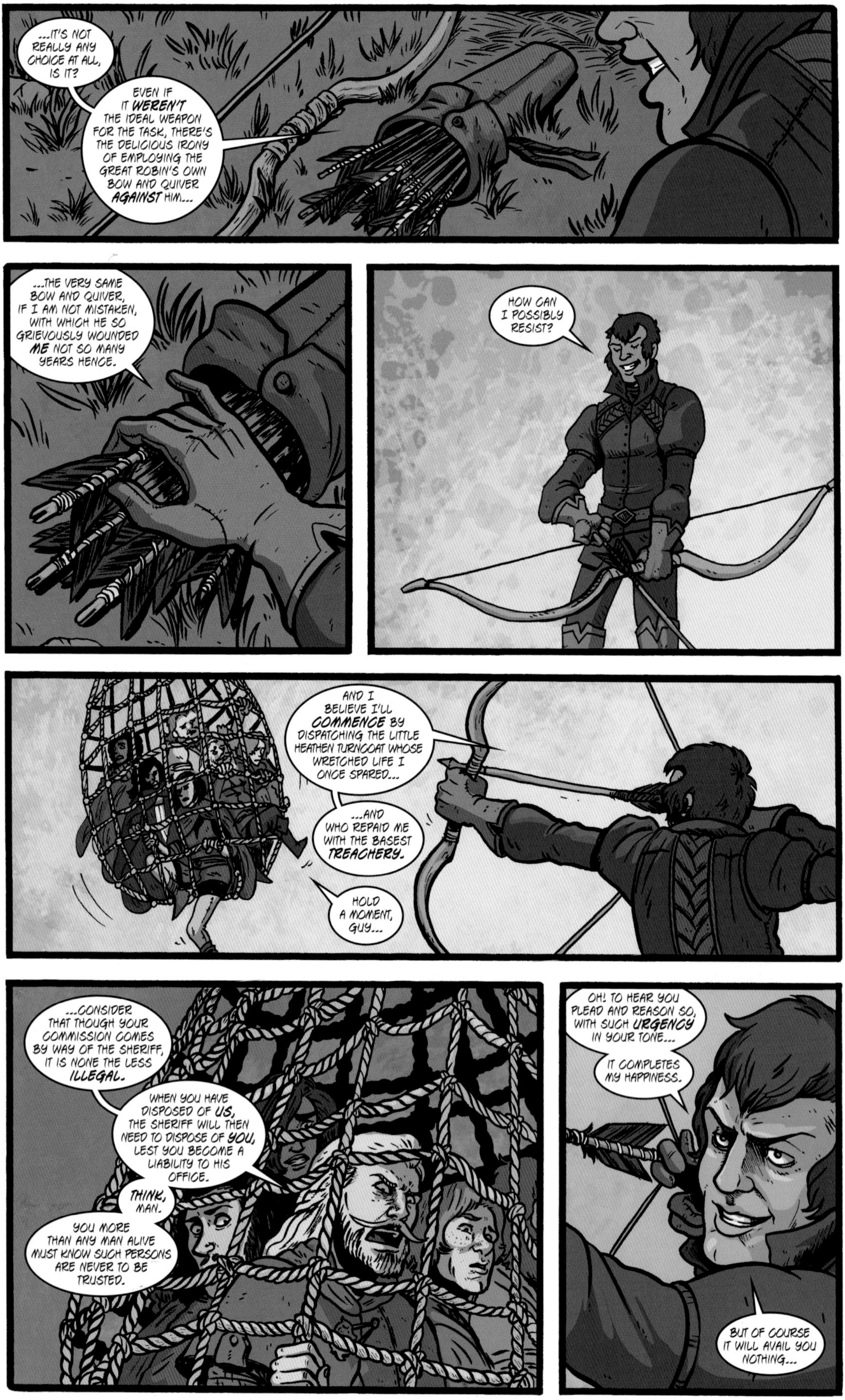
...IT'S NOT REALLY ANY CHOICE AT ALL, IS IT?
EVEN IF IT WEREN'T THE IDEAL WEAPON FOR THE TASK, THERE'S THE DELICIOUS IRONY OF EMPLOYING THE GREAT ROBIN'S OWN BOW AND QUIVER AGAINST HIM...
...THE VERY SAME BOW AND QUIVER, IF I AM NOT MISTAKEN, WITH WHICH HE SO GRIEVOUSLY WOUNDED ME NOT SO MANY YEARS HENCE.
HOW CAN I POSSIBLY RESIST?
AND I BELIEVE I'LL COMMENCE BY DISPATCHING THE LITTLE HEATHEN TURNCOAT WHOSE WRETCHED LIFE I ONCE SPARED...
...AND WHO REPAID ME WITH THE BASEST TREACHERY.
HOLD A MOMENT, GUY...
...CONSIDER THAT THOUGH YOUR COMMISSION COMES BY WAY OF THE SHERIFF, IT IS NONE THE LESS ILLEGAL.
WHEN YOU HAVE DISPOSED OF US, THE SHERIFF WILL THEN NEED TO DISPOSE OF YOU, LEST YOU BECOME A LIABILITY TO HIS OFFICE.
THINK, MAN.
YOU MORE THAN ANY MAN ALIVE MUST KNOW SUCH PERSONS ARE NEVER TO BE TRUSTED.
OH! TO HEAR YOU PLEAD AND REASON SO, WITH SUCH URGENCY IN YOUR TONE...
IT COMPLETES MY HAPPINESS.
BUT OF COURSE IT WILL AVAIL YOU NOTHING...

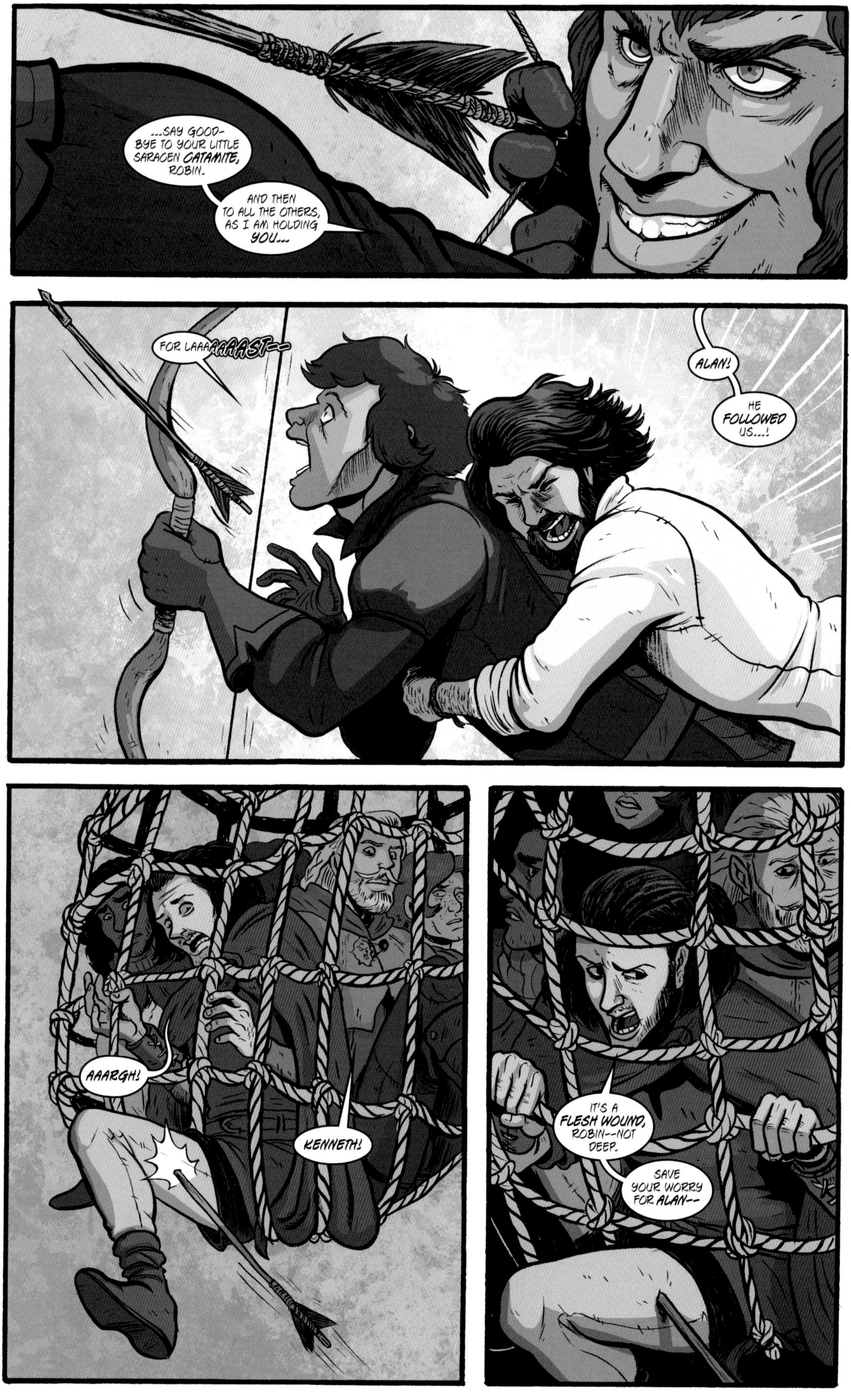
...SAY GOOD-BYE TO YOUR LITTLE SARACEN CATAMITE, ROBIN.
AND THEN TO ALL THE OTHERS, AS I AM HOLDING YOU...
FOR LAAAAAAAST--
ALAN!
HE FOLLOWED US...!
AAARGH!
KENNETH!
IT'S A FLESH WOUND, ROBIN--NOT DEEP.
SAVE YOUR WORRY FOR ALAN--

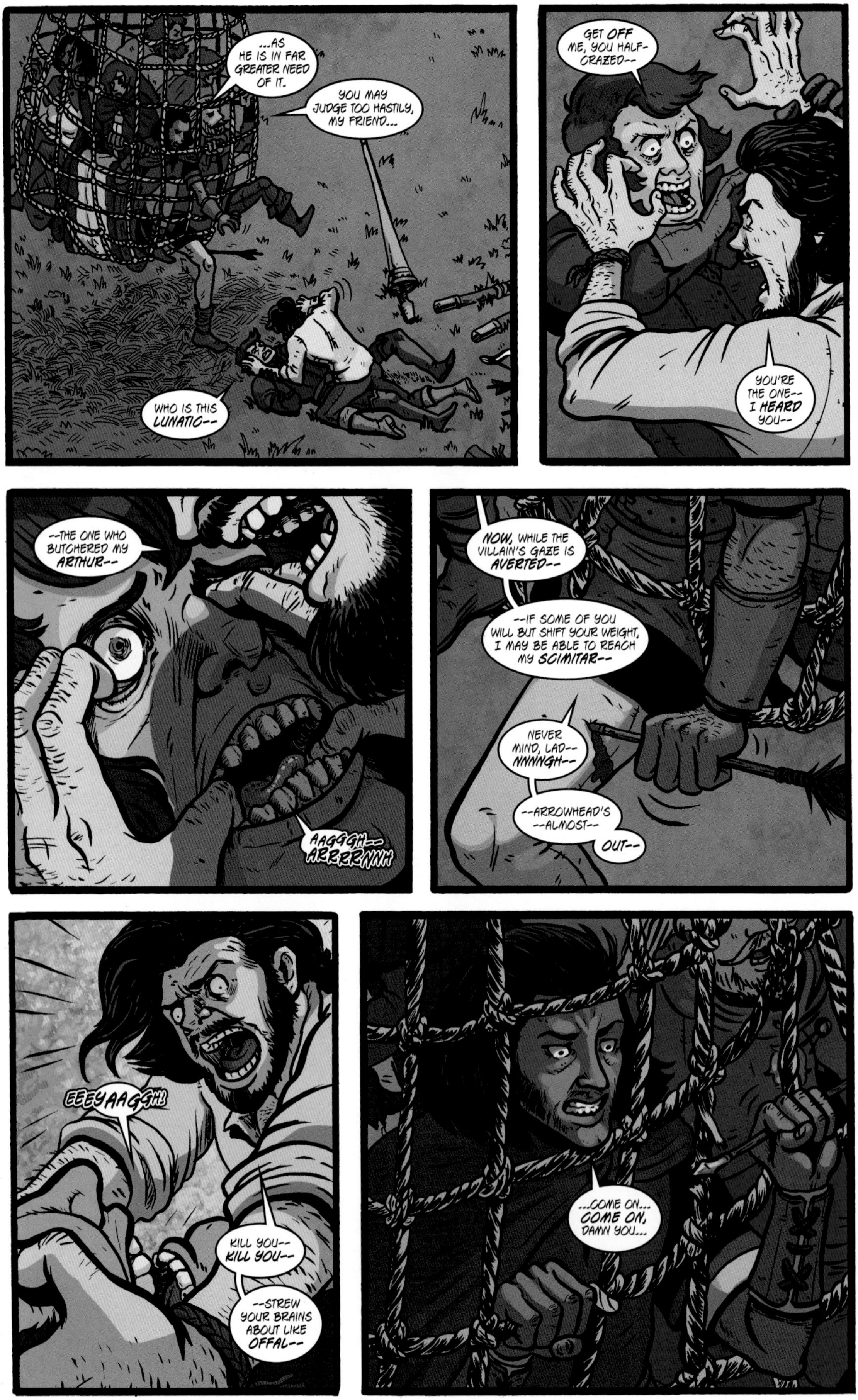
...AS HE IS IN FAR GREATER NEED OF IT.
YOU MAY JUDGE TOO HASTILY, MY FRIEND...
WHO IS THIS LUNATIC--
GET OFF ME, YOU HALF-CRAZED--
YOU'RE THE ONE-- I HEARD YOU--
--THE ONE WHO BUTCHERED MY ARTHUR--
AAGGGH-- ARRRRNNH
NOW, WHILE THE VILLAIN'S GAZE IS AVERTED--
--IF SOME OF YOU WILL BUT SHIFT YOUR WEIGHT, I MAY BE ABLE TO REACH MY SCIMITAR--
NEVER MIND, LAD-- NNNNGH--
--ARROWHEAD'S --ALMOST--
OUT--
EEEYAAGGH!
KILL YOU-- KILL YOU--
--STREW YOUR BRAINS ABOUT LIKE OFFAL--
...COME ON... COME ON, DAMN YOU...

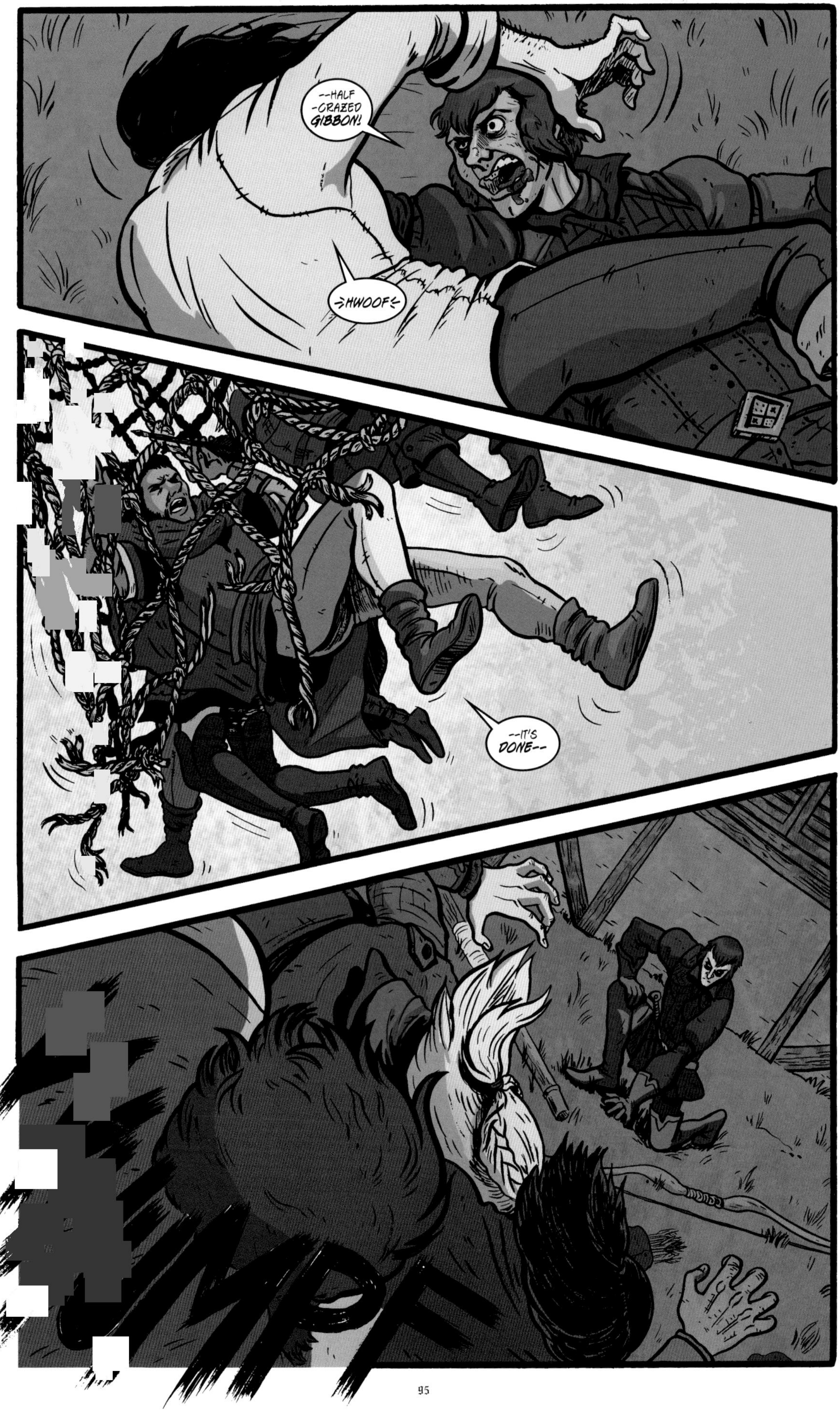
--HALF
-CRAZED
GIBBON!
HWOOF
--IT'S
DONE--

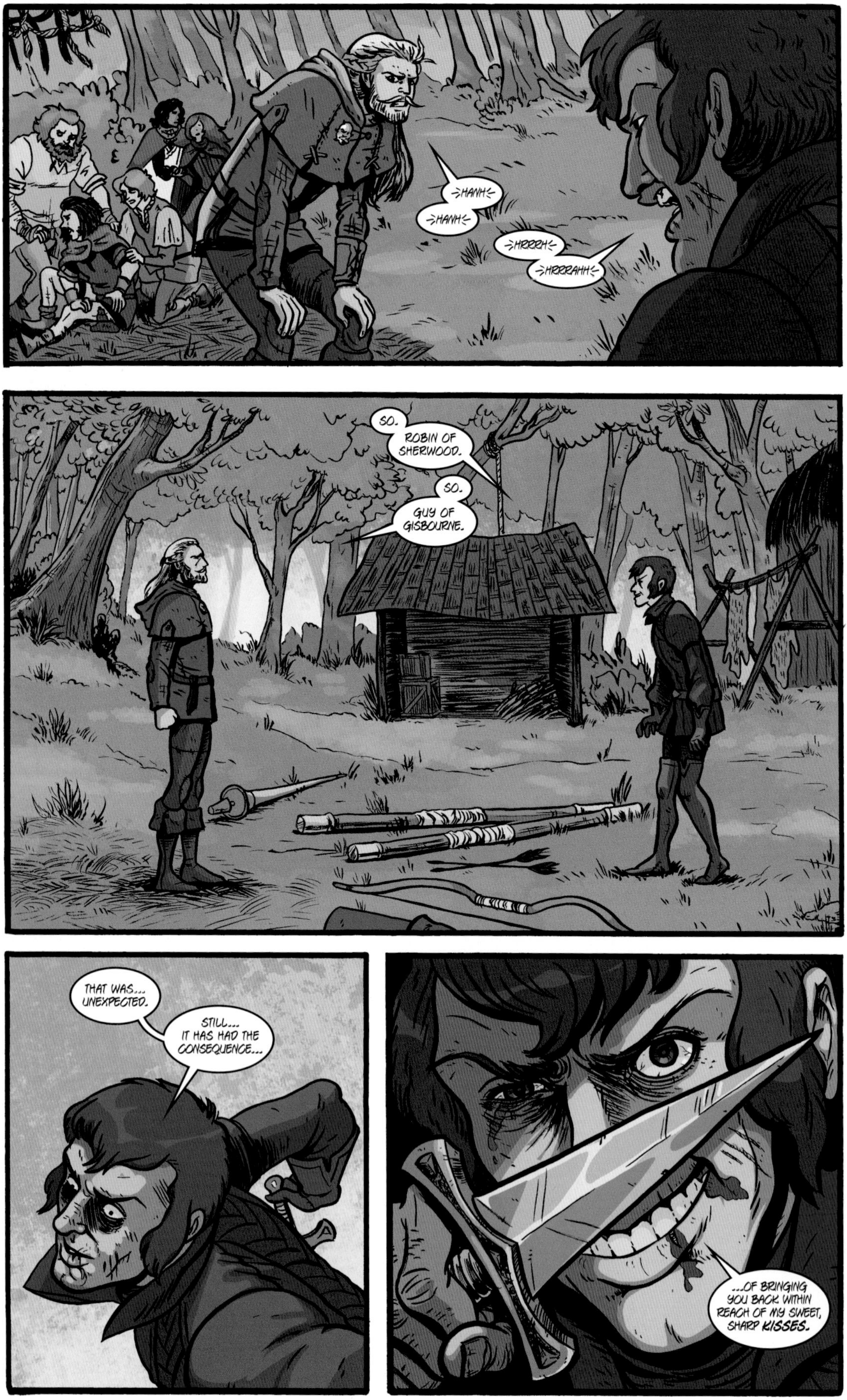
HANH
HANH
HRRRH
HRRRAHH
SO.
ROBIN OF SHERWOOD.
SO.
GUY OF GISBOURNE.
THAT WAS... UNEXPECTED.
STILL... IT HAS HAD THE CONSEQUENCE...
...OF BRINGING YOU BACK WITHIN REACH OF MY SWEET, SHARP KISSES.

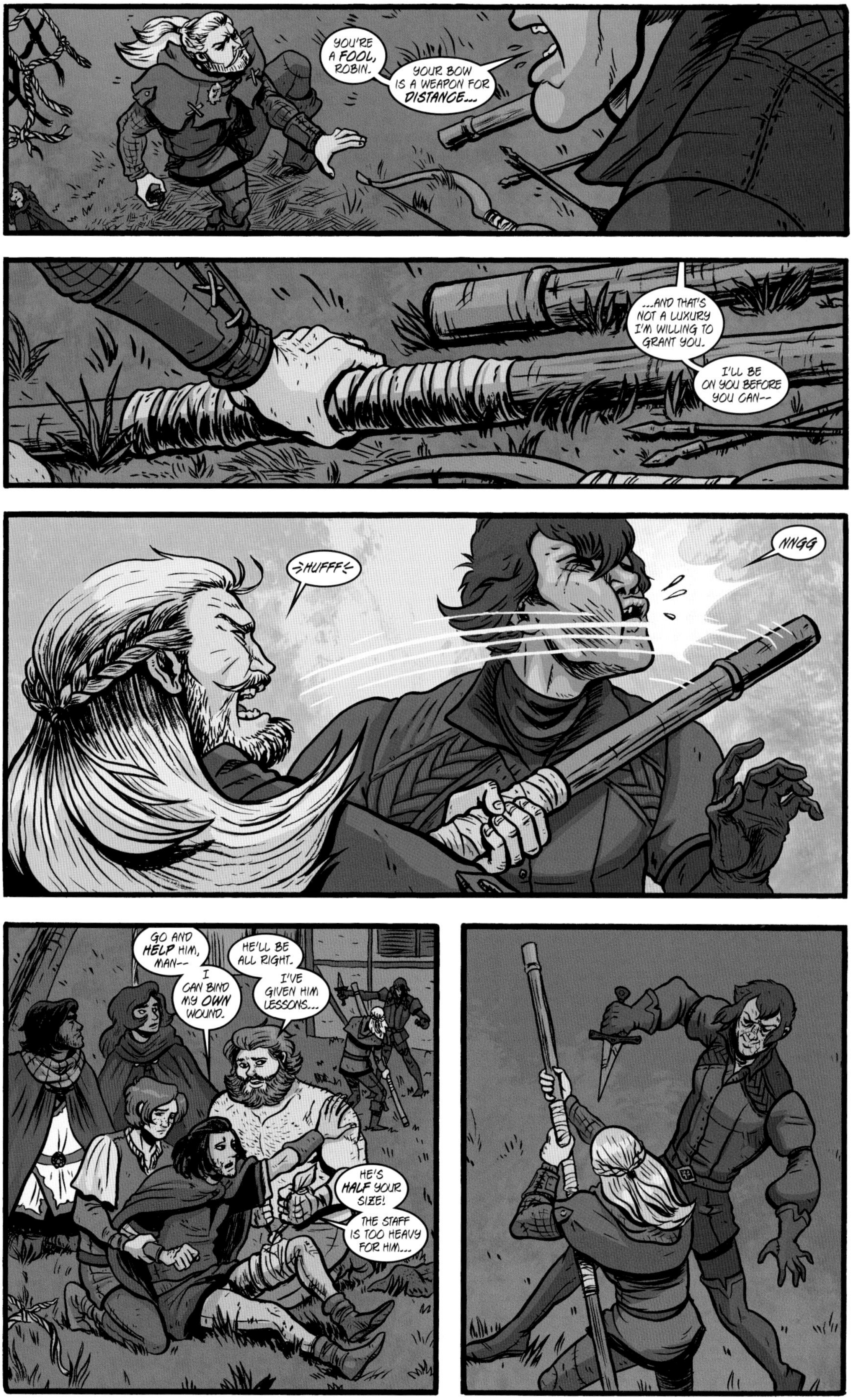

YOU'RE A FOOL, ROBIN.
YOUR BOW IS A WEAPON FOR DISTANCE...
...AND THAT'S NOT A LUXURY I'M WILLING TO GRANT YOU.
I'LL BE ON YOU BEFORE YOU CAN--
HUFFF
NNGG
GO AND HELP HIM, MAN--
I CAN BIND MY OWN WOUND.
HE'LL BE ALL RIGHT.
I'VE GIVEN HIM LESSONS...
HE'S HALF YOUR SIZE!
THE STAFF IS TOO HEAVY FOR HIM...

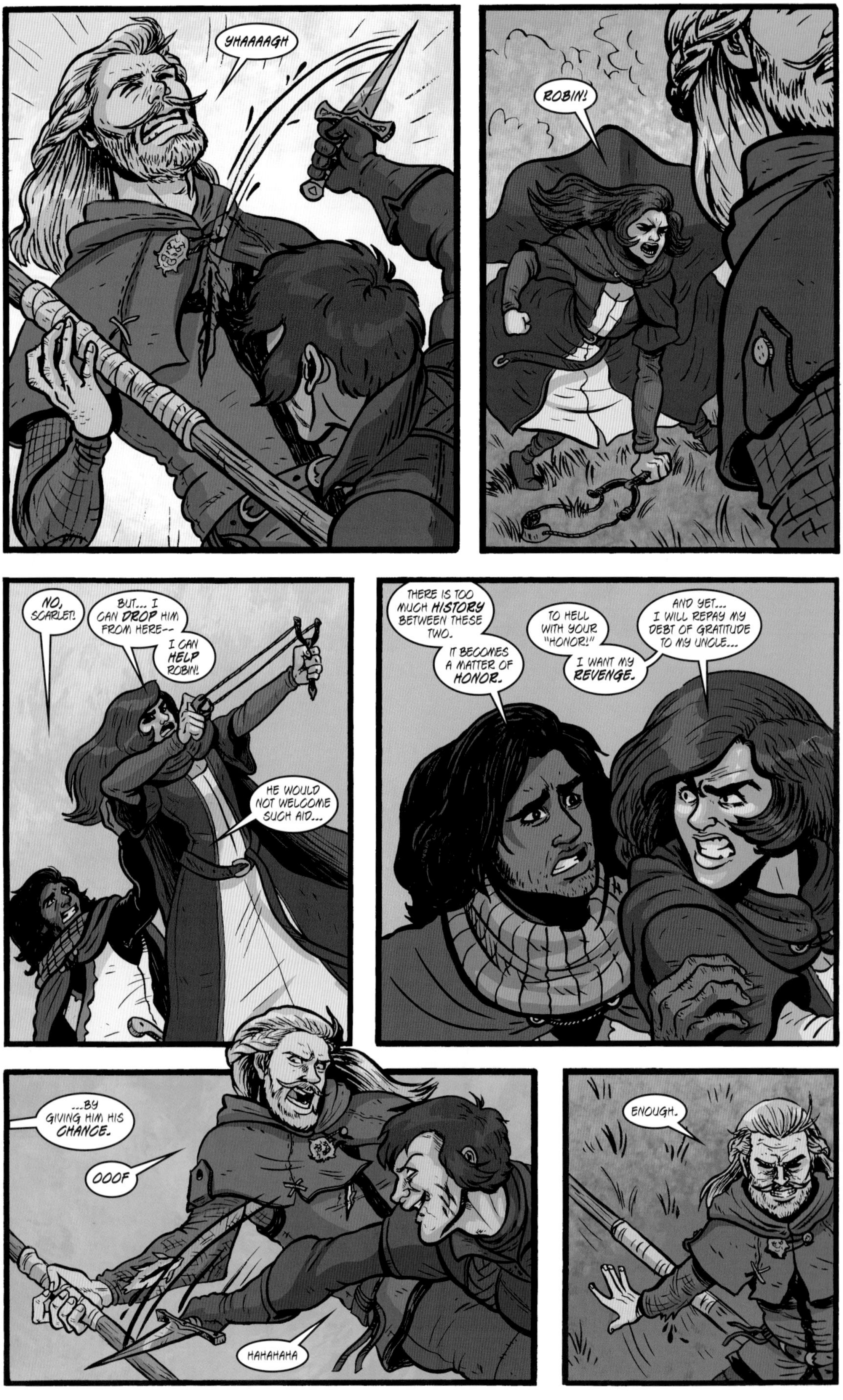
YHAAAAGH
ROBIN!
NO, SCARLET!
BUT... I CAN DROP HIM FROM HERE--
I CAN HELP ROBIN!
HE WOULD NOT WELCOME SUCH AID...
THERE IS TOO MUCH HISTORY BETWEEN THESE TWO.
IT BECOMES A MATTER OF HONOR.
TO HELL WITH YOUR "HONOR!"
I WANT MY REVENGE.
AND YET... I WILL REPAY MY DEBT OF GRATITUDE TO MY UNCLE...
...BY GIVING HIM HIS CHANCE.
OOOF
HAHAHAHA
ENOUGH.

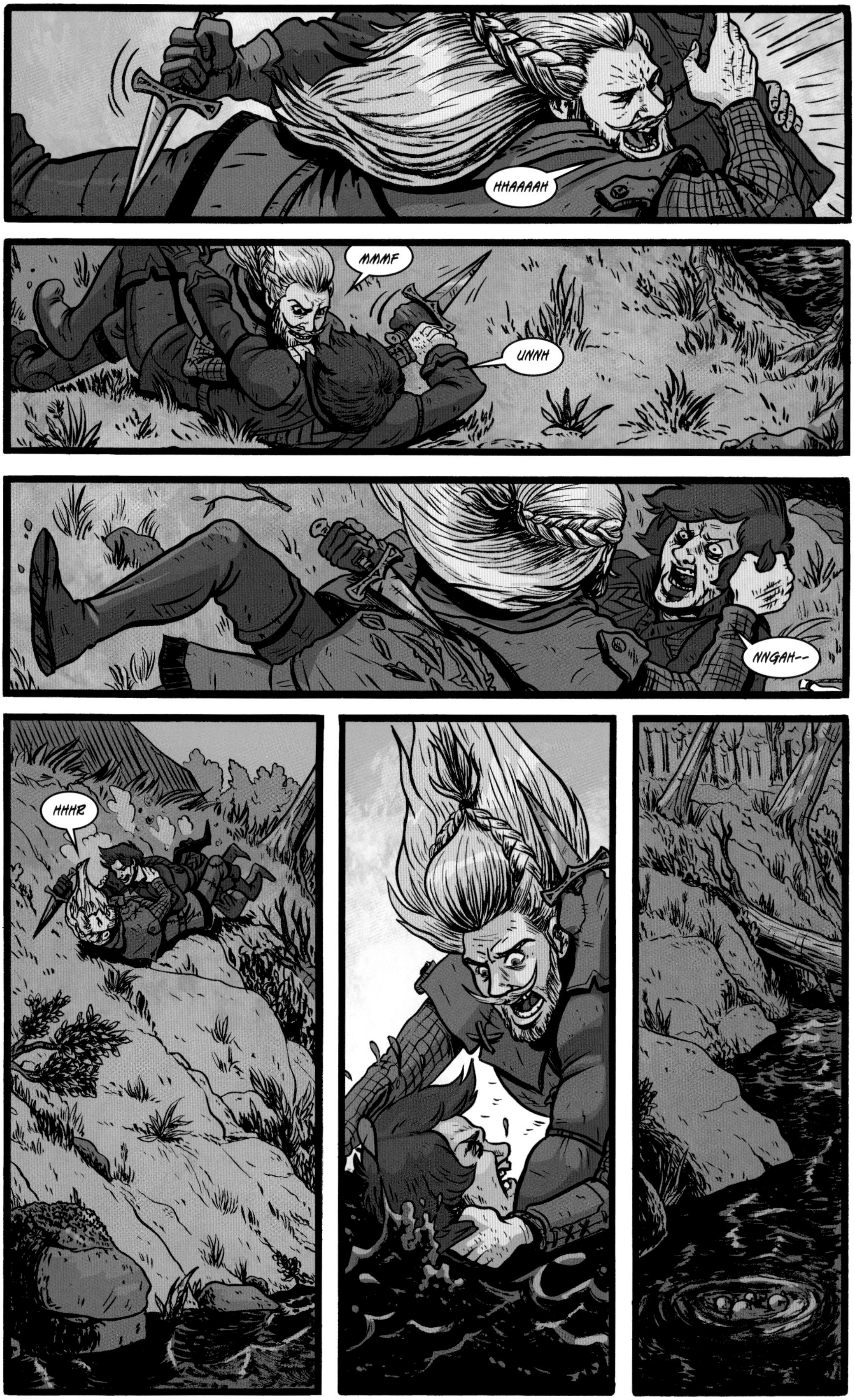
HHAAAAH
MMMF
UNNH
NNGAH--
HHHR

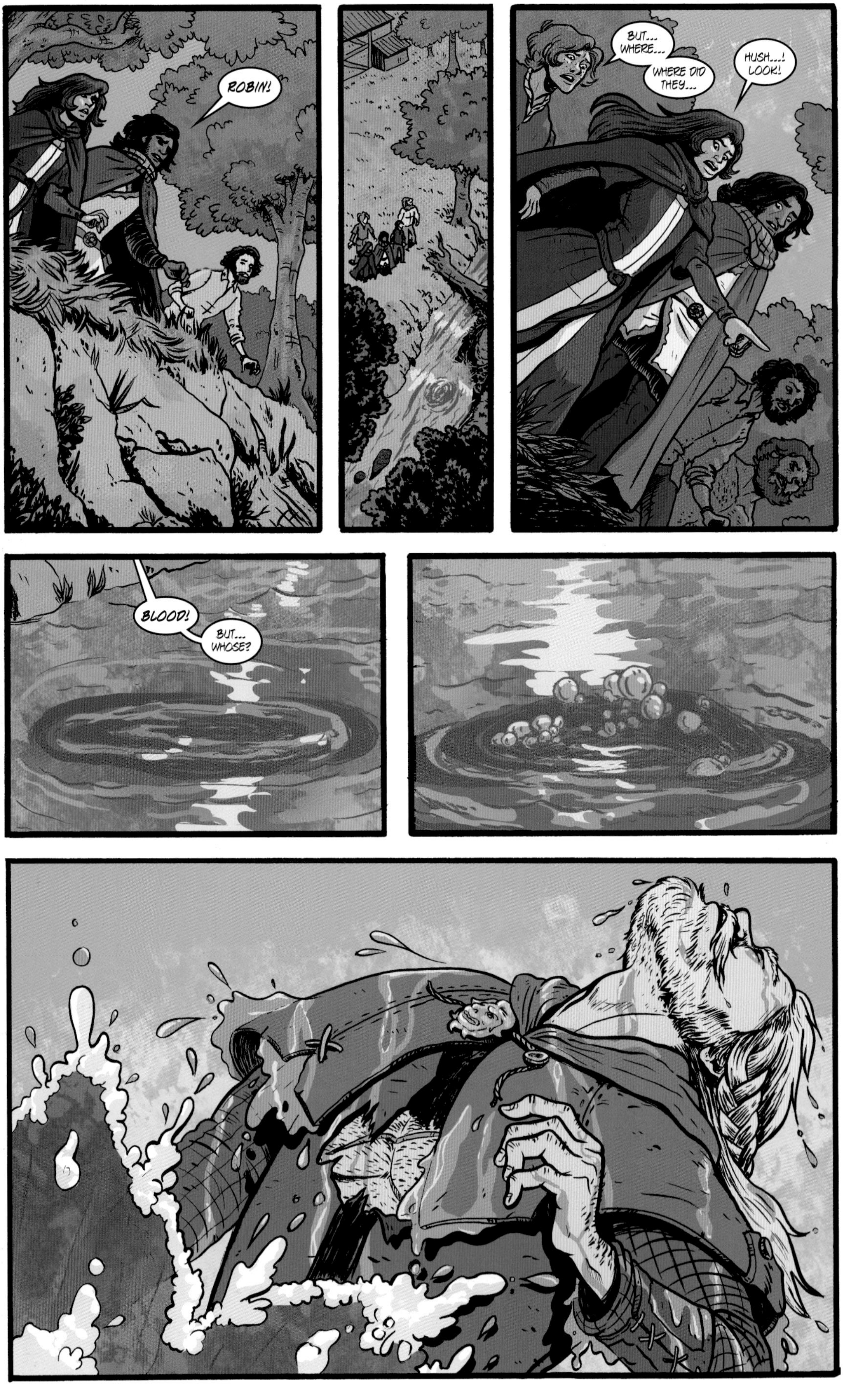
ROBIN!
BUT... WHERE...
WHERE DID THEY...
HUSH...! LOOK!
BLOOD!
BUT... WHOSE?

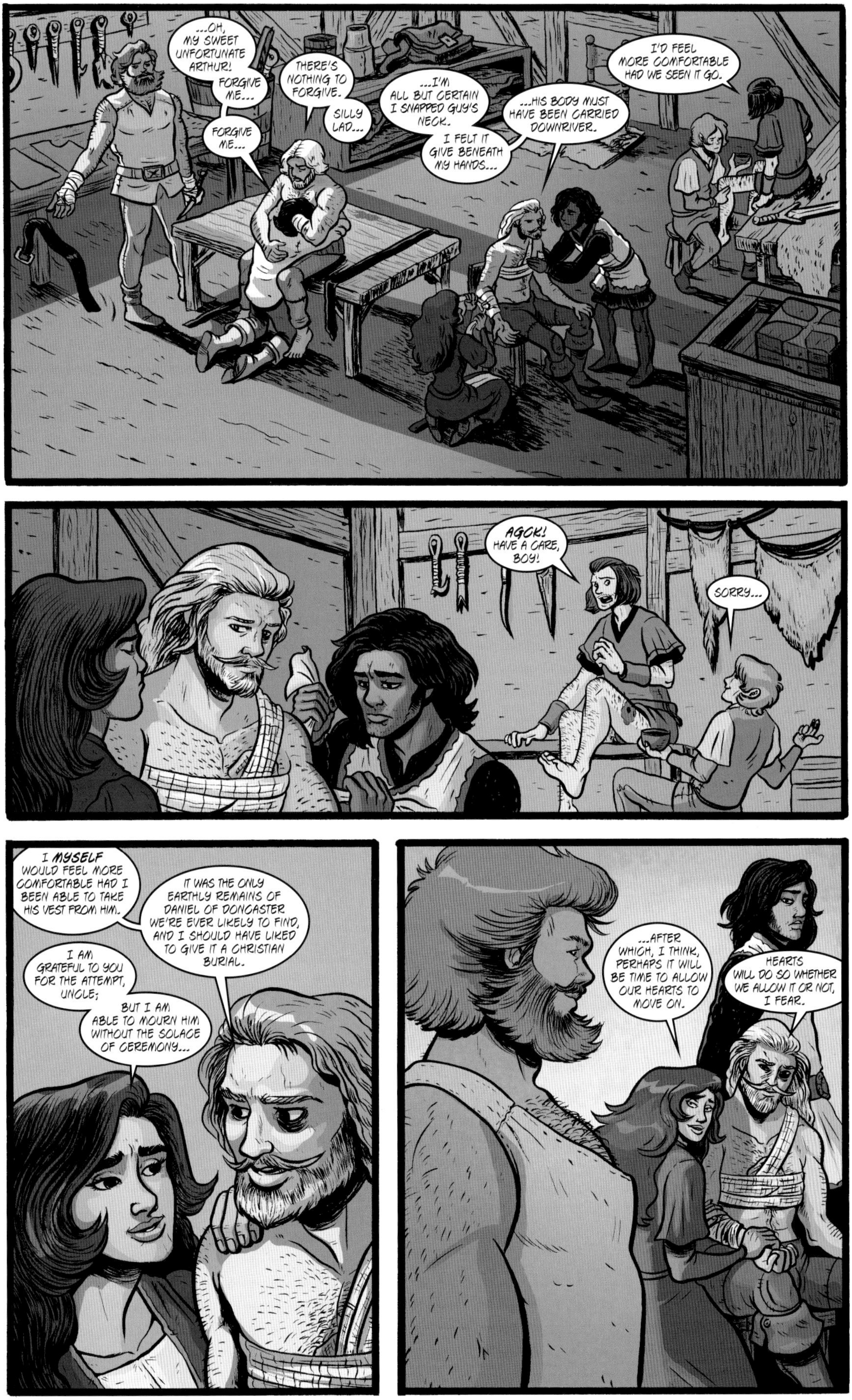
...OH, MY SWEET UNFORTUNATE ARTHUR!
FORGIVE ME...
FORGIVE ME...
THERE'S NOTHING TO FORGIVE.
SILLY LAD...
...I'M ALL BUT CERTAIN I SNAPPED GUY'S NECK.
I FELT IT GIVE BENEATH MY HANDS...
...HIS BODY MUST HAVE BEEN CARRIED DOWNRIVER.
I'D FEEL MORE COMFORTABLE HAD WE SEEN IT GO.
AGOK! HAVE A CARE, BOY!
SORRY...
I MYSELF WOULD FEEL MORE COMFORTABLE HAD I BEEN ABLE TO TAKE HIS VEST FROM HIM.
IT WAS THE ONLY EARTHLY REMAINS OF DANIEL OF DONCASTER WE'RE EVER LIKELY TO FIND, AND I SHOULD HAVE LIKED TO GIVE IT A CHRISTIAN BURIAL.
I AM GRATEFUL TO YOU FOR THE ATTEMPT, UNCLE;
BUT I AM ABLE TO MOURN HIM WITHOUT THE SOLACE OF CEREMONY...
...AFTER WHICH, I THINK, PERHAPS IT WILL BE TIME TO ALLOW OUR HEARTS TO MOVE ON.
HEARTS WILL DO SO WHETHER WE ALLOW IT OR NOT, I FEAR.

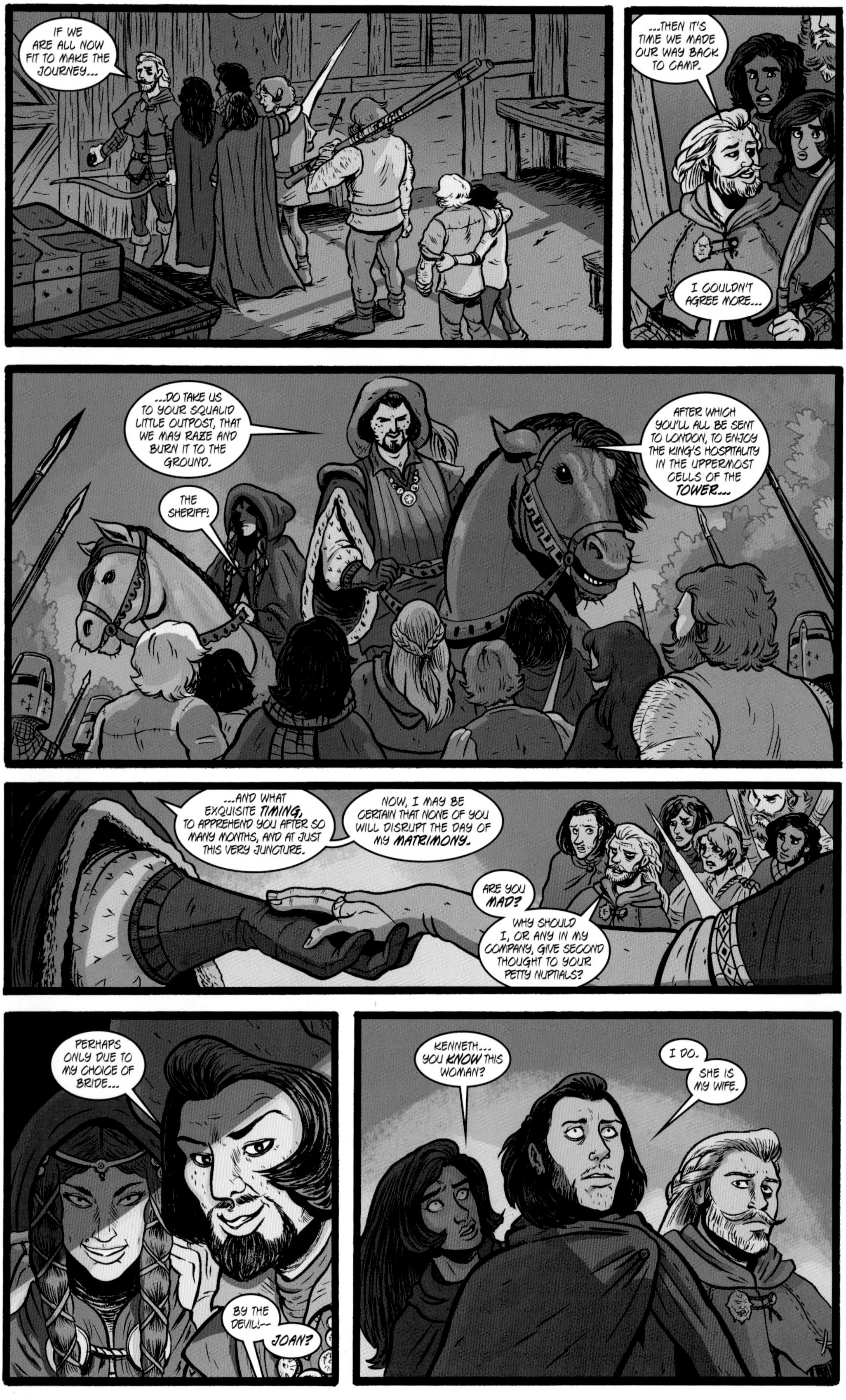

IF WE ARE ALL NOW FIT TO MAKE THE JOURNEY...
...THEN IT'S TIME WE MADE OUR WAY BACK TO CAMP.
I COULDN'T AGREE MORE...
...DO TAKE US TO YOUR SQUALID LITTLE OUTPOST, THAT WE MAY RAZE AND BURN IT TO THE GROUND.
AFTER WHICH YOU'LL ALL BE SENT TO LONDON, TO ENJOY THE KING'S HOSPITALITY IN THE UPPERMOST CELLS OF THE TOWER...
THE SHERIFF!
...AND WHAT EXQUISITE TIMING, TO APPREHEND YOU AFTER SO MANY MONTHS, AND AT JUST THIS VERY JUNCTURE.
NOW, I MAY BE CERTAIN THAT NONE OF YOU WILL DISRUPT THE DAY OF MY MATRIMONY.
ARE YOU MAD?
WHY SHOULD I, OR ANY IN MY COMPANY, GIVE SECOND THOUGHT TO YOUR PETTY NUPTIALS?
PERHAPS ONLY DUE TO MY CHOICE OF BRIDE...
BY THE DEVIL!-- JOAN?
KENNETH... YOU KNOW THIS WOMAN?
I DO.
SHE IS MY WIFE.

Chapter 8

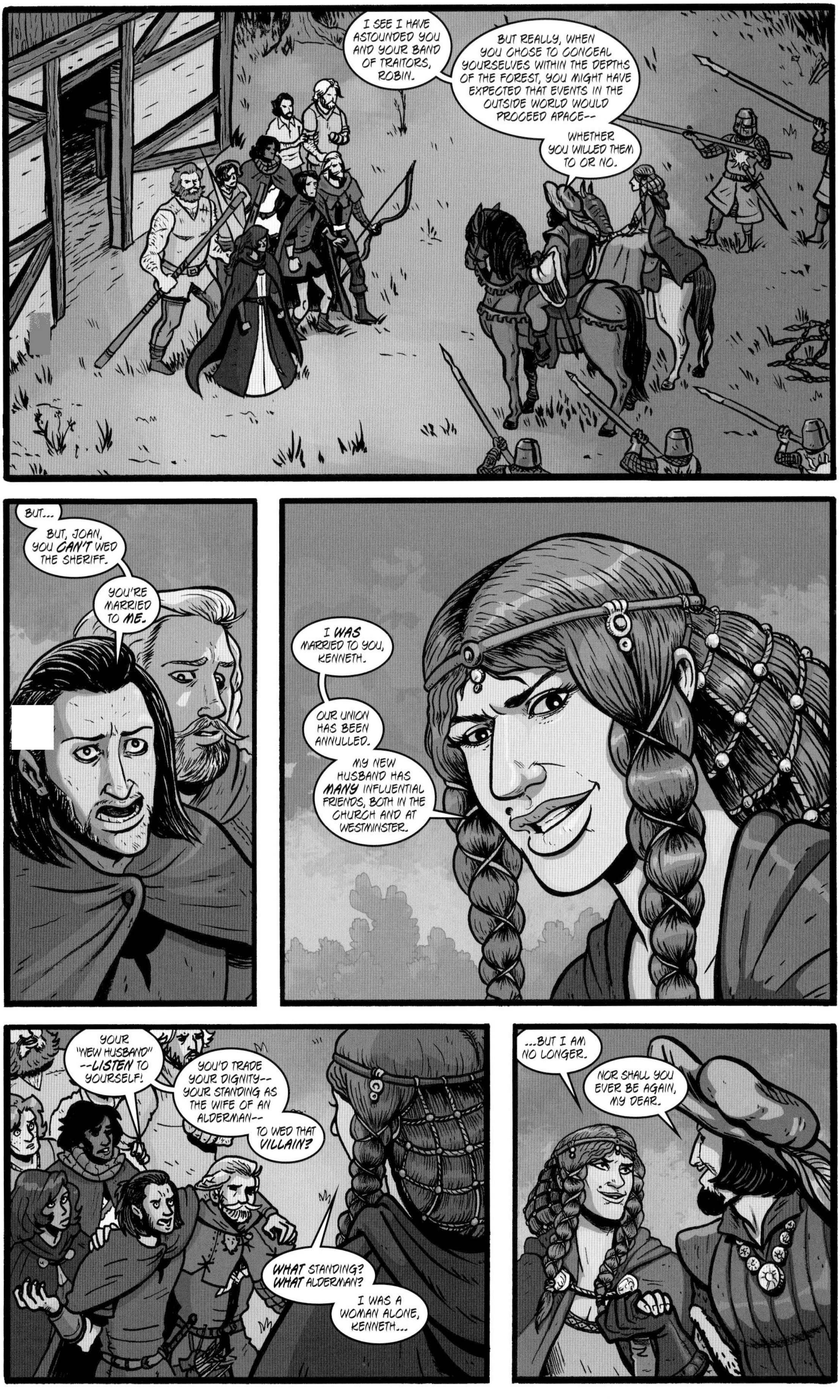
I SEE I HAVE ASTOUNDED YOU AND YOUR BAND OF TRAITORS, ROBIN.
BUT REALLY, WHEN YOU CHOSE TO CONCEAL YOURSELVES WITHIN THE DEPTHS OF THE FOREST, YOU MIGHT HAVE EXPECTED THAT EVENTS IN THE OUTSIDE WORLD WOULD PROCEED APACE--
WHETHER YOU WILLED THEM TO OR NO.
BUT...
BUT, JOAN, YOU CAN'T WED THE SHERIFF.
YOU'RE MARRIED TO ME.
I WAS MARRIED TO YOU, KENNETH.
OUR UNION HAS BEEN ANNULLED.
MY NEW HUSBAND HAS MANY INFLUENTIAL FRIENDS, BOTH IN THE CHURCH AND AT WESTMINSTER.
YOUR "NEW HUSBAND" --LISTEN TO YOURSELF!
YOU'D TRADE YOUR DIGNITY-- YOUR STANDING AS THE WIFE OF AN ALDERMAN--
TO WED THAT VILLAIN?
WHAT STANDING? WHAT ALDERMAN?
I WAS A WOMAN ALONE, KENNETH...
...BUT I AM NO LONGER.
NOR SHALL YOU EVER BE AGAIN, MY DEAR.

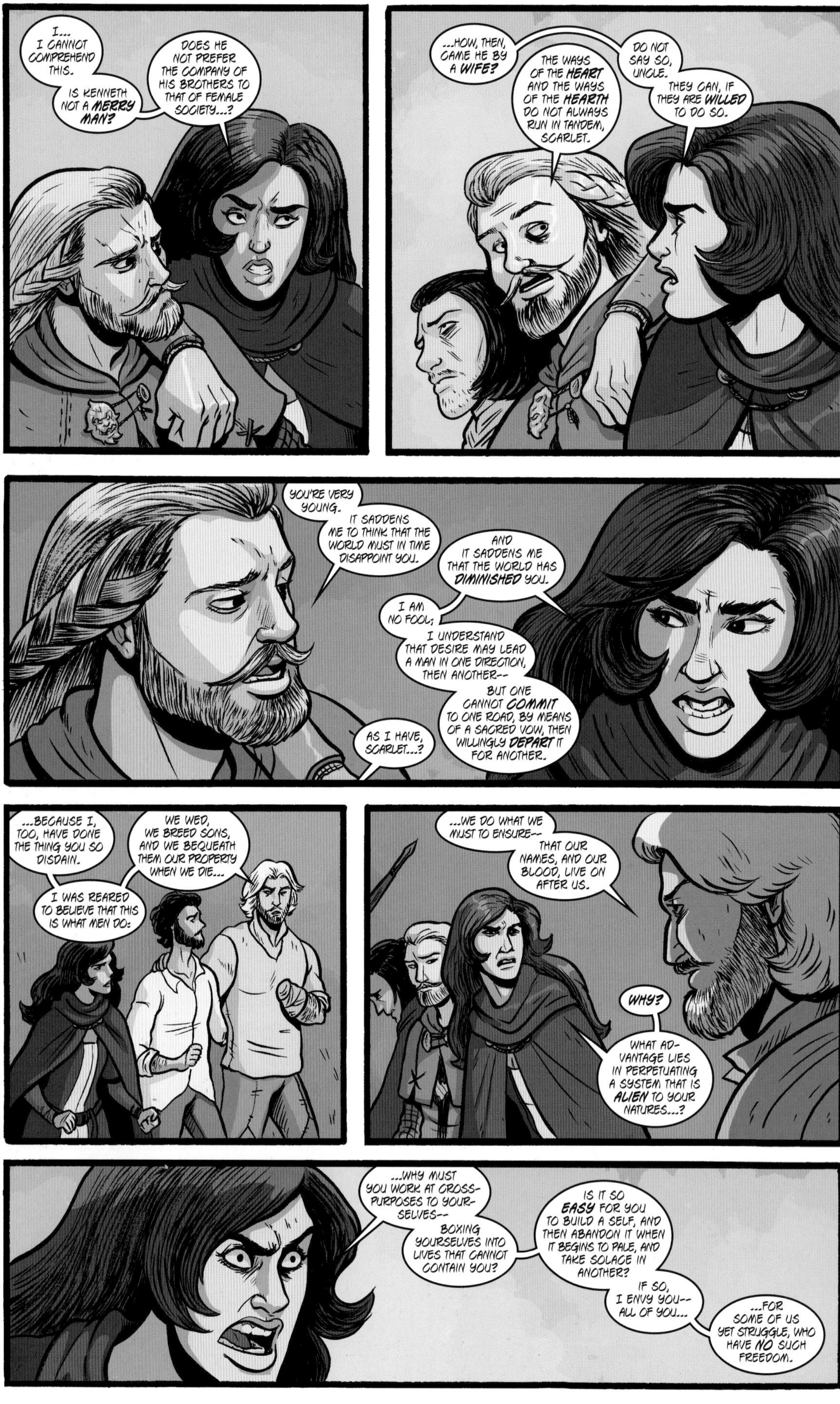
I... I CANNOT COMPREHEND THIS.
IS KENNETH NOT A MERRY MAN?
DOES HE NOT PREFER THE COMPANY OF HIS BROTHERS TO THAT OF FEMALE SOCIETY...?
...HOW, THEN, CAME HE BY A WIFE?
THE WAYS OF THE HEART AND THE WAYS OF THE HEARTH DO NOT ALWAYS RUN IN TANDEM, SCARLET.
DO NOT SAY SO, UNCLE.
THEY CAN, IF THEY ARE WILLED TO DO SO.
YOU'RE VERY YOUNG.
IT SADDENS ME TO THINK THAT THE WORLD MUST IN TIME DISAPPOINT YOU.
AND IT SADDENS ME THAT THE WORLD HAS DIMINISHED YOU.
I AM NO FOOL;
I UNDERSTAND THAT DESIRE MAY LEAD A MAN IN ONE DIRECTION, THEN ANOTHER--
BUT ONE CANNOT COMMIT TO ONE ROAD, BY MEANS OF A SACRED VOW, THEN WILLINGLY DEPART IT FOR ANOTHER.
AS I HAVE, SCARLET...?
...BECAUSE I, TOO, HAVE DONE THE THING YOU SO DISDAIN.
I WAS REARED TO BELIEVE THAT THIS IS WHAT MEN DO:
WE WED, WE BREED SONS, AND WE BEQUEATH THEM OUR PROPERTY WHEN WE DIE...
...WE DO WHAT WE MUST TO ENSURE--
THAT OUR NAMES, AND OUR BLOOD, LIVE ON AFTER US.
WHY?
WHAT ADVANTAGE LIES IN PERPETUATING A SYSTEM THAT IS ALIEN TO YOUR NATURES...?
...WHY MUST YOU WORK AT CROSS-PURPOSES TO YOURSELVES--
BOXING YOURSELVES INTO LIVES THAT CANNOT CONTAIN YOU?
IS IT SO EASY FOR YOU TO BUILD A SELF, AND THEN ABANDON IT WHEN IT BEGINS TO PALE, AND TAKE SOLACE IN ANOTHER?
IF SO, I ENVY YOU-- ALL OF YOU...
...FOR SOME OF US YET STRUGGLE, WHO HAVE NO SUCH FREEDOM.

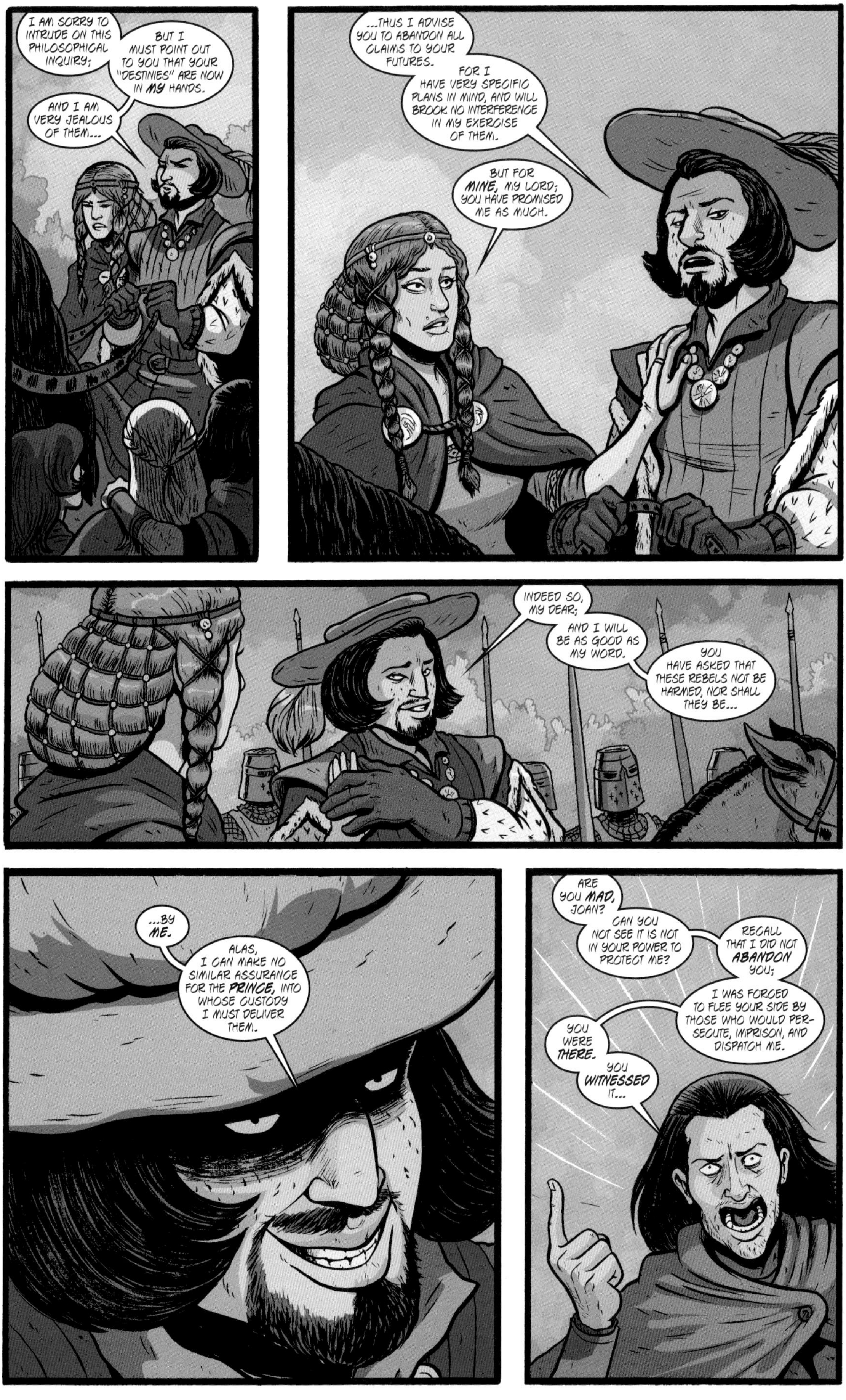
I AM SORRY TO INTRUDE ON THIS PHILOSOPHICAL INQUIRY;
BUT I MUST POINT OUT TO YOU THAT YOUR "DESTINIES" ARE NOW IN MY HANDS.
AND I AM VERY JEALOUS OF THEM...
...THUS I ADVISE YOU TO ABANDON ALL CLAIMS TO YOUR FUTURES.
FOR I HAVE VERY SPECIFIC PLANS IN MIND, AND WILL BROOK NO INTERFERENCE IN MY EXERCISE OF THEM.
BUT FOR MINE, MY LORD; YOU HAVE PROMISED ME AS MUCH.
INDEED SO, MY DEAR;
AND I WILL BE AS GOOD AS MY WORD.
YOU HAVE ASKED THAT THESE REBELS NOT BE HARMED, NOR SHALL THEY BE...
...BY ME.
ALAS, I CAN MAKE NO SIMILAR ASSURANCE FOR THE PRINCE, INTO WHOSE CUSTODY I MUST DELIVER THEM.
ARE YOU MAD, JOAN?
CAN YOU NOT SEE IT IS NOT IN YOUR POWER TO PROTECT ME?
RECALL THAT I DID NOT ABANDON YOU;
I WAS FORCED TO FLEE YOUR SIDE BY THOSE WHO WOULD PERSECUTE, IMPRISON, AND DISPATCH ME.
YOU WERE THERE.
YOU WITNESSED IT...

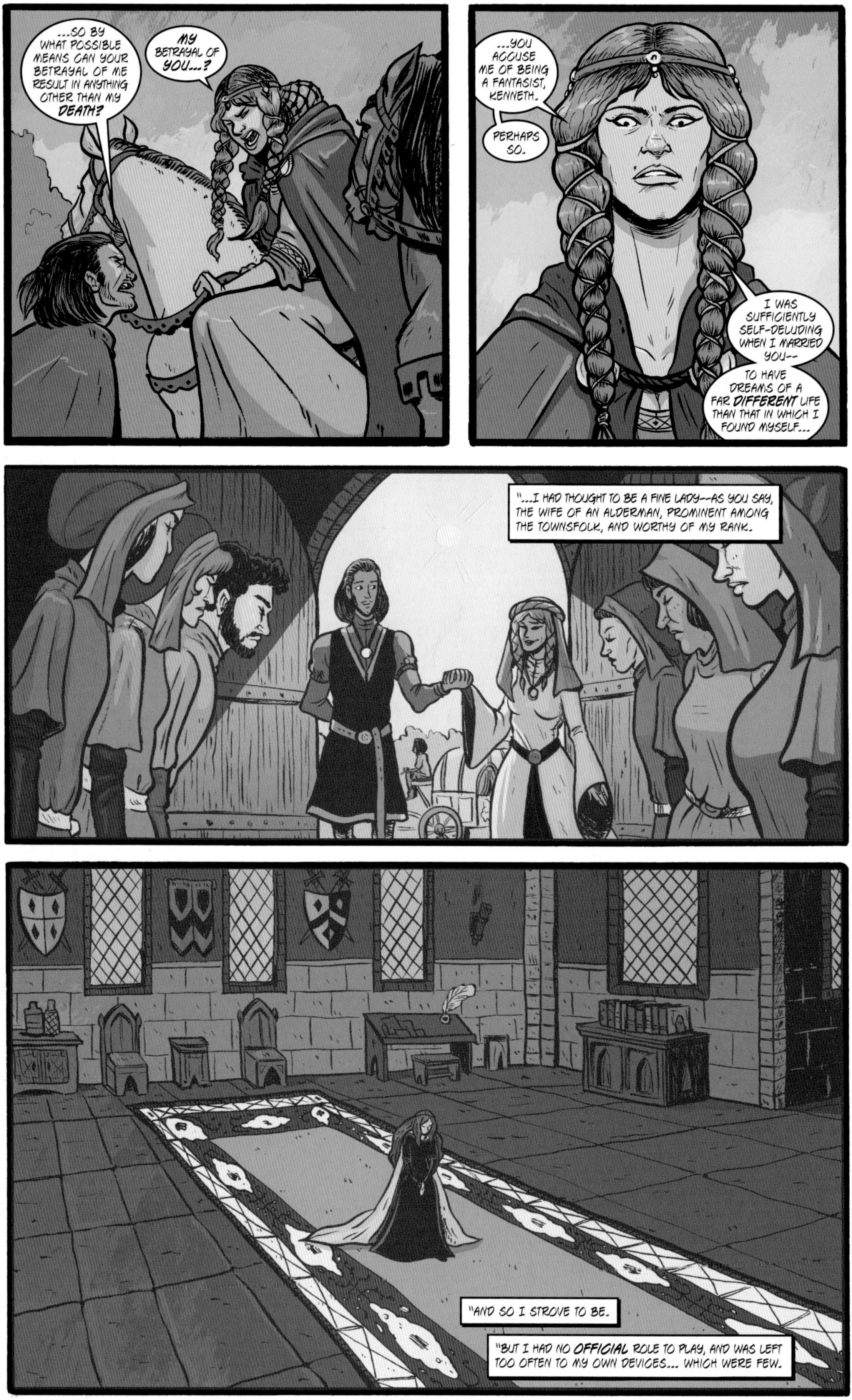
...SO BY WHAT POSSIBLE MEANS CAN YOUR BETRAYAL OF ME RESULT IN ANYTHING OTHER THAN MY DEATH?
MY BETRAYAL OF YOU...?
...YOU ACCUSE ME OF BEING A FANTASIST, KENNETH.
PERHAPS SO.
I WAS SUFFICIENTLY SELF-DELUDING WHEN I MARRIED YOU--
TO HAVE DREAMS OF A FAR DIFFERENT LIFE THAN THAT IN WHICH I FOUND MYSELF...
"...I HAD THOUGHT TO BE A FINE LADY--AS YOU SAY, THE WIFE OF AN ALDERMAN, PROMINENT AMONG THE TOWNSFOLK, AND WORTHY OF MY RANK.
"AND SO I STROVE TO BE.
"BUT I HAD NO OFFICIAL ROLE TO PLAY, AND WAS LEFT TOO OFTEN TO MY OWN DEVICES... WHICH WERE FEW.

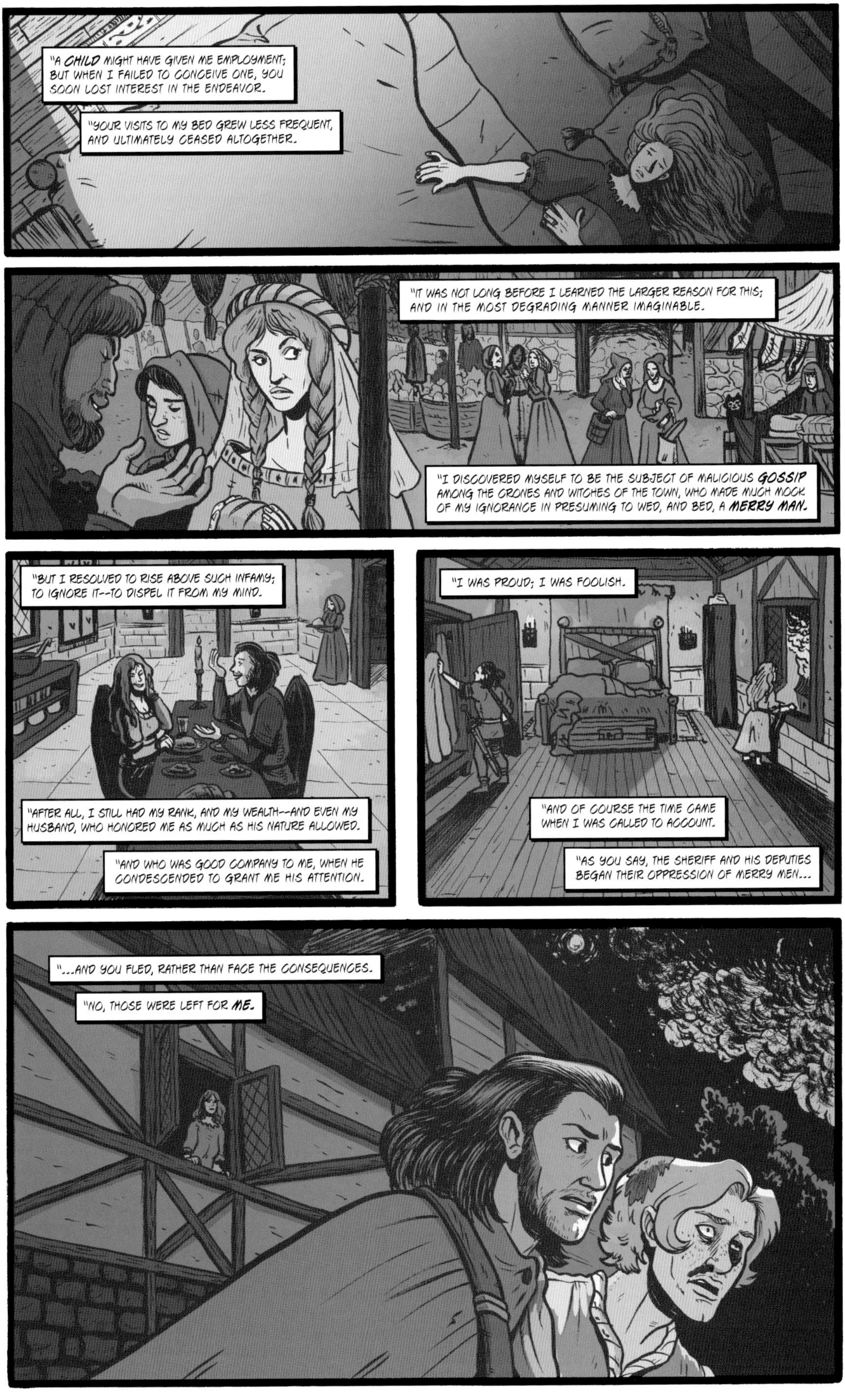
"A CHILD MIGHT HAVE GIVEN ME EMPLOYMENT; BUT WHEN I FAILED TO CONCEIVE ONE, YOU SOON LOST INTEREST IN THE ENDEAVOR.
"YOUR VISITS TO MY BED GREW LESS FREQUENT, AND ULTIMATELY CEASED ALTOGETHER.
"IT WAS NOT LONG BEFORE I LEARNED THE LARGER REASON FOR THIS; AND IN THE MOST DEGRADING MANNER IMAGINABLE.
"I DISCOVERED MYSELF TO BE THE SUBJECT OF MALICIOUS GOSSIP AMONG THE CRONES AND WITCHES OF THE TOWN, WHO MADE MUCH MOCK OF MY IGNORANCE IN PRESUMING TO WED, AND BED, A MERRY MAN.
"BUT I RESOLVED TO RISE ABOVE SUCH INFAMY; TO IGNORE IT--TO DISPEL IT FROM MY MIND.
"AFTER ALL, I STILL HAD MY RANK, AND MY WEALTH--AND EVEN MY HUSBAND, WHO HONORED ME AS MUCH AS HIS NATURE ALLOWED.
"AND WHO WAS GOOD COMPANY TO ME, WHEN HE CONDESCENDED TO GRANT ME HIS ATTENTION.
"I WAS PROUD; I WAS FOOLISH.
"AND OF COURSE THE TIME CAME WHEN I WAS CALLED TO ACCOUNT.
"AS YOU SAY, THE SHERIFF AND HIS DEPUTIES BEGAN THEIR OPPRESSION OF MERRY MEN...
"...AND YOU FLED, RATHER THAN FACE THE CONSEQUENCES.
"NO, THOSE WERE LEFT FOR ME.

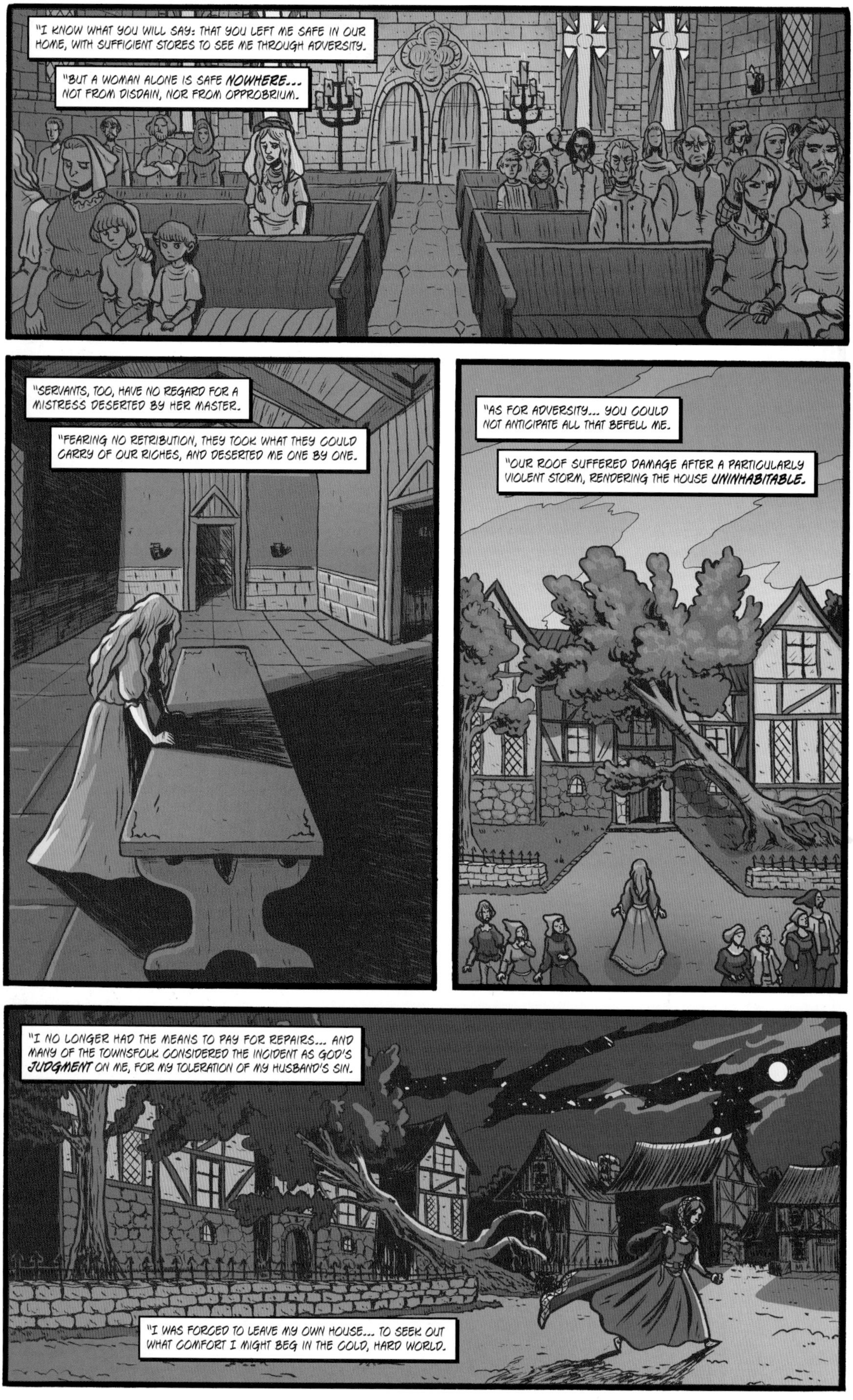
"I KNOW WHAT YOU WILL SAY: THAT YOU LEFT ME SAFE IN OUR HOME, WITH SUFFICIENT STORES TO SEE ME THROUGH ADVERSITY.
"BUT A WOMAN ALONE IS SAFE NOWHERE... NOT FROM DISDAIN, NOR FROM OPPROBRIUM.
"SERVANTS, TOO, HAVE NO REGARD FOR A MISTRESS DESERTED BY HER MASTER.
"FEARING NO RETRIBUTION, THEY TOOK WHAT THEY COULD CARRY OF OUR RICHES, AND DESERTED ME ONE BY ONE.
"AS FOR ADVERSITY... YOU COULD NOT ANTICIPATE ALL THAT BEFELL ME.
"OUR ROOF SUFFERED DAMAGE AFTER A PARTICULARLY VIOLENT STORM, RENDERING THE HOUSE UNINHABITABLE.
"I NO LONGER HAD THE MEANS TO PAY FOR REPAIRS... AND MANY OF THE TOWNSFOLK CONSIDERED THE INCIDENT AS GOD'S JUDGMENT ON ME, FOR MY TOLERATION OF MY HUSBAND'S SIN.
"I WAS FORCED TO LEAVE MY OWN HOUSE... TO SEEK OUT WHAT COMFORT I MIGHT BEG IN THE COLD, HARD WORLD.

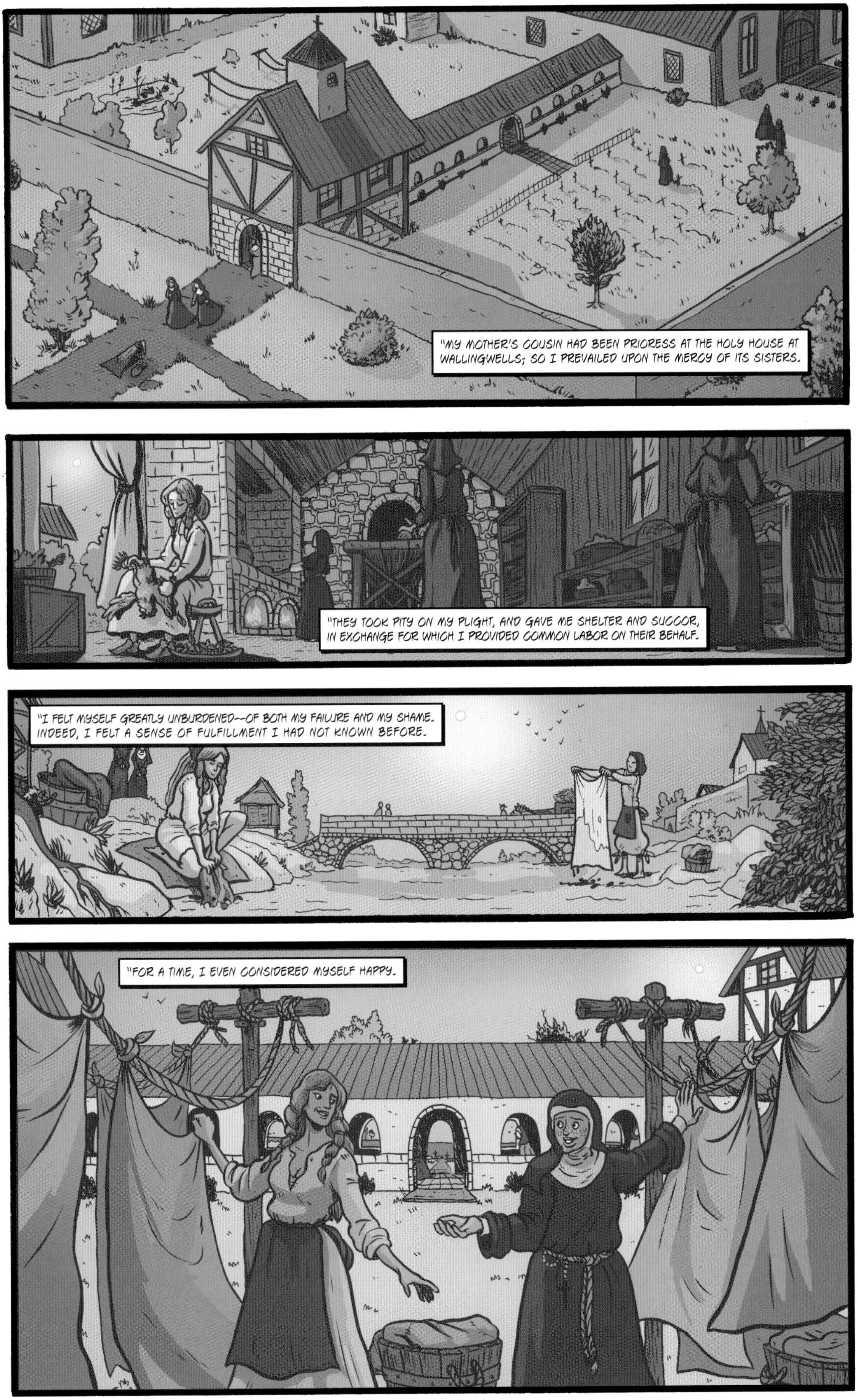
"MY MOTHER'S COUSIN HAD BEEN PRIORESS AT THE HOLY HOUSE AT WALLINGWELLS; SO I PREVAILED UPON THE MERCY OF ITS SISTERS.
"THEY TOOK PITY ON MY PLIGHT, AND GAVE ME SHELTER AND SUCCOR, IN EXCHANGE FOR WHICH I PROVIDED COMMON LABOR ON THEIR BEHALF.
"I FELT MYSELF GREATLY UNBURDENED--OF BOTH MY FAILURE AND MY SHAME. INDEED, I FELT A SENSE OF FULFILLMENT I HAD NOT KNOWN BEFORE.
"FOR A TIME, I EVEN CONSIDERED MYSELF HAPPY.

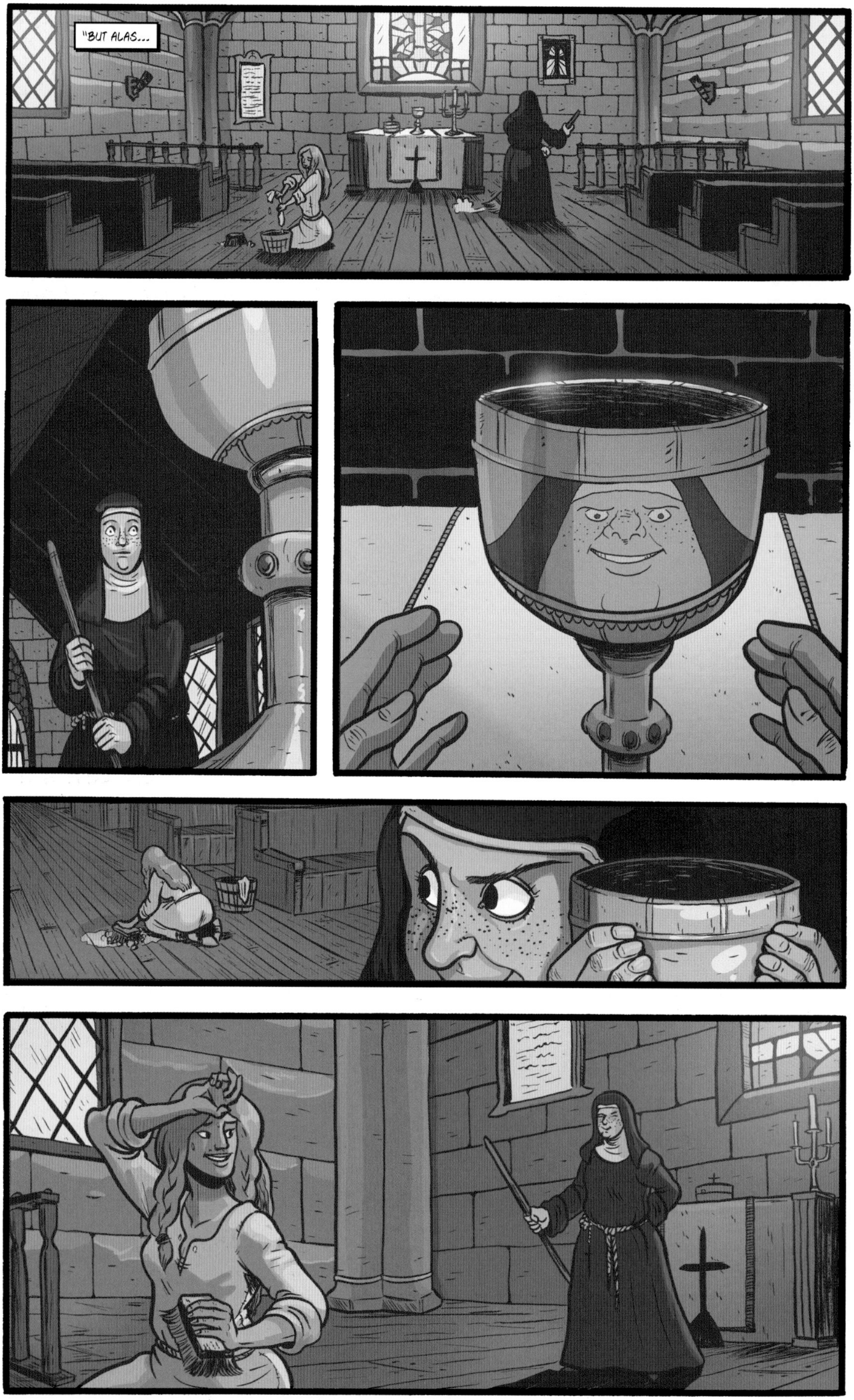
"BUT ALAS...

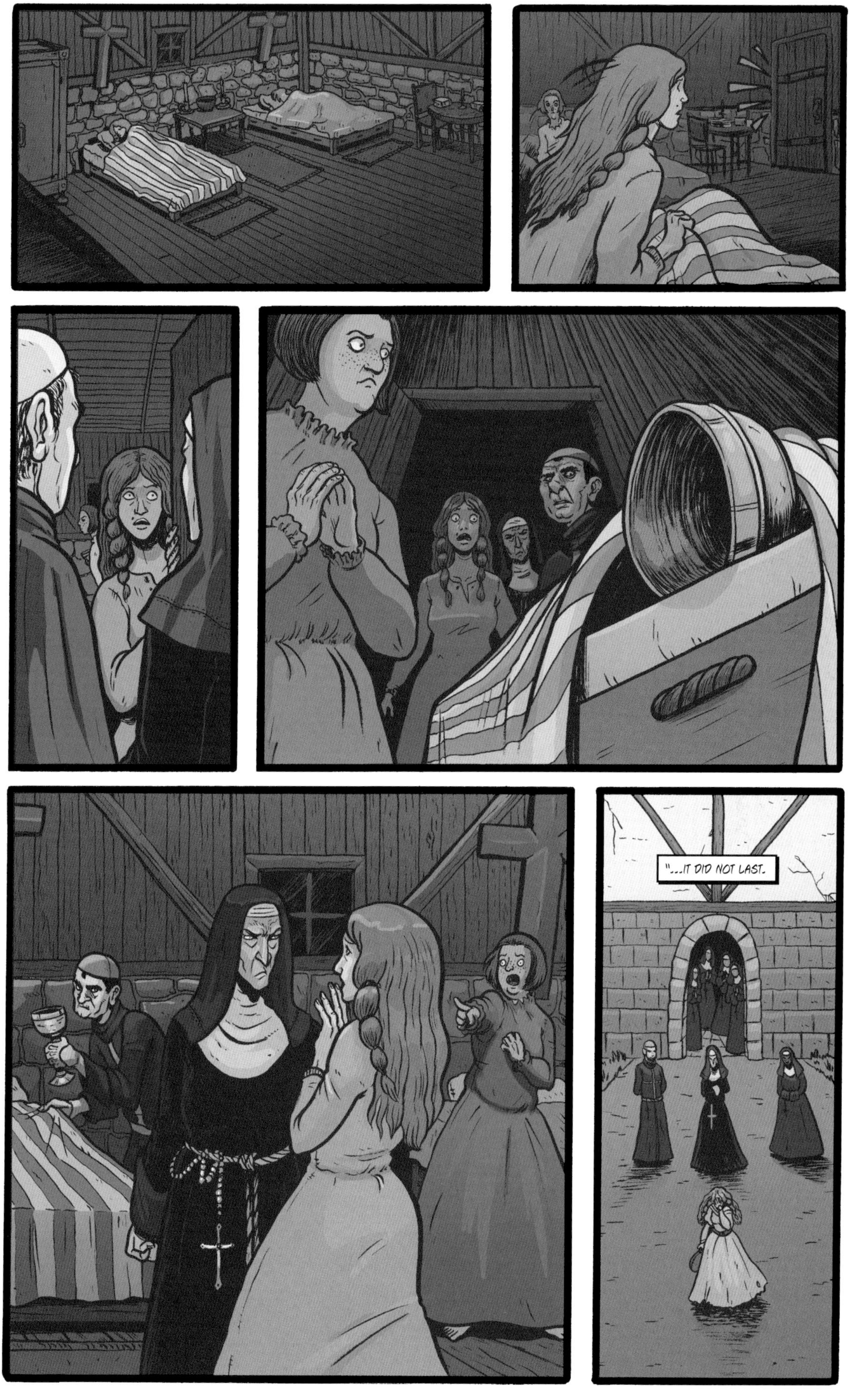
"...IT DID NOT LAST.

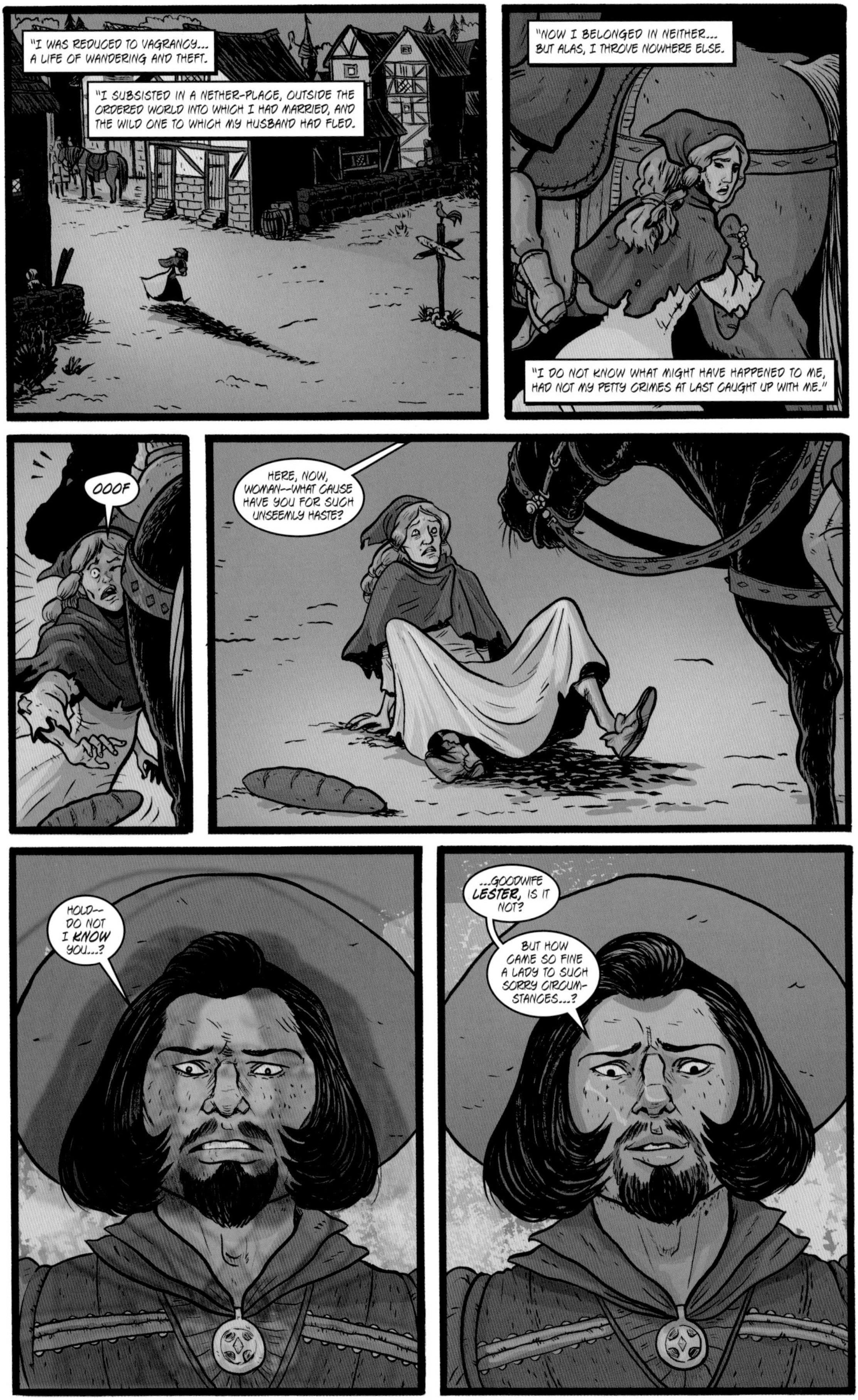
"I WAS REDUCED TO VAGRANCY... A LIFE OF WANDERING AND THEFT.
"I SUBSISTED IN A NETHER-PLACE, OUTSIDE THE ORDERED WORLD INTO WHICH I HAD MARRIED, AND THE WILD ONE TO WHICH MY HUSBAND HAD FLED.
"NOW I BELONGED IN NEITHER... BUT ALAS, I THROVE NOWHERE ELSE.
"I DO NOT KNOW WHAT MIGHT HAVE HAPPENED TO ME, HAD NOT MY PETTY CRIMES AT LAST CAUGHT UP WITH ME."
OOOF
HERE, NOW, WOMAN--WHAT CAUSE HAVE YOU FOR SUCH UNSEEMLY HASTE?
HOLD-- DO NOT I KNOW YOU...?
...GOODWIFE LESTER, IS IT NOT?
BUT HOW CAME SO FINE A LADY TO SUCH SORRY CIRCUM-STANCES...?

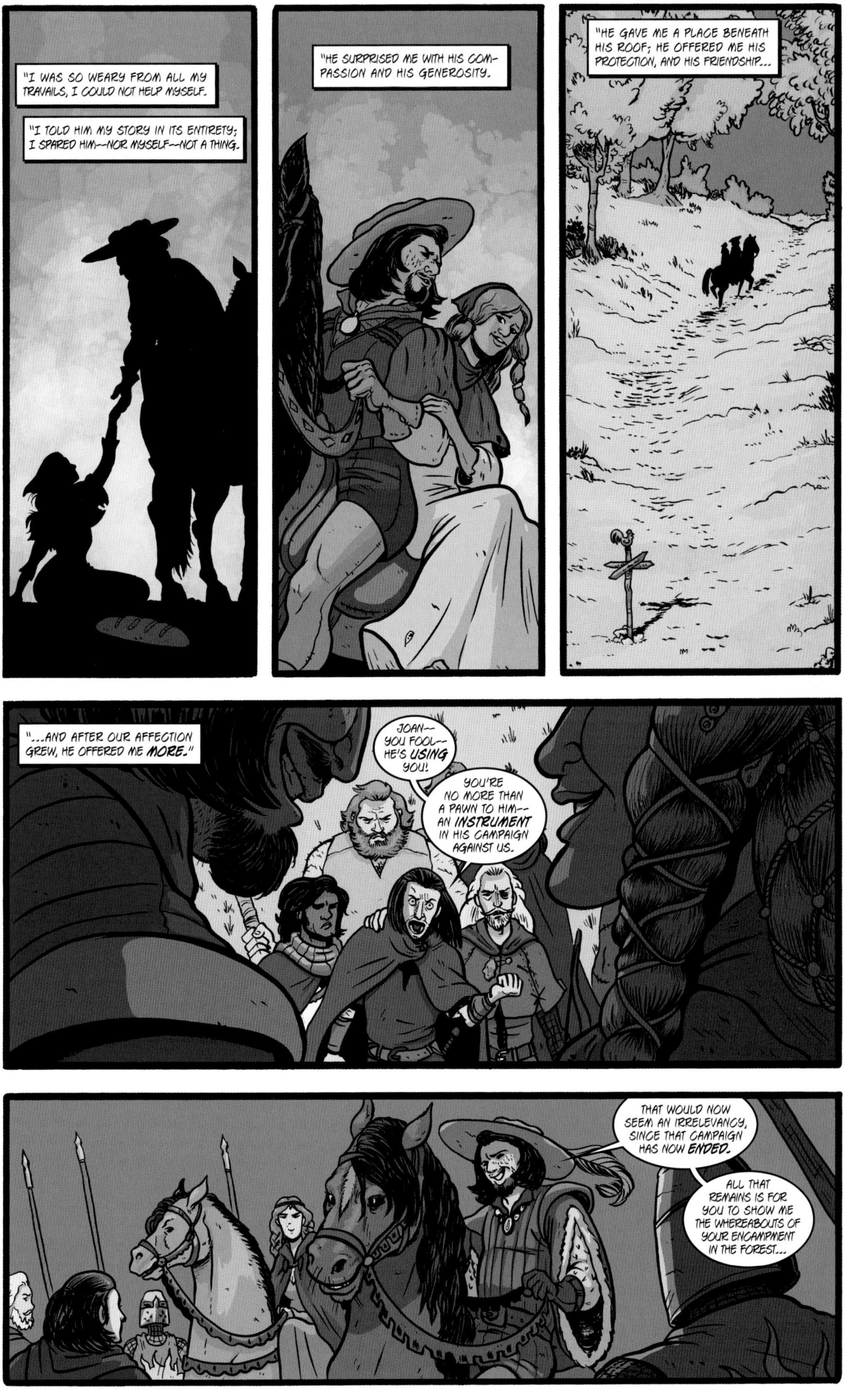
"I WAS SO WEARY FROM ALL MY TRAVAILS, I COULD NOT HELP MYSELF.
"I TOLD HIM MY STORY IN ITS ENTIRETY; I SPARED HIM--NOR MYSELF--NOT A THING.
"HE SURPRISED ME WITH HIS COMPASSION AND HIS GENEROSITY.
"HE GAVE ME A PLACE BENEATH HIS ROOF; HE OFFERED ME HIS PROTECTION, AND HIS FRIENDSHIP...
"...AND AFTER OUR AFFECTION GREW, HE OFFERED ME MORE."
JOAN-- YOU FOOL-- HE'S USING YOU!
YOU'RE NO MORE THAN A PAWN TO HIM-- AN INSTRUMENT IN HIS CAMPAIGN AGAINST US.
THAT WOULD NOW SEEM AN IRRELEVANCY, SINCE THAT CAMPAIGN HAS NOW ENDED.
ALL THAT REMAINS IS FOR YOU TO SHOW ME THE WHEREABOUTS OF YOUR ENCAMPMENT IN THE FOREST...

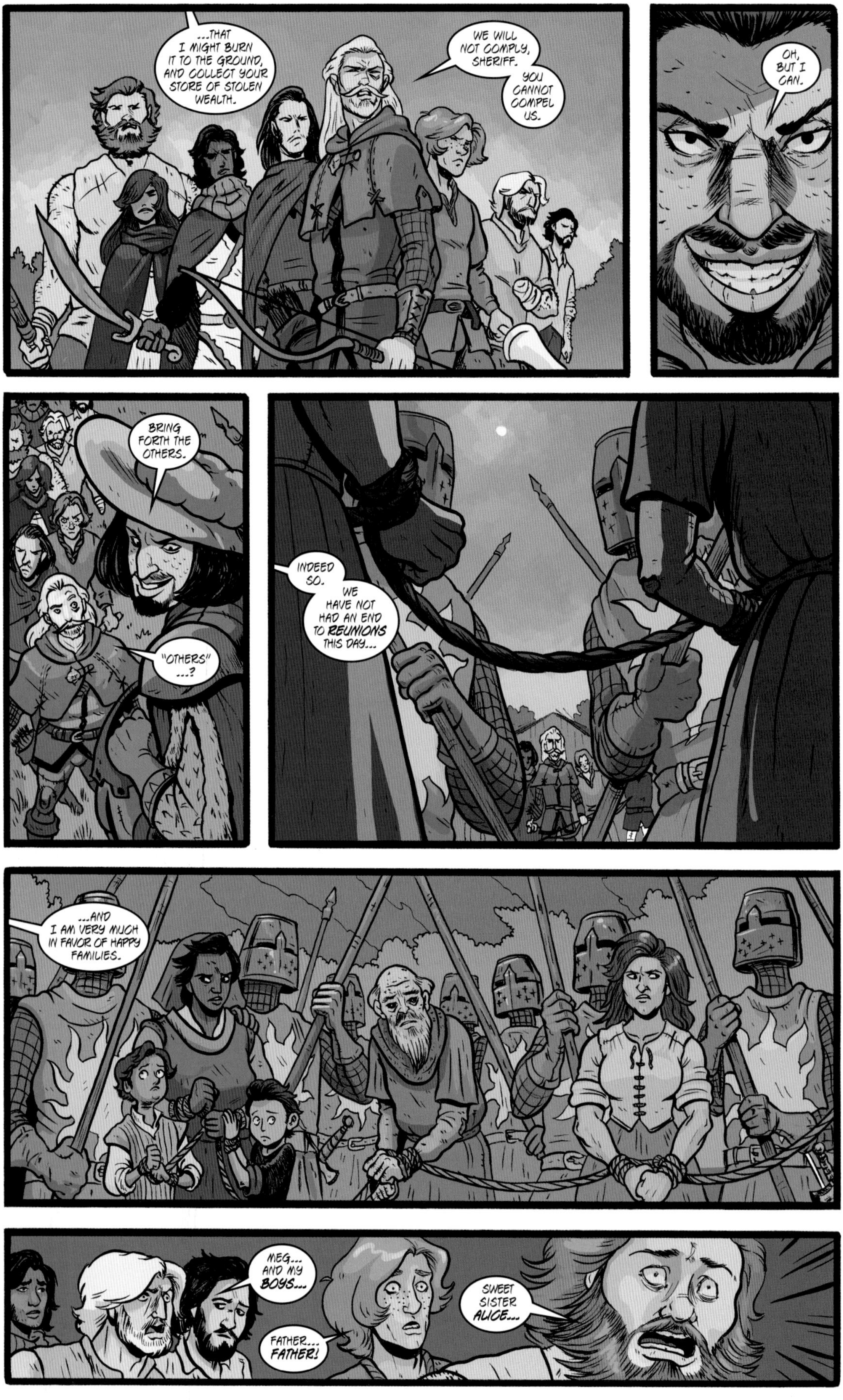
...THAT I MIGHT BURN IT TO THE GROUND, AND COLLECT YOUR STORE OF STOLEN WEALTH.
WE WILL NOT COMPLY, SHERIFF.
YOU CANNOT COMPEL US.
OH, BUT I CAN.
BRING FORTH THE OTHERS.
"OTHERS" ...?
INDEED SO.
WE HAVE NOT HAD AN END TO REUNIONS THIS DAY...
...AND I AM VERY MUCH IN FAVOR OF HAPPY FAMILIES.
MEG... AND MY BOYS...
FATHER... FATHER!
SWEET SISTER ALICE...

Chapter
9

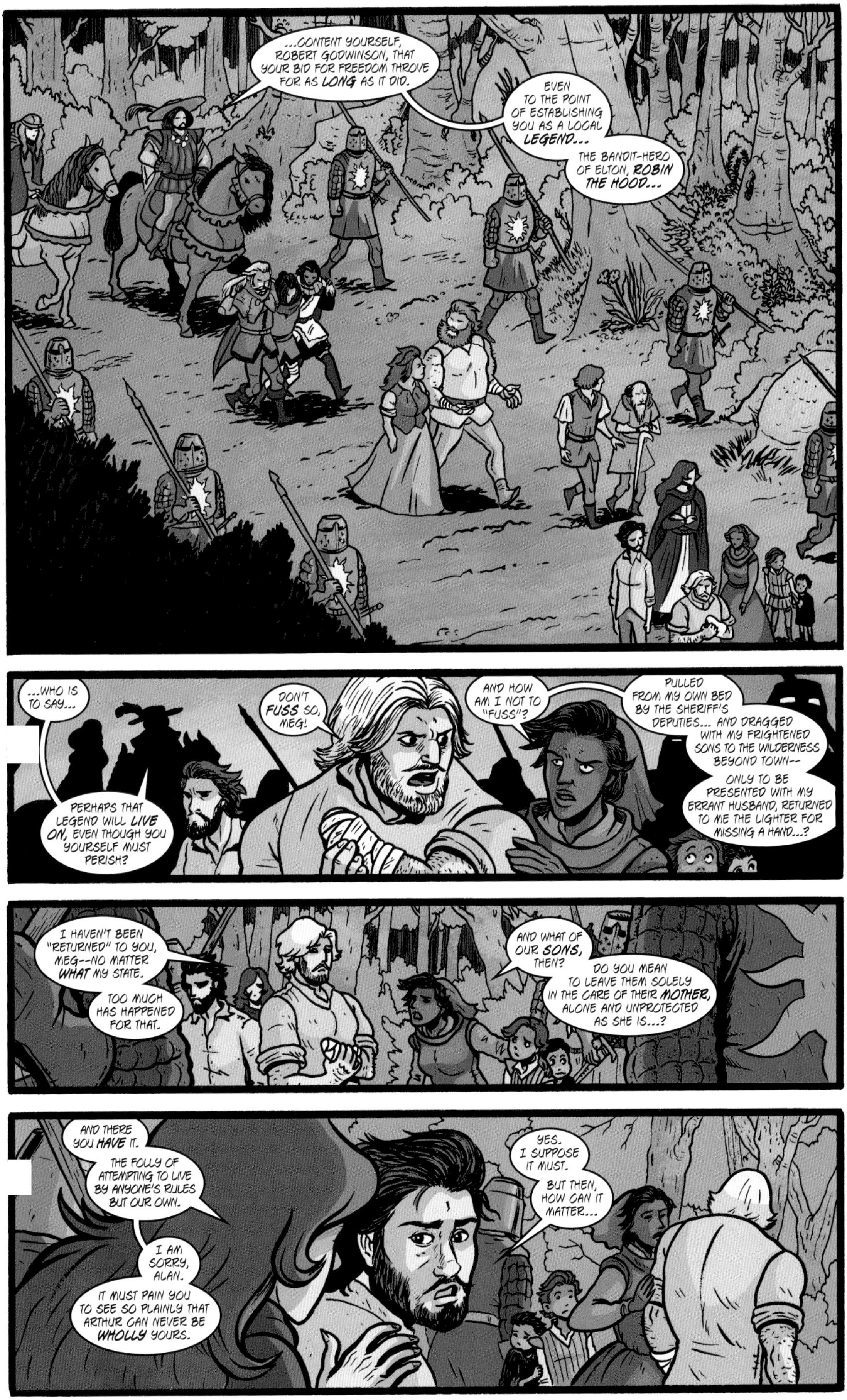
...CONTENT YOURSELF, ROBERT GODWINSON, THAT YOUR BID FOR FREEDOM THROVE FOR AS LONG AS IT DID.
EVEN TO THE POINT OF ESTABLISHING YOU AS A LOCAL LEGEND...
THE BANDIT-HERO OF ELTON, ROBIN THE HOOD...
...WHO IS TO SAY...
PERHAPS THAT LEGEND WILL LIVE ON, EVEN THOUGH YOU YOURSELF MUST PERISH?
DON'T FUSS SO, MEG!
AND HOW AM I NOT TO "FUSS"?
PULLED FROM MY OWN BED BY THE SHERIFF'S DEPUTIES... AND DRAGGED WITH MY FRIGHTENED SONS TO THE WILDERNESS BEYOND TOWN--
ONLY TO BE PRESENTED WITH MY ERRANT HUSBAND, RETURNED TO ME THE LIGHTER FOR MISSING A HAND...?
I HAVEN'T BEEN "RETURNED" TO YOU, MEG--NO MATTER WHAT MY STATE.
TOO MUCH HAS HAPPENED FOR THAT.
AND WHAT OF OUR SONS, THEN?
DO YOU MEAN TO LEAVE THEM SOLELY IN THE CARE OF THEIR MOTHER, ALONE AND UNPROTECTED AS SHE IS...?
AND THERE YOU HAVE IT.
THE FOLLY OF ATTEMPTING TO LIVE BY ANYONE'S RULES BUT OUR OWN.
I AM SORRY, ALAN.
IT MUST PAIN YOU TO SEE SO PLAINLY THAT ARTHUR CAN NEVER BE WHOLLY YOURS.
YES. I SUPPOSE IT MUST.
BUT THEN, HOW CAN IT MATTER...

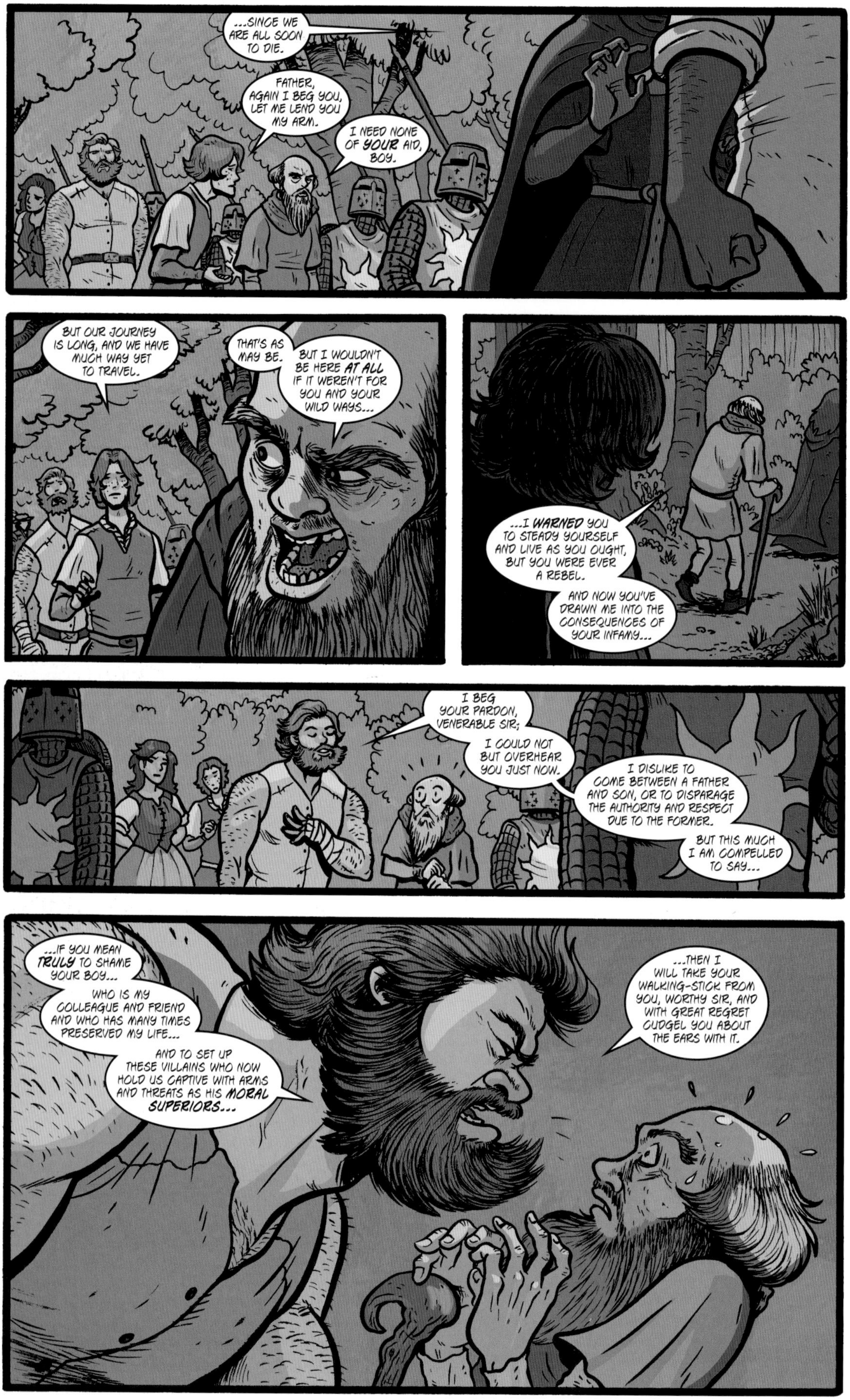
...SINCE WE ARE ALL SOON TO DIE.
FATHER, AGAIN I BEG YOU, LET ME LEND YOU MY ARM.
I NEED NONE OF YOUR AID, BOY.
BUT OUR JOURNEY IS LONG, AND WE HAVE MUCH WAY YET TO TRAVEL.
THAT'S AS MAY BE.
BUT I WOULDN'T BE HERE AT ALL IF IT WEREN'T FOR YOU AND YOUR WILD WAYS...
...I WARNED YOU TO STEADY YOURSELF AND LIVE AS YOU OUGHT, BUT YOU WERE EVER A REBEL.
AND NOW YOU'VE DRAWN ME INTO THE CONSEQUENCES OF YOUR INFAMY...
I BEG YOUR PARDON, VENERABLE SIR;
I COULD NOT BUT OVERHEAR YOU JUST NOW.
I DISLIKE TO COME BETWEEN A FATHER AND SON, OR TO DISPARAGE THE AUTHORITY AND RESPECT DUE TO THE FORMER.
BUT THIS MUCH I AM COMPELLED TO SAY...
...IF YOU MEAN TRULY TO SHAME YOUR BOY...
WHO IS MY COLLEAGUE AND FRIEND AND WHO HAS MANY TIMES PRESERVED MY LIFE...
AND TO SET UP THESE VILLAINS WHO NOW HOLD US CAPTIVE WITH ARMS AND THREATS AS HIS MORAL SUPERIORS...
...THEN I WILL TAKE YOUR WALKING-STICK FROM YOU, WORTHY SIR, AND WITH GREAT REGRET CUDGEL YOU ABOUT THE EARS WITH IT.

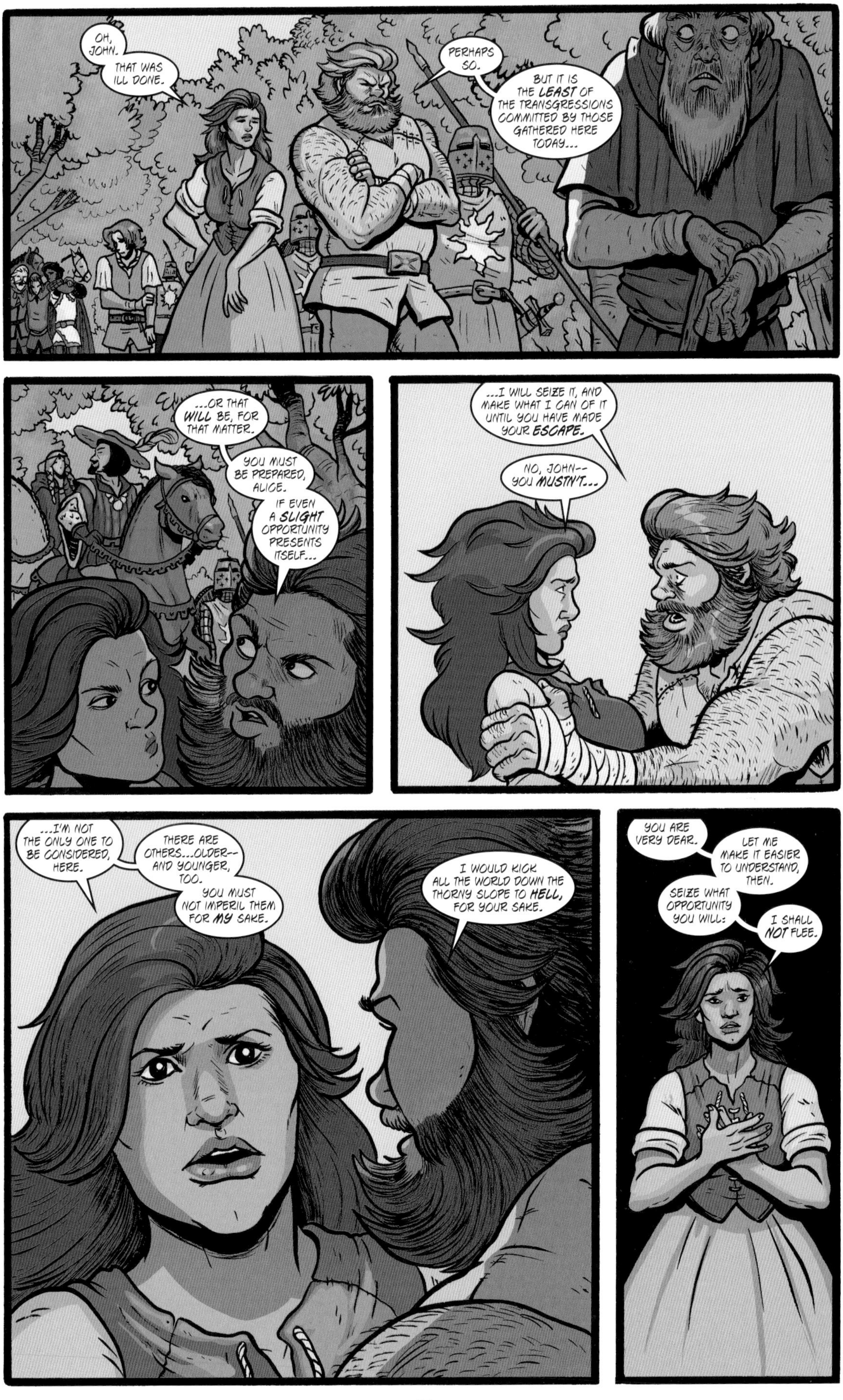
OH, JOHN.
THAT WAS ILL DONE.
PERHAPS SO.
BUT IT IS THE LEAST OF THE TRANSGRESSIONS COMMITTED BY THOSE GATHERED HERE TODAY...
...OR THAT WILL BE, FOR THAT MATTER.
YOU MUST BE PREPARED, ALICE.
IF EVEN A SLIGHT OPPORTUNITY PRESENTS ITSELF...
...I WILL SEIZE IT, AND MAKE WHAT I CAN OF IT UNTIL YOU HAVE MADE YOUR ESCAPE.
NO, JOHN--YOU MUSTN'T...
...I'M NOT THE ONLY ONE TO BE CONSIDERED, HERE.
THERE ARE OTHERS...OLDER--AND YOUNGER, TOO.
YOU MUST NOT IMPERIL THEM FOR MY SAKE.
I WOULD KICK ALL THE WORLD DOWN THE THORNY SLOPE TO HELL, FOR YOUR SAKE.
YOU ARE VERY DEAR.
LET ME MAKE IT EASIER TO UNDERSTAND, THEN.
SEIZE WHAT OPPORTUNITY YOU WILL:
I SHALL NOT FLEE.

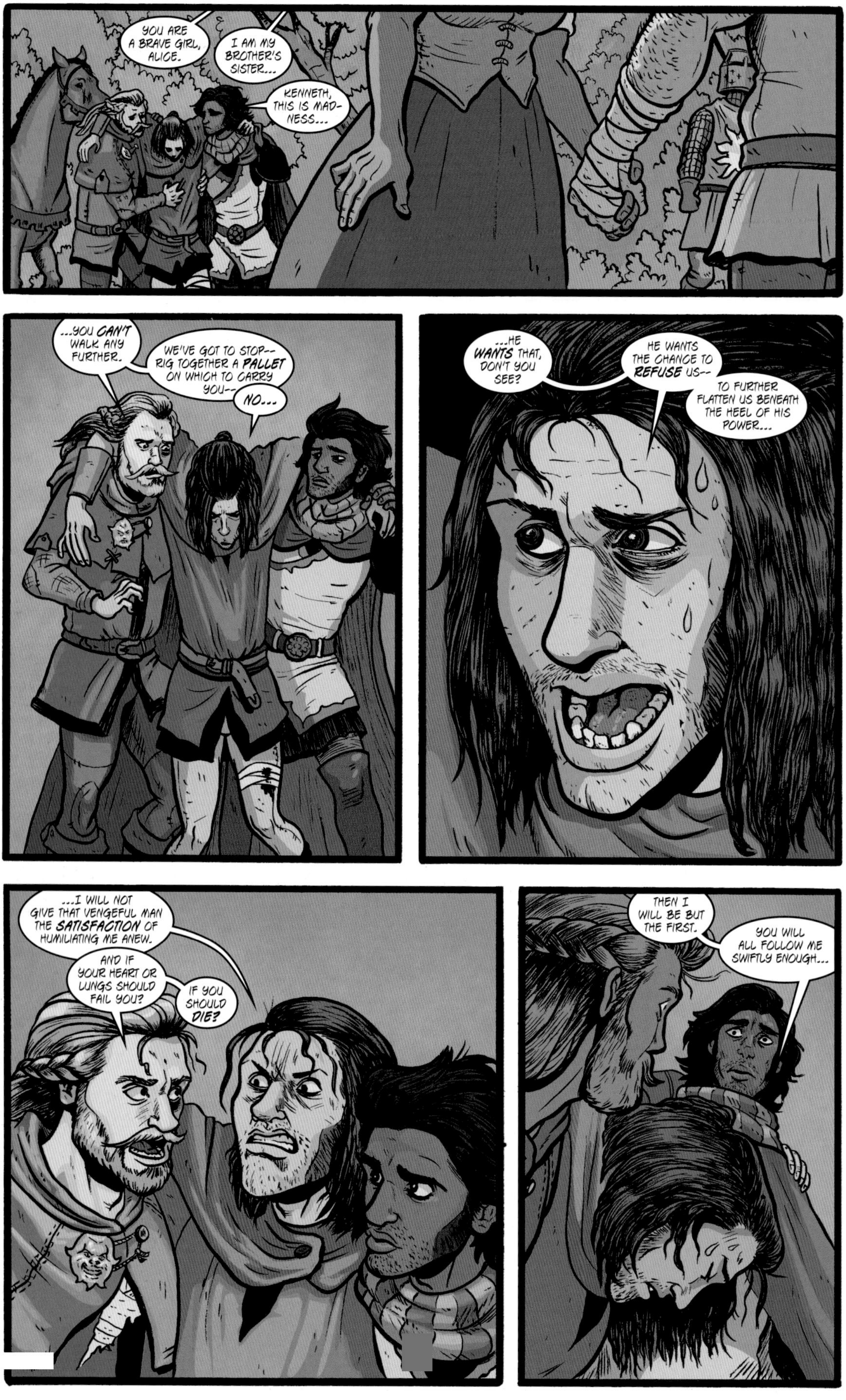
YOU ARE A BRAVE GIRL, ALICE.
I AM MY BROTHER'S SISTER...
KENNETH, THIS IS MADNESS...
...YOU CAN'T WALK ANY FURTHER.
WE'VE GOT TO STOP-- RIG TOGETHER A PALLET ON WHICH TO CARRY YOU--
NO...
...HE WANTS THAT, DON'T YOU SEE?
HE WANTS THE CHANCE TO REFUSE US--
TO FURTHER FLATTEN US BENEATH THE HEEL OF HIS POWER...
...I WILL NOT GIVE THAT VENGEFUL MAN THE SATISFACTION OF HUMILIATING ME ANEW.
AND IF YOUR HEART OR LUNGS SHOULD FAIL YOU?
IF YOU SHOULD DIE?
THEN I WILL BE BUT THE FIRST.
YOU WILL ALL FOLLOW ME SWIFTLY ENOUGH...

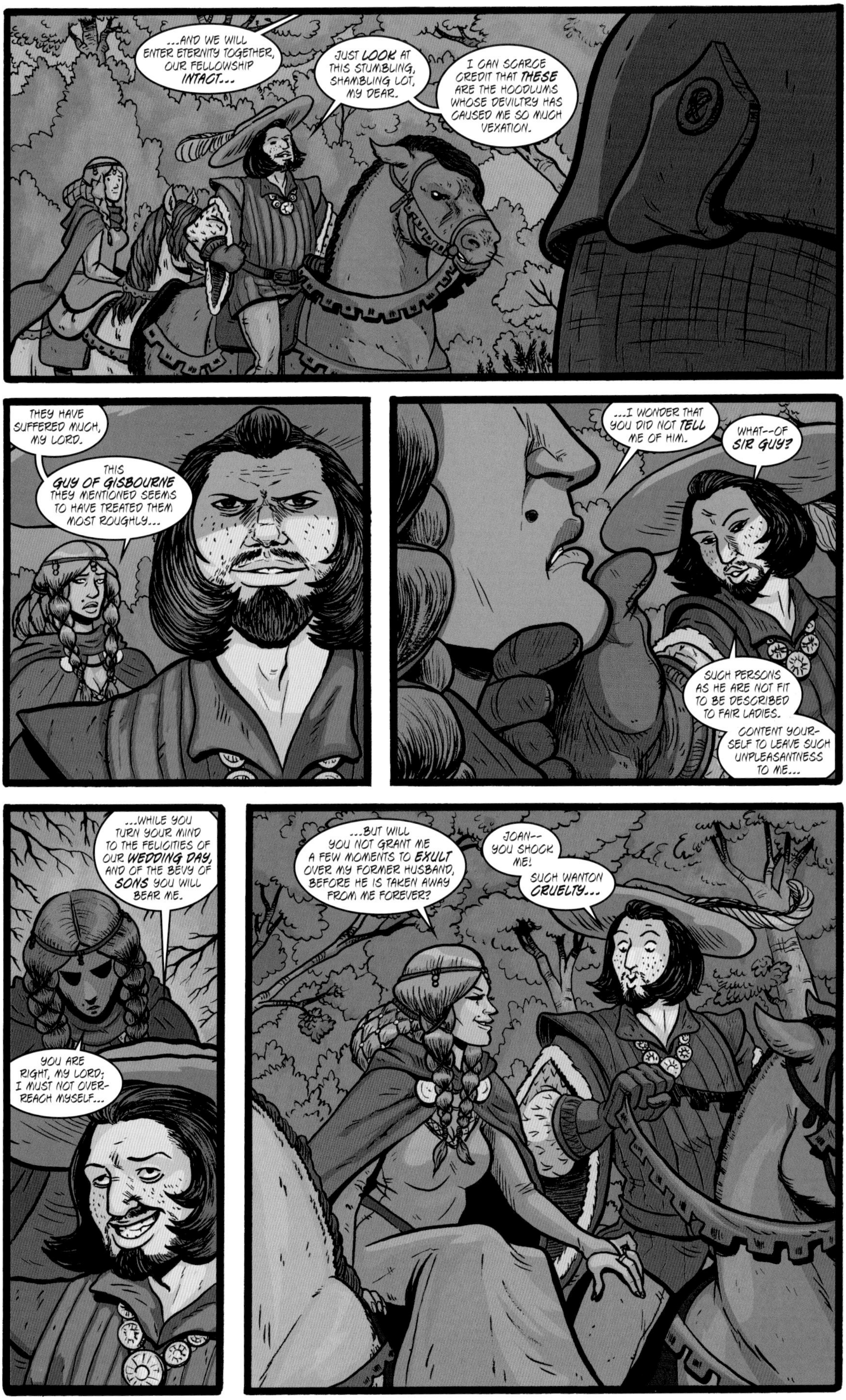
...AND WE WILL ENTER ETERNITY TOGETHER, OUR FELLOWSHIP INTACT...
JUST LOOK AT THIS STUMBLING, SHAMBLING LOT, MY DEAR.
I CAN SCARCE CREDIT THAT THESE ARE THE HOODLUMS WHOSE DEVILTRY HAS CAUSED ME SO MUCH VEXATION.
THEY HAVE SUFFERED MUCH, MY LORD.
THIS GUY OF GISBOURNE THEY MENTIONED SEEMS TO HAVE TREATED THEM MOST ROUGHLY...
...I WONDER THAT YOU DID NOT TELL ME OF HIM.
WHAT--OF SIR GUY?
SUCH PERSONS AS HE ARE NOT FIT TO BE DESCRIBED TO FAIR LADIES.
CONTENT YOURSELF TO LEAVE SUCH UNPLEASANTNESS TO ME...
...WHILE YOU TURN YOUR MIND TO THE FELICITIES OF OUR WEDDING DAY, AND OF THE BEVY OF SONS YOU WILL BEAR ME.
YOU ARE RIGHT, MY LORD; I MUST NOT OVERREACH MYSELF...
...BUT WILL YOU NOT GRANT ME A FEW MOMENTS TO EXULT OVER MY FORMER HUSBAND, BEFORE HE IS TAKEN AWAY FROM ME FOREVER?
JOAN-- YOU SHOCK ME!
SUCH WANTON CRUELTY...

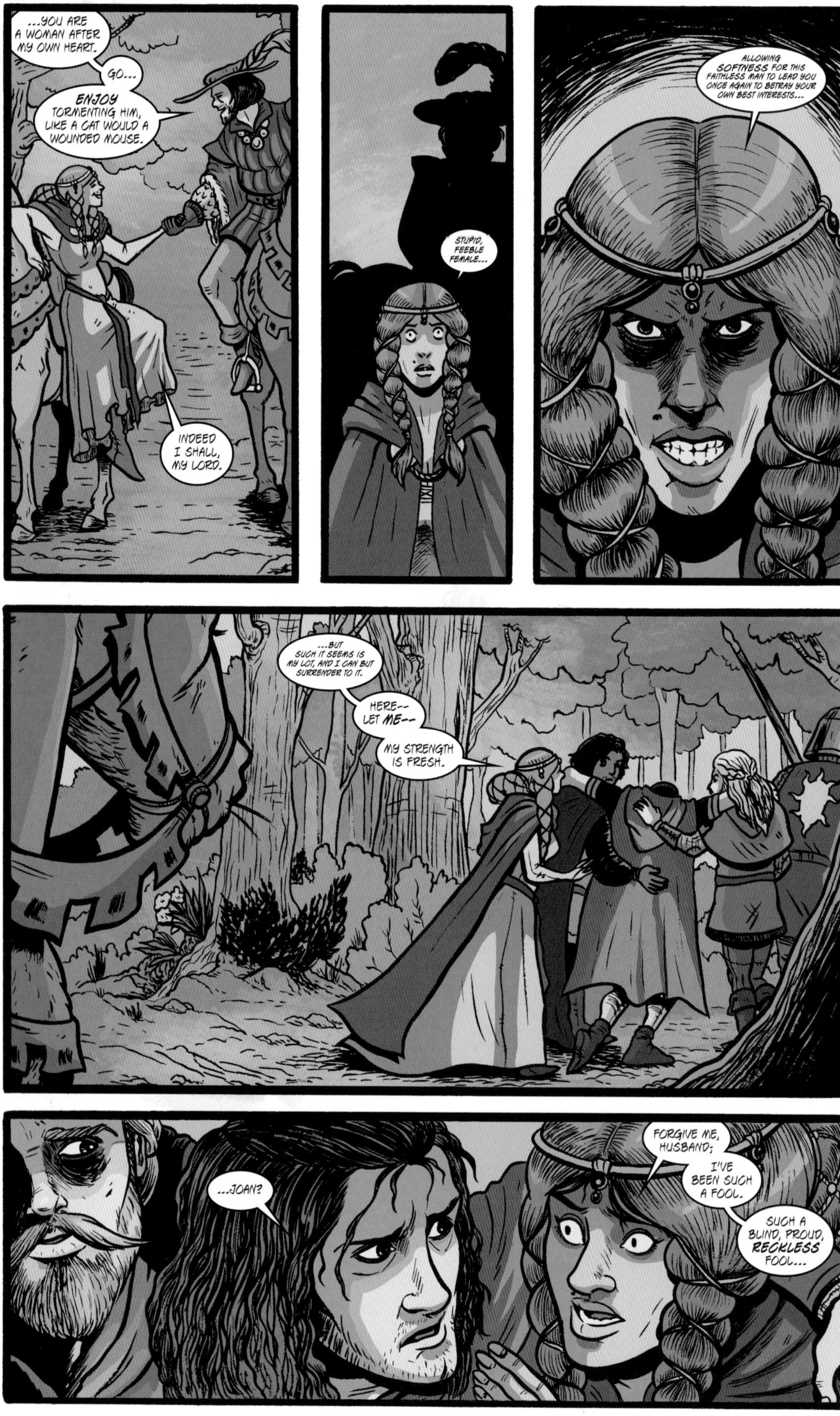
...YOU ARE A WOMAN AFTER MY OWN HEART.
GO...
ENJOY TORMENTING HIM, LIKE A CAT WOULD A WOUNDED MOUSE.
INDEED I SHALL, MY LORD.
STUPID, FEEBLE FEMALE...
ALLOWING SOFTNESS FOR THIS FAITHLESS MAN TO LEAD YOU ONCE AGAIN TO BETRAY YOUR OWN BEST INTERESTS...
...BUT SUCH IT SEEMS IS MY LOT, AND I CAN BUT SURRENDER TO IT.
HERE-- LET ME--
MY STRENGTH IS FRESH.
...JOAN?
FORGIVE ME, HUSBAND;
I'VE BEEN SUCH A FOOL.
SUCH A BLIND, PROUD, RECKLESS FOOL...

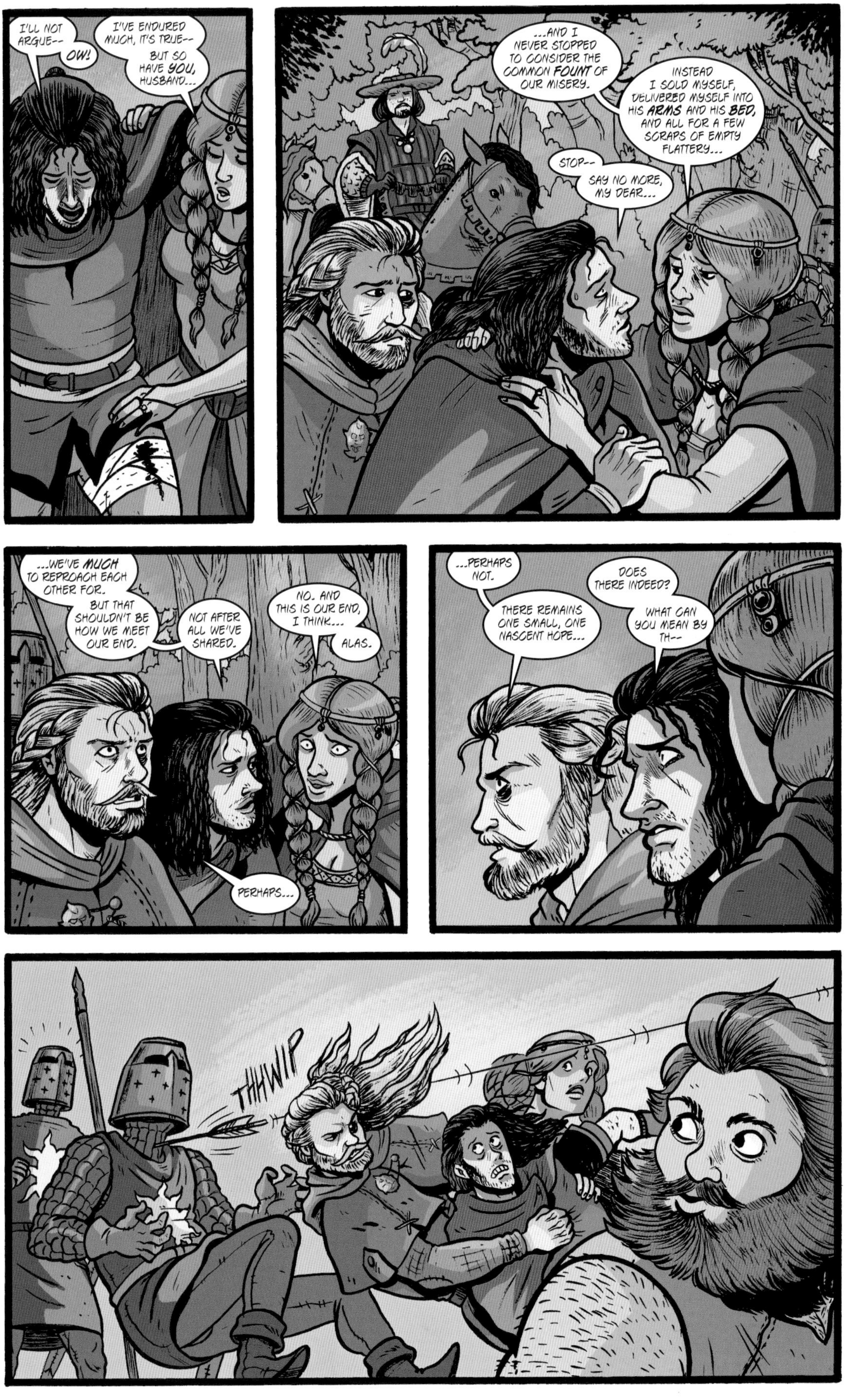

I'LL NOT ARGUE-- OW!
I'VE ENDURED MUCH, IT'S TRUE-- BUT SO HAVE YOU, HUSBAND...
...AND I NEVER STOPPED TO CONSIDER THE COMMON FOUNT OF OUR MISERY.
INSTEAD I SOLD MYSELF, DELIVERED MYSELF INTO HIS ARMS AND HIS BED, AND ALL FOR A FEW SCRAPS OF EMPTY FLATTERY...
STOP--
SAY NO MORE, MY DEAR...
...WE'VE MUCH TO REPROACH EACH OTHER FOR.
BUT THAT SHOULDN'T BE HOW WE MEET OUR END.
NOT AFTER ALL WE'VE SHARED.
NO. AND THIS IS OUR END, I THINK...
ALAS.
PERHAPS...
...PERHAPS NOT.
THERE REMAINS ONE SMALL, ONE NASCENT HOPE...
DOES THERE INDEED?
WHAT CAN YOU MEAN BY TH--
THHWIP

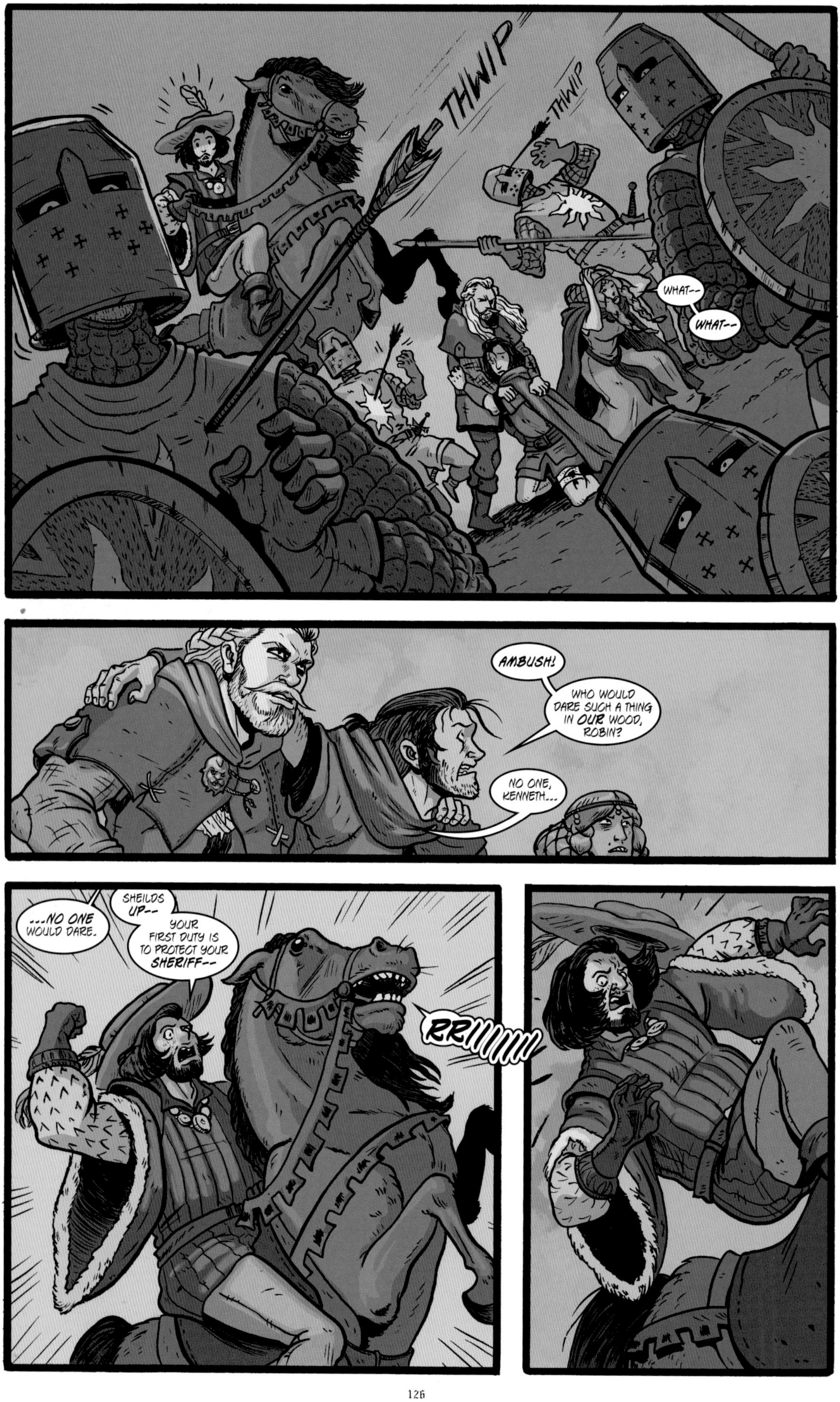
THWIP
THWIP
WHAT--
WHAT--
AMBUSH!
WHO WOULD DARE SUCH A THING IN OUR WOOD, ROBIN?
NO ONE, KENNETH...
...NO ONE WOULD DARE.
SHEILDS UP--
YOUR FIRST DUTY IS TO PROTECT YOUR SHERIFF--
RRIIIIIII

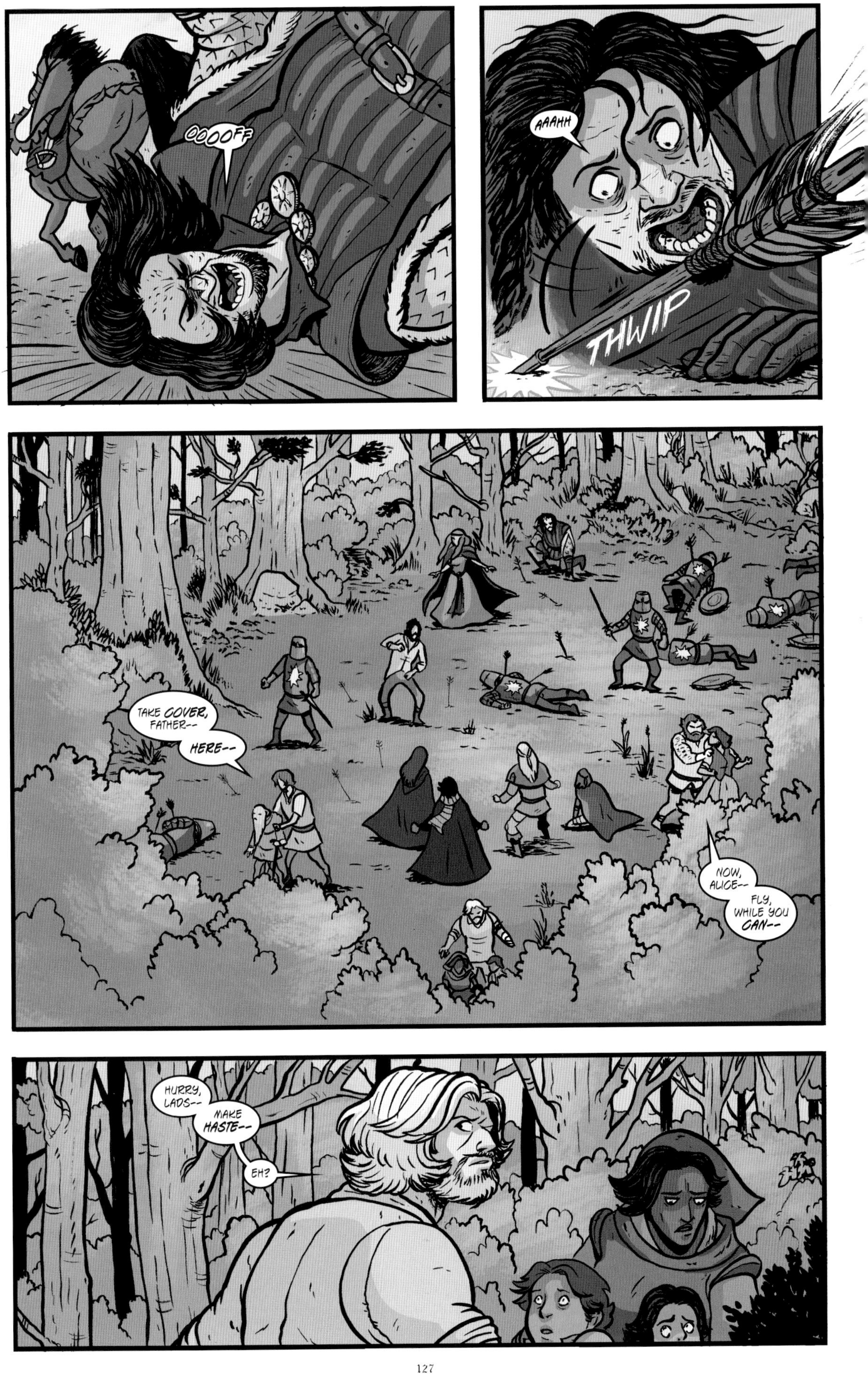
OOOOFF
AAAHH
THWIP
TAKE COVER, FATHER--
HERE--
NOW, ALICE--
FLY, WHILE YOU CAN--
HURRY, LADS--
MAKE HASTE--
EH?

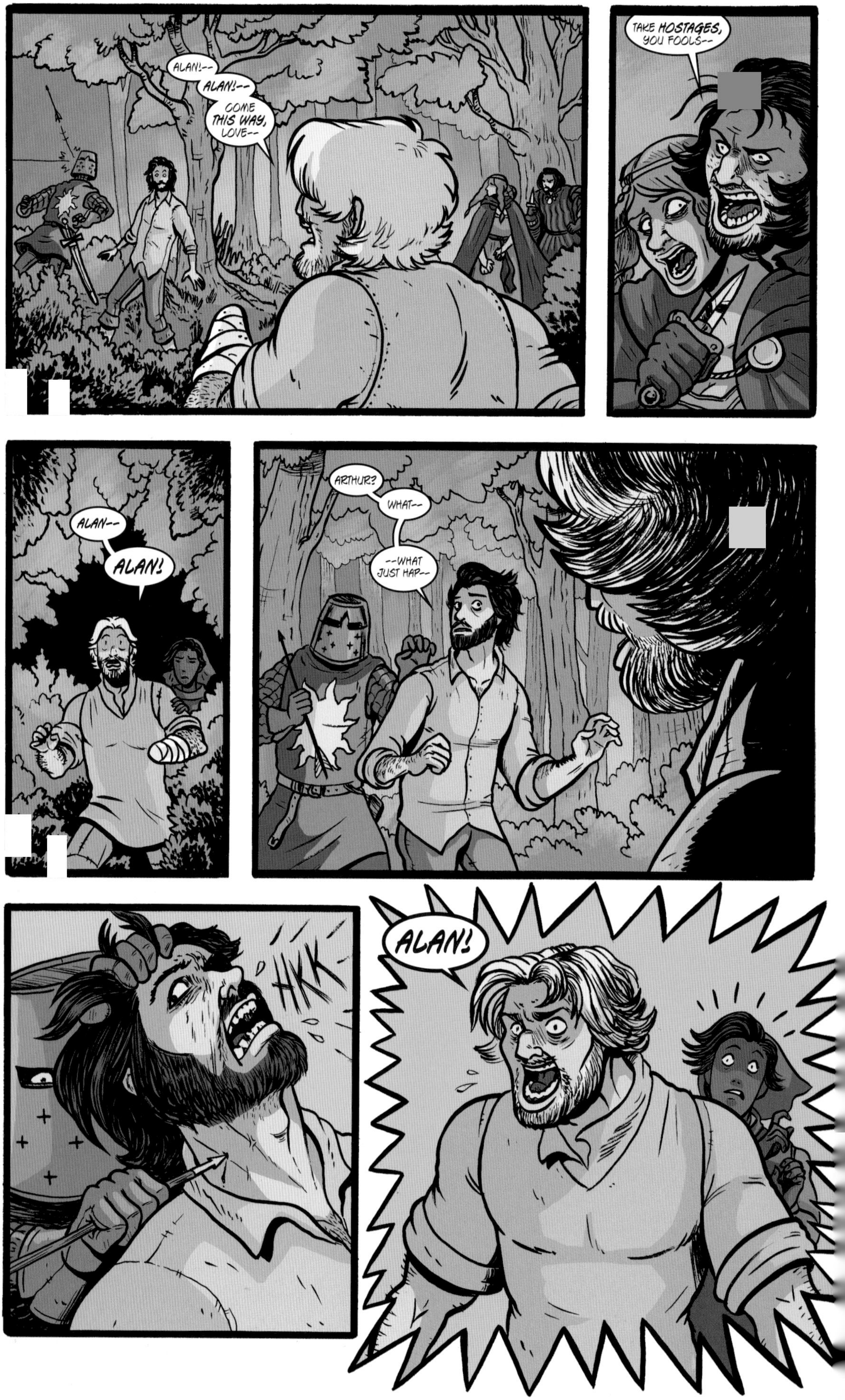
ALAN!--
ALAN!--
COME THIS WAY, LOVE--
TAKE HOSTAGES, YOU FOOLS--
ALAN--
ALAN!
ARTHUR?
WHAT--
--WHAT JUST HAP--
HKK
ALAN!

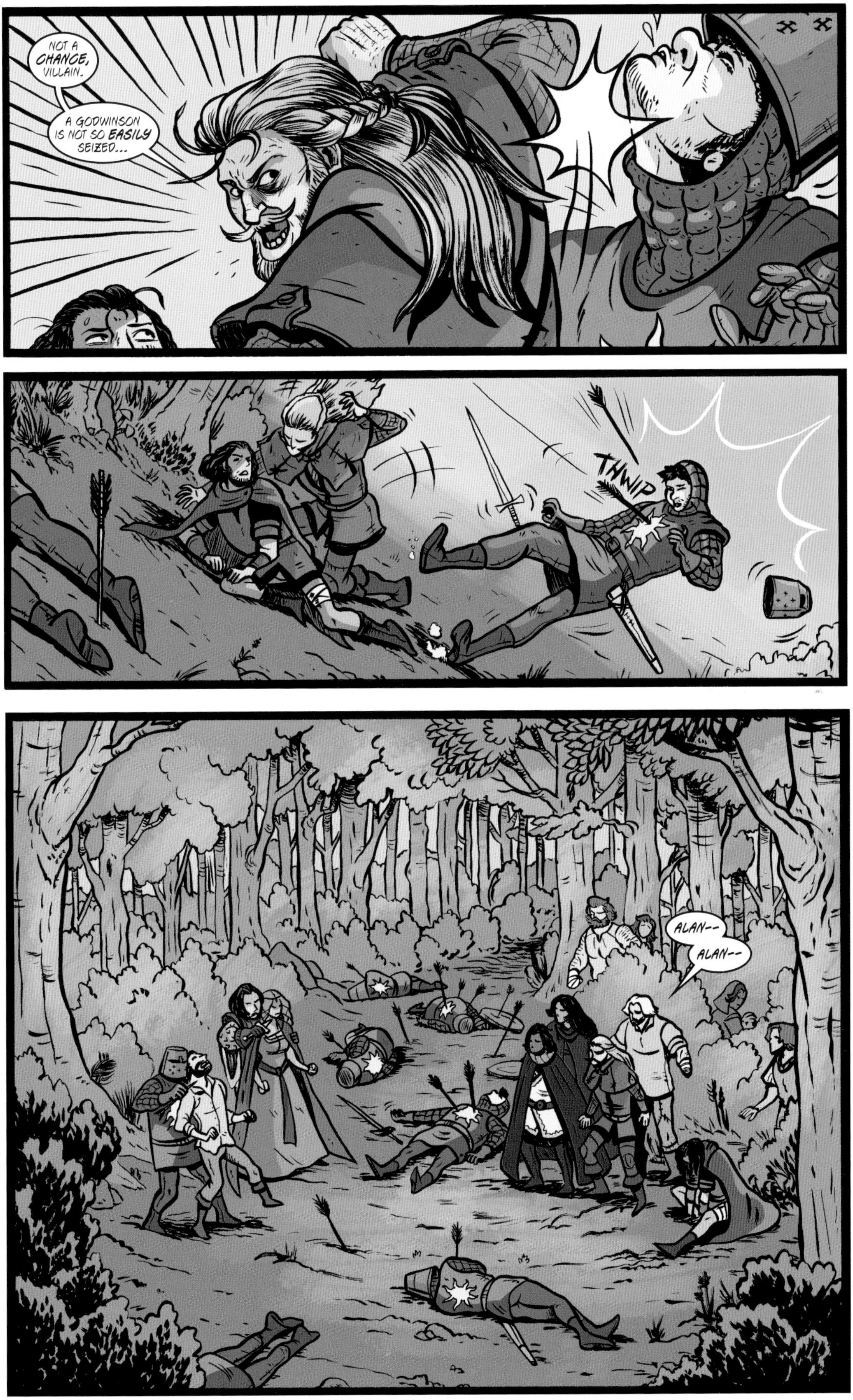
NOT A CHANCE, VILLAIN.
A GODWINSON IS NOT SO EASILY SEIZED...
THWIP
ALAN--
ALAN--

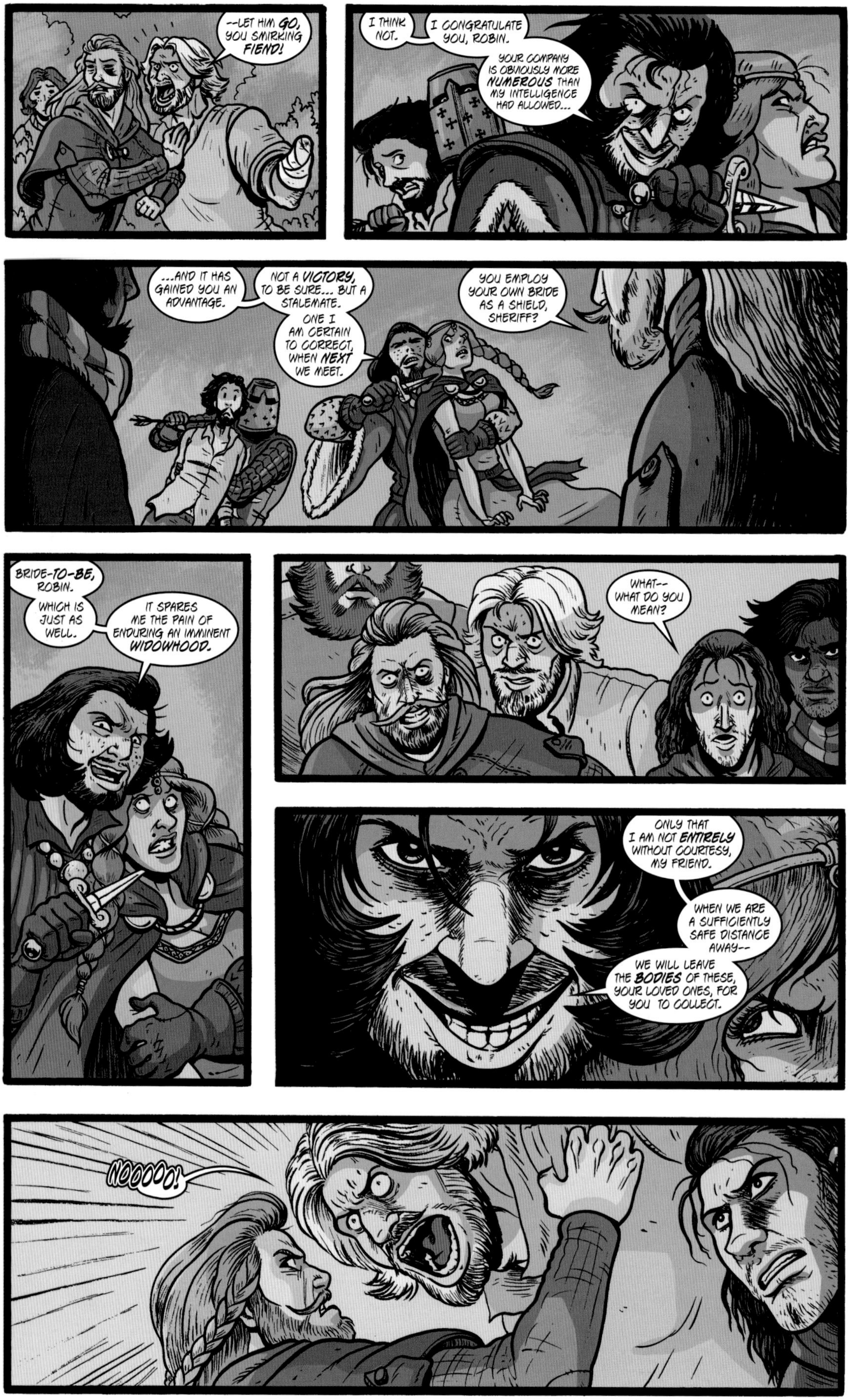
--LET HIM GO, YOU SMIRKING FIEND!
I THINK NOT.
I CONGRATULATE YOU, ROBIN.
YOUR COMPANY IS OBVIOUSLY MORE NUMEROUS THAN MY INTELLIGENCE HAD ALLOWED...
...AND IT HAS GAINED YOU AN ADVANTAGE.
NOT A VICTORY, TO BE SURE... BUT A STALEMATE.
ONE I AM CERTAIN TO CORRECT, WHEN NEXT WE MEET.
YOU EMPLOY YOUR OWN BRIDE AS A SHIELD, SHERIFF?
BRIDE-TO-BE, ROBIN.
WHICH IS JUST AS WELL.
IT SPARES ME THE PAIN OF ENDURING AN IMMINENT WIDOWHOOD.
WHAT-- WHAT DO YOU MEAN?
ONLY THAT I AM NOT ENTIRELY WITHOUT COURTESY, MY FRIEND.
WHEN WE ARE A SUFFICIENTLY SAFE DISTANCE AWAY--
WE WILL LEAVE THE BODIES OF THESE, YOUR LOVED ONES, FOR YOU TO COLLECT.
NOOOOO!

Chapter
10

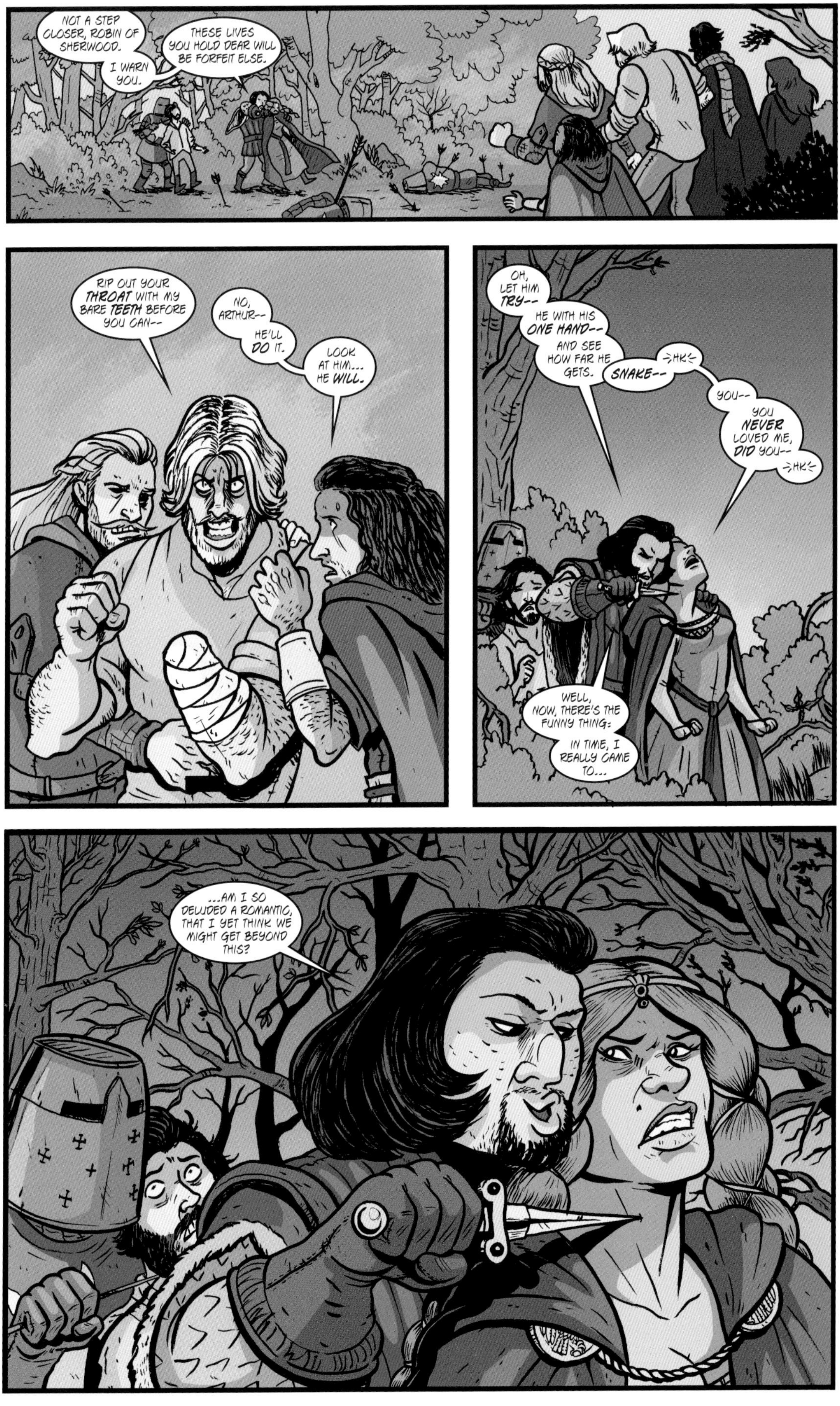

NOT A STEP CLOSER, ROBIN OF SHERWOOD.
I WARN YOU.
THESE LIVES YOU HOLD DEAR WILL BE FORFEIT ELSE.
RIP OUT YOUR THROAT WITH MY BARE TEETH BEFORE YOU CAN--
NO, ARTHUR--
HE'LL DO IT.
LOOK AT HIM... HE WILL.
OH, LET HIM TRY--
HE WITH HIS ONE HAND--
AND SEE HOW FAR HE GETS.
SNAKE--
HK
YOU--
YOU NEVER LOVED ME, DID YOU--
HK
WELL, NOW, THERE'S THE FUNNY THING:
IN TIME, I REALLY CAME TO...
...AM I SO DELUDED A ROMANTIC, THAT I YET THINK WE MIGHT GET BEYOND THIS?

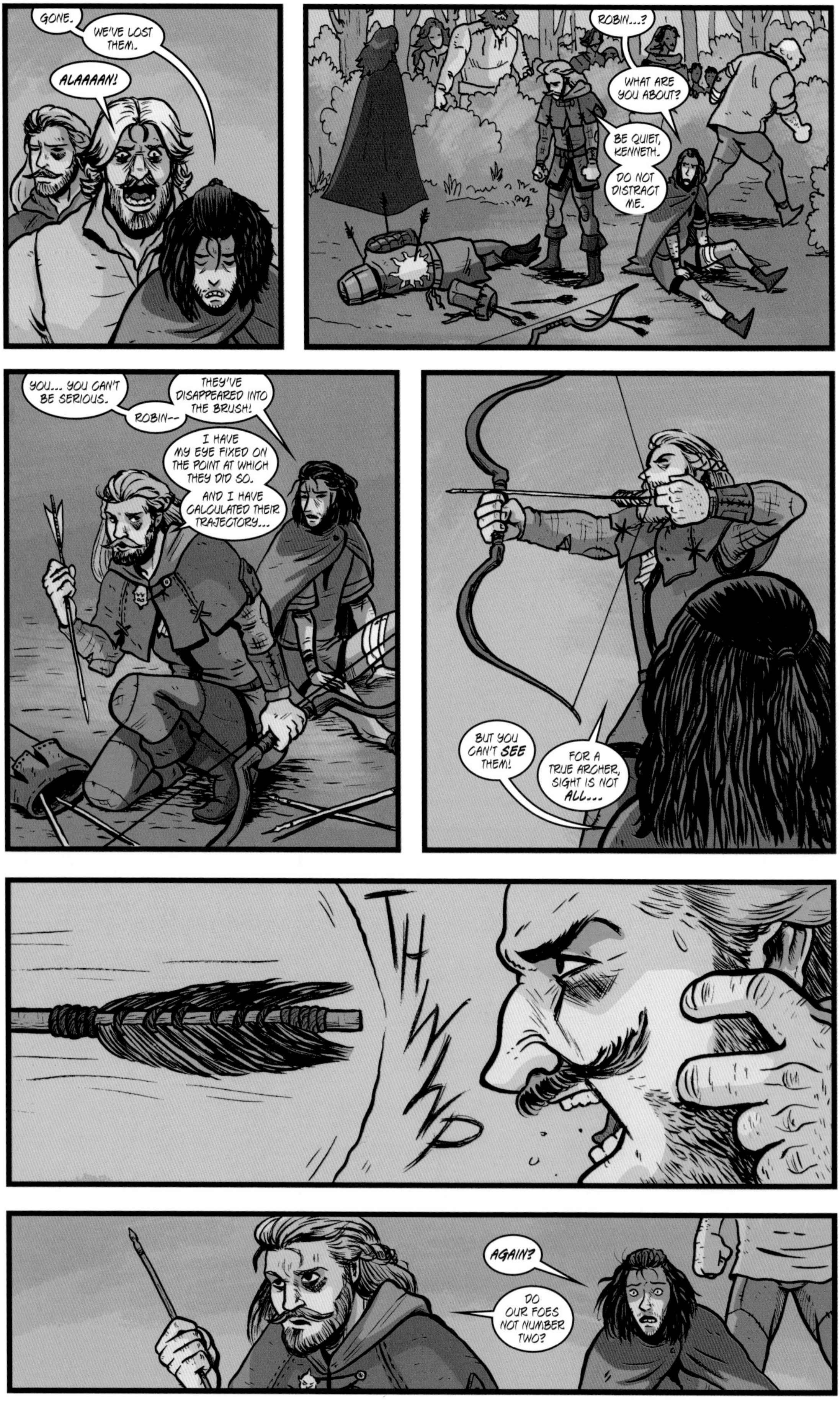
GONE.
WE'VE LOST THEM.
ALAAAAN!
ROBIN...?
WHAT ARE YOU ABOUT?
BE QUIET, KENNETH.
DO NOT DISTRACT ME.
YOU... YOU CAN'T BE SERIOUS.
ROBIN--
THEY'VE DISAPPEARED INTO THE BRUSH!
I HAVE MY EYE FIXED ON THE POINT AT WHICH THEY DID SO.
AND I HAVE CALCULATED THEIR TRAJECTORY...
BUT YOU CAN'T SEE THEM!
FOR A TRUE ARCHER, SIGHT IS NOT ALL...
THWMP
AGAIN?
DO OUR FOES NOT NUMBER TWO?

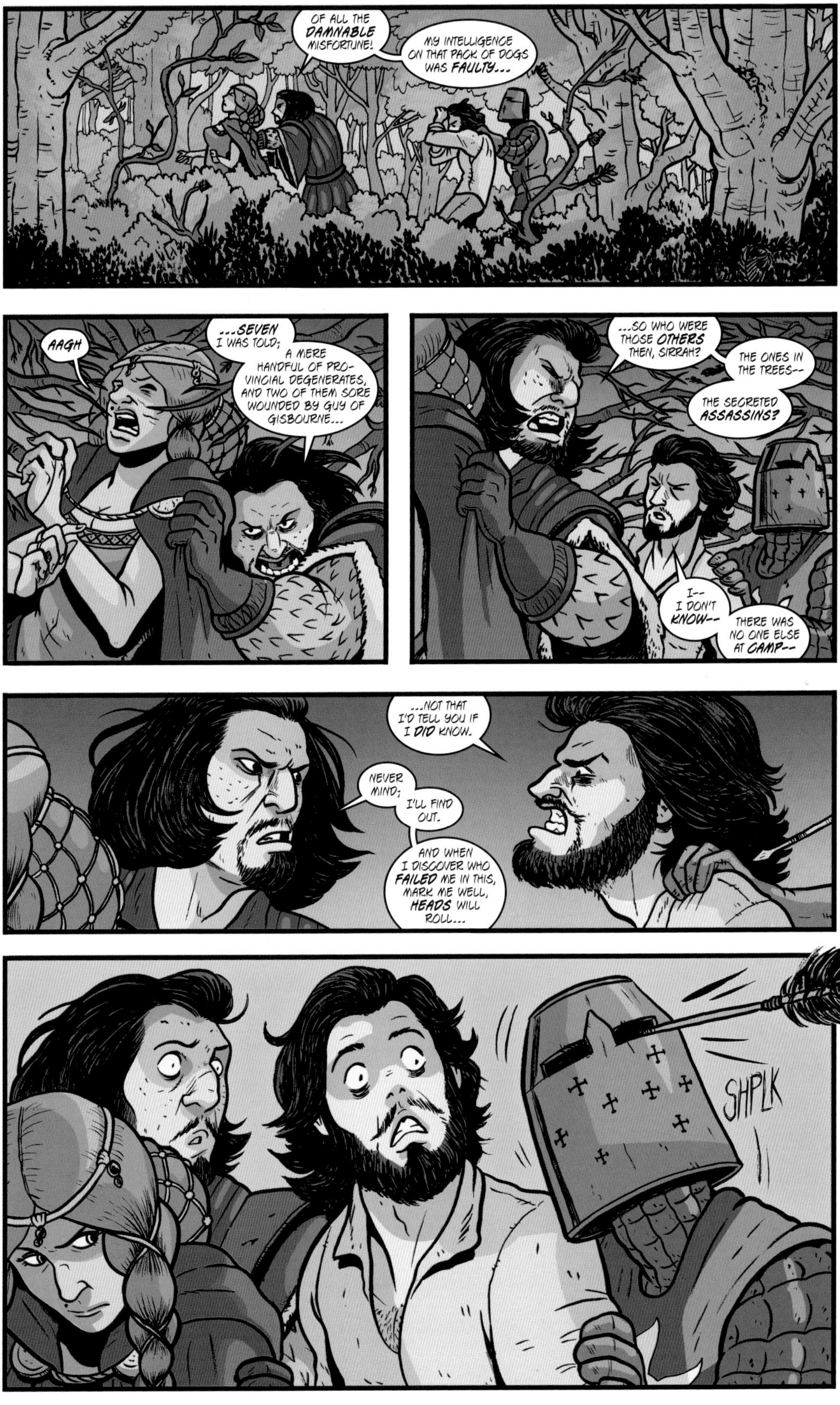
OF ALL THE DAMNABLE MISFORTUNE!
MY INTELLIGENCE ON THAT PACK OF DOGS WAS FAULTY...
AAGH
...SEVEN I WAS TOLD;
A MERE HANDFUL OF PROVINCIAL DEGENERATES, AND TWO OF THEM SORE WOUNDED BY GUY OF GISBOURNE...
...SO WHO WERE THOSE OTHERS THEN, SIRRAH?
THE ONES IN THE TREES--
THE SECRETED ASSASSINS?
I-- I DON'T KNOW--
THERE WAS NO ONE ELSE AT CAMP--
...NOT THAT I'D TELL YOU IF I DID KNOW.
NEVER MIND;
I'LL FIND OUT.
AND WHEN I DISCOVER WHO FAILED ME IN THIS, MARK ME WELL, HEADS WILL ROLL...
SHPLK

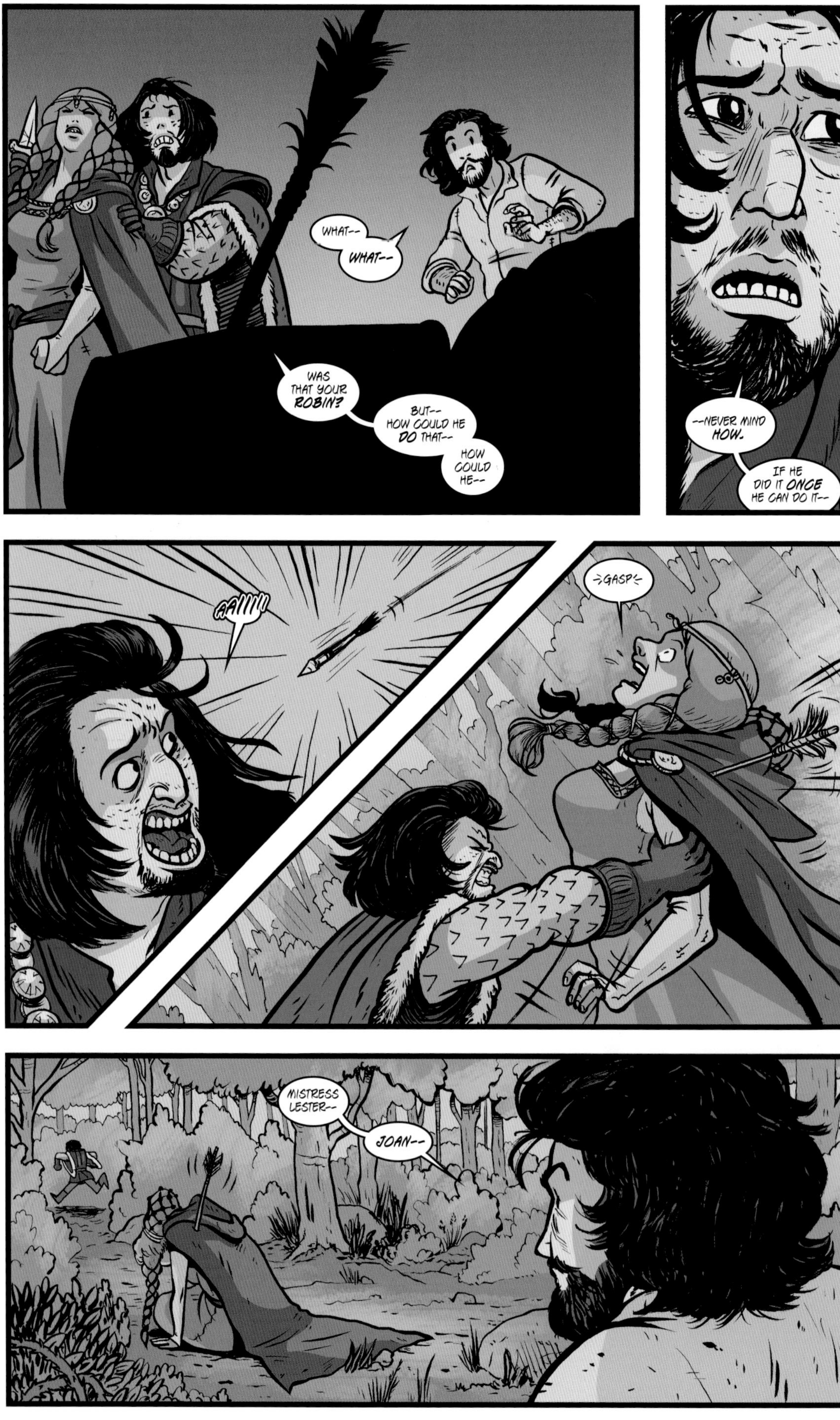
WHAT--
WHAT--
WAS THAT YOUR ROBIN?
BUT-- HOW COULD HE DO THAT--
HOW COULD HE--
--NEVER MIND HOW.
IF HE DID IT ONCE HE CAN DO IT--
AA!!!!!
GASP
MISTRESS LESTER--
JOAN--

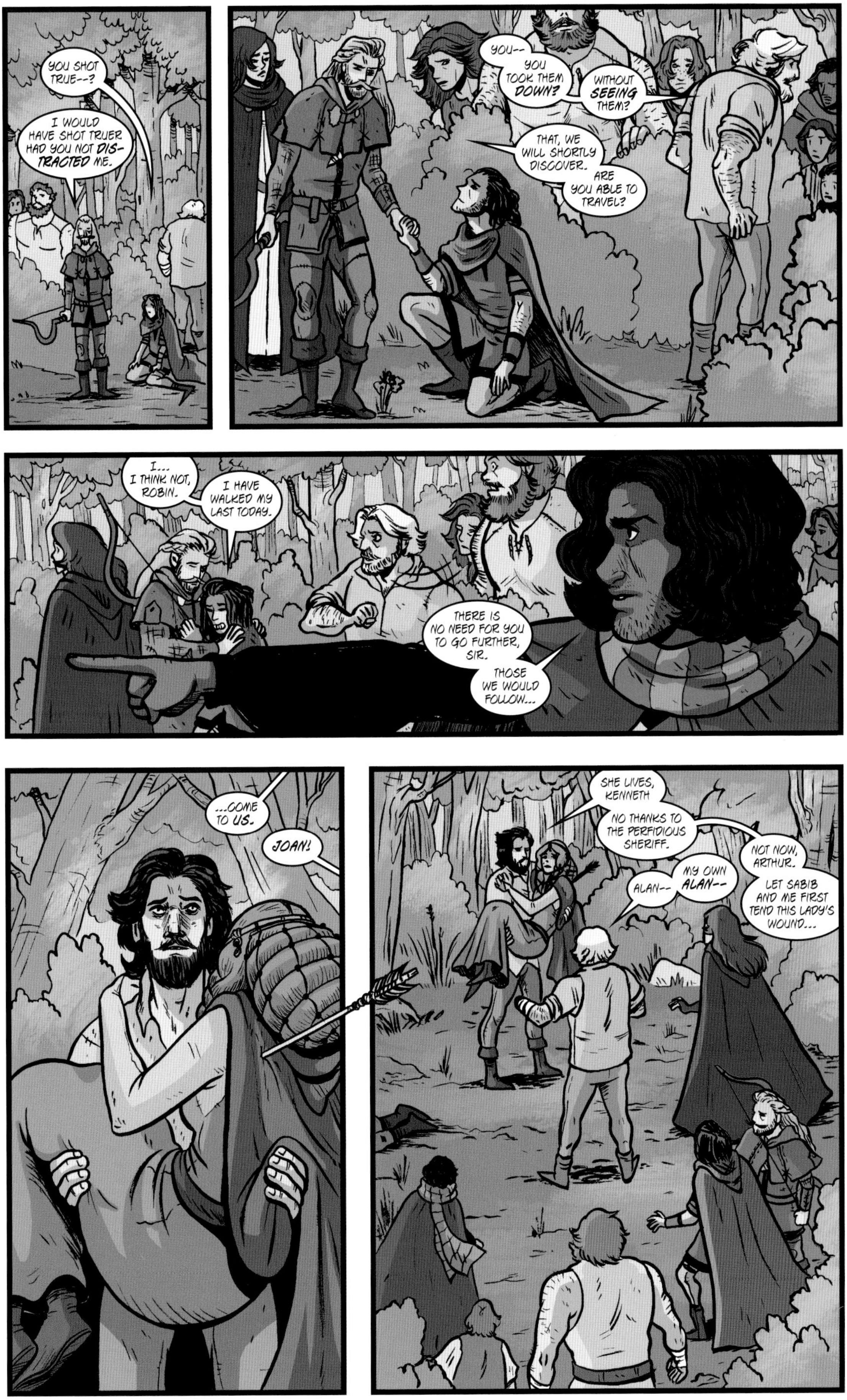

YOU SHOT TRUE--?
I WOULD HAVE SHOT TRUER HAD YOU NOT DIS-TRACTED ME.
YOU-- YOU TOOK THEM DOWN?
WITHOUT SEEING THEM?
THAT, WE WILL SHORTLY DISCOVER.
ARE YOU ABLE TO TRAVEL?
I... I THINK NOT, ROBIN.
I HAVE WALKED MY LAST TODAY.
THERE IS NO NEED FOR YOU TO GO FURTHER, SIR.
THOSE WE WOULD FOLLOW...
...COME TO US.
JOAN!
SHE LIVES, KENNETH
NO THANKS TO THE PERFIDIOUS SHERIFF.
NOT NOW, ARTHUR.
LET SABIB AND ME FIRST TEND THIS LADY'S WOUND...
ALAN--
MY OWN ALAN--

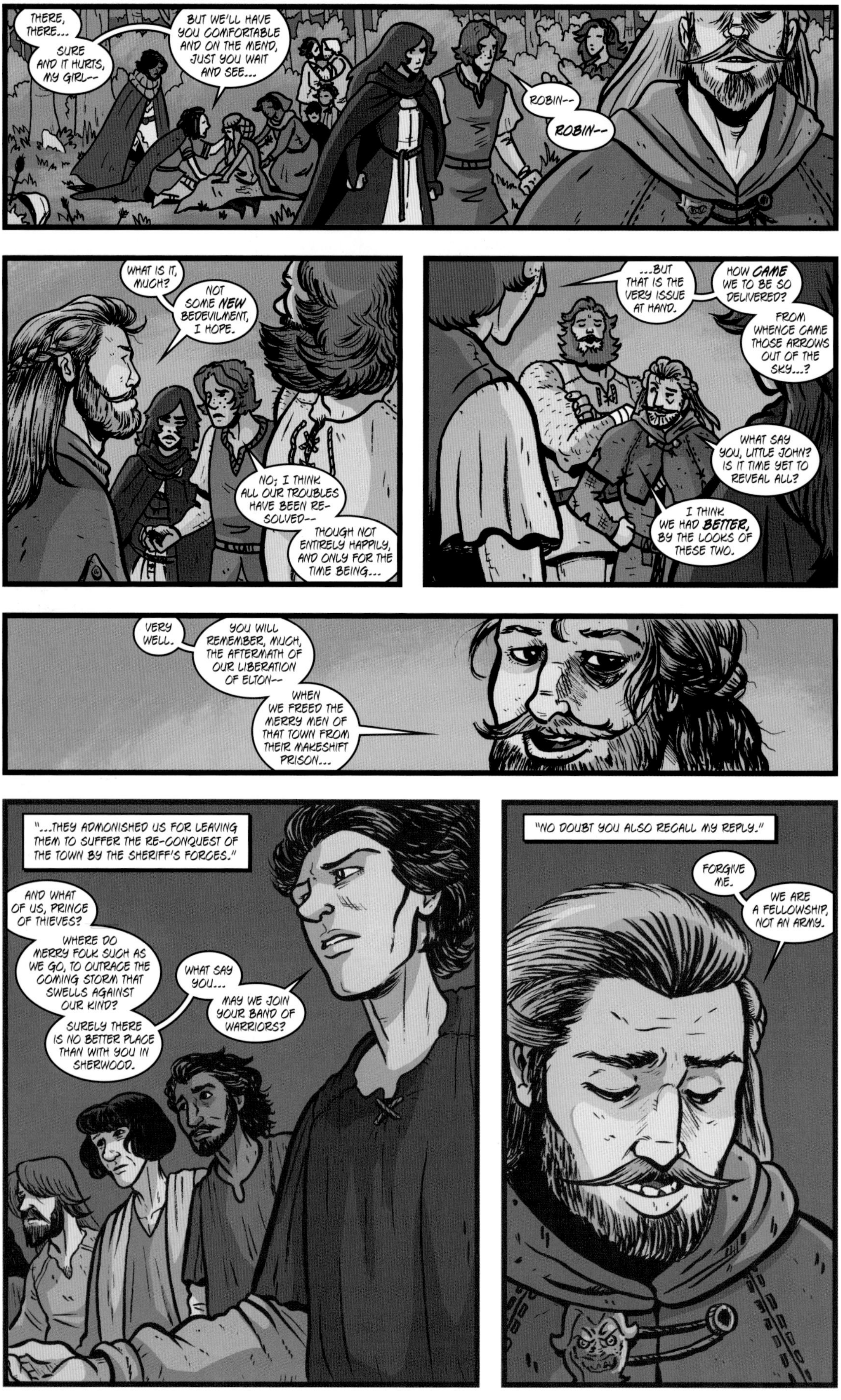
THERE, THERE...
SURE AND IT HURTS, MY GIRL--
BUT WE'LL HAVE YOU COMFORTABLE AND ON THE MEND, JUST YOU WAIT AND SEE...
ROBIN--
ROBIN--
WHAT IS IT, MUCH?
NOT SOME NEW BEDEVILMENT, I HOPE.
NO; I THINK ALL OUR TROUBLES HAVE BEEN RE-SOLVED--
THOUGH NOT ENTIRELY HAPPILY, AND ONLY FOR THE TIME BEING...
...BUT THAT IS THE VERY ISSUE AT HAND.
HOW CAME WE TO BE SO DELIVERED?
FROM WHENCE CAME THOSE ARROWS OUT OF THE SKY...?
WHAT SAY YOU, LITTLE JOHN? IS IT TIME YET TO REVEAL ALL?
I THINK WE HAD BETTER, BY THE LOOKS OF THESE TWO.
VERY WELL.
YOU WILL REMEMBER, MUCH, THE AFTERMATH OF OUR LIBERATION OF ELTON--
WHEN WE FREED THE MERRY MEN OF THAT TOWN FROM THEIR MAKESHIFT PRISON...
"...THEY ADMONISHED US FOR LEAVING THEM TO SUFFER THE RE-CONQUEST OF THE TOWN BY THE SHERIFF'S FORCES."
AND WHAT OF US, PRINCE OF THIEVES?
WHERE DO MERRY FOLK SUCH AS WE GO, TO OUTRACE THE COMING STORM THAT SWELLS AGAINST OUR KIND?
SURELY THERE IS NO BETTER PLACE THAN WITH YOU IN SHERWOOD.
WHAT SAY YOU...
MAY WE JOIN YOUR BAND OF WARRIORS?
"NO DOUBT YOU ALSO RECALL MY REPLY."
FORGIVE ME.
WE ARE A FELLOWSHIP, NOT AN ARMY.

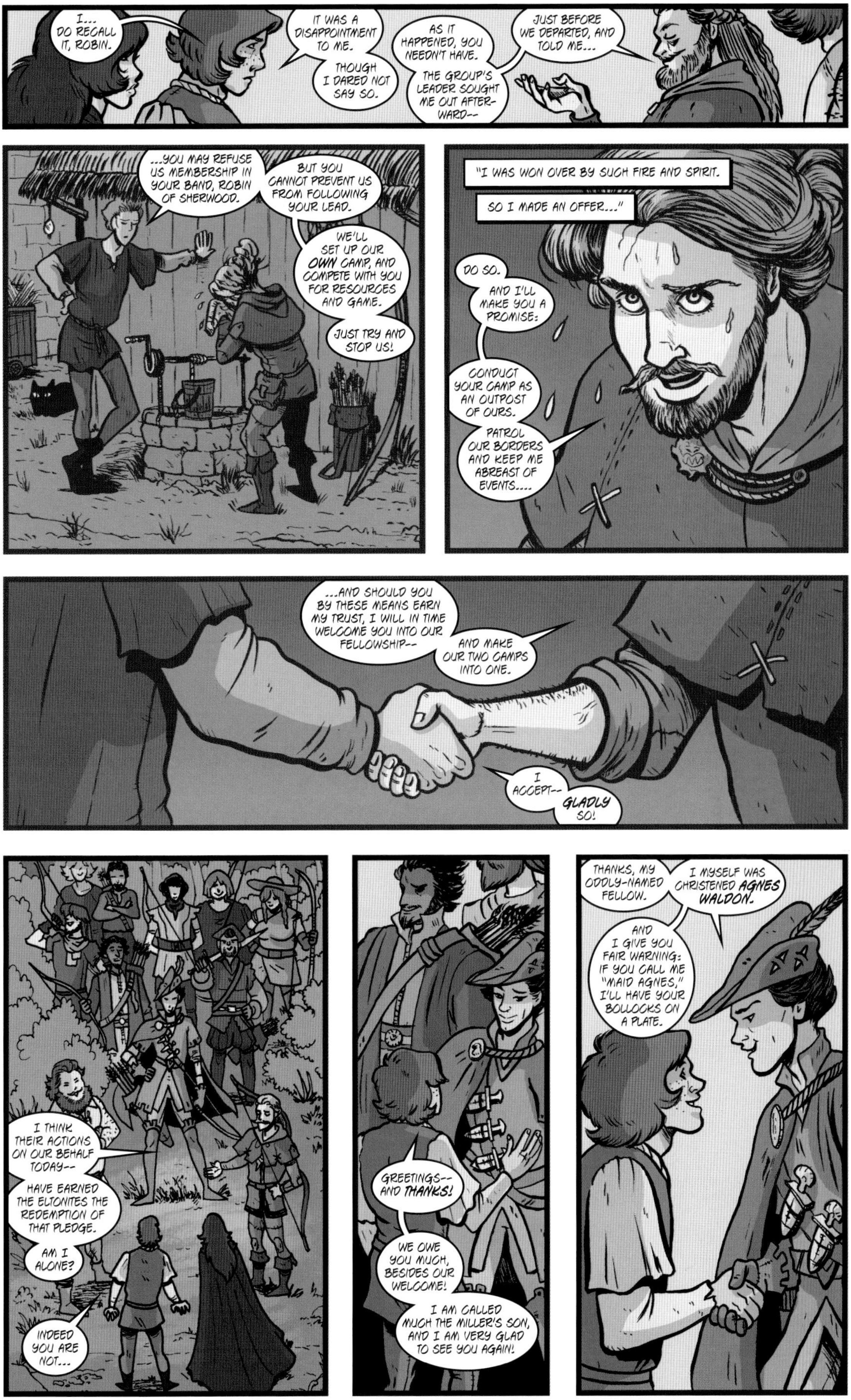
I... DO RECALL IT, ROBIN.
IT WAS A DISAPPOINTMENT TO ME.
THOUGH I DARED NOT SAY SO.
AS IT HAPPENED, YOU NEEDN'T HAVE.
THE GROUP'S LEADER SOUGHT ME OUT AFTER-WARD--
JUST BEFORE WE DEPARTED, AND TOLD ME...
...YOU MAY REFUSE US MEMBERSHIP IN YOUR BAND, ROBIN OF SHERWOOD.
BUT YOU CANNOT PREVENT US FROM FOLLOWING YOUR LEAD.
WE'LL SET UP OUR OWN CAMP, AND COMPETE WITH YOU FOR RESOURCES AND GAME.
JUST TRY AND STOP US!
"I WAS WON OVER BY SUCH FIRE AND SPIRIT.
SO I MADE AN OFFER..."
DO SO.
AND I'LL MAKE YOU A PROMISE:
CONDUCT YOUR CAMP AS AN OUTPOST OF OURS.
PATROL OUR BORDERS AND KEEP ME ABREAST OF EVENTS....
...AND SHOULD YOU BY THESE MEANS EARN MY TRUST, I WILL IN TIME WELCOME YOU INTO OUR FELLOWSHIP--
AND MAKE OUR TWO CAMPS INTO ONE.
I ACCEPT-- GLADLY SO!
I THINK THEIR ACTIONS ON OUR BEHALF TODAY--
HAVE EARNED THE ELTONITES THE REDEMPTION OF THAT PLEDGE.
AM I ALONE?
INDEED YOU ARE NOT...
GREETINGS-- AND THANKS!
WE OWE YOU MUCH, BESIDES OUR WELCOME!
I AM CALLED MUCH THE MILLER'S SON, AND I AM VERY GLAD TO SEE YOU AGAIN!
THANKS, MY ODDLY-NAMED FELLOW.
I MYSELF WAS CHRISTENED AGNES WALDON.
AND I GIVE YOU FAIR WARNING: IF YOU CALL ME "MAID AGNES," I'LL HAVE YOUR BOLLOCKS ON A PLATE.

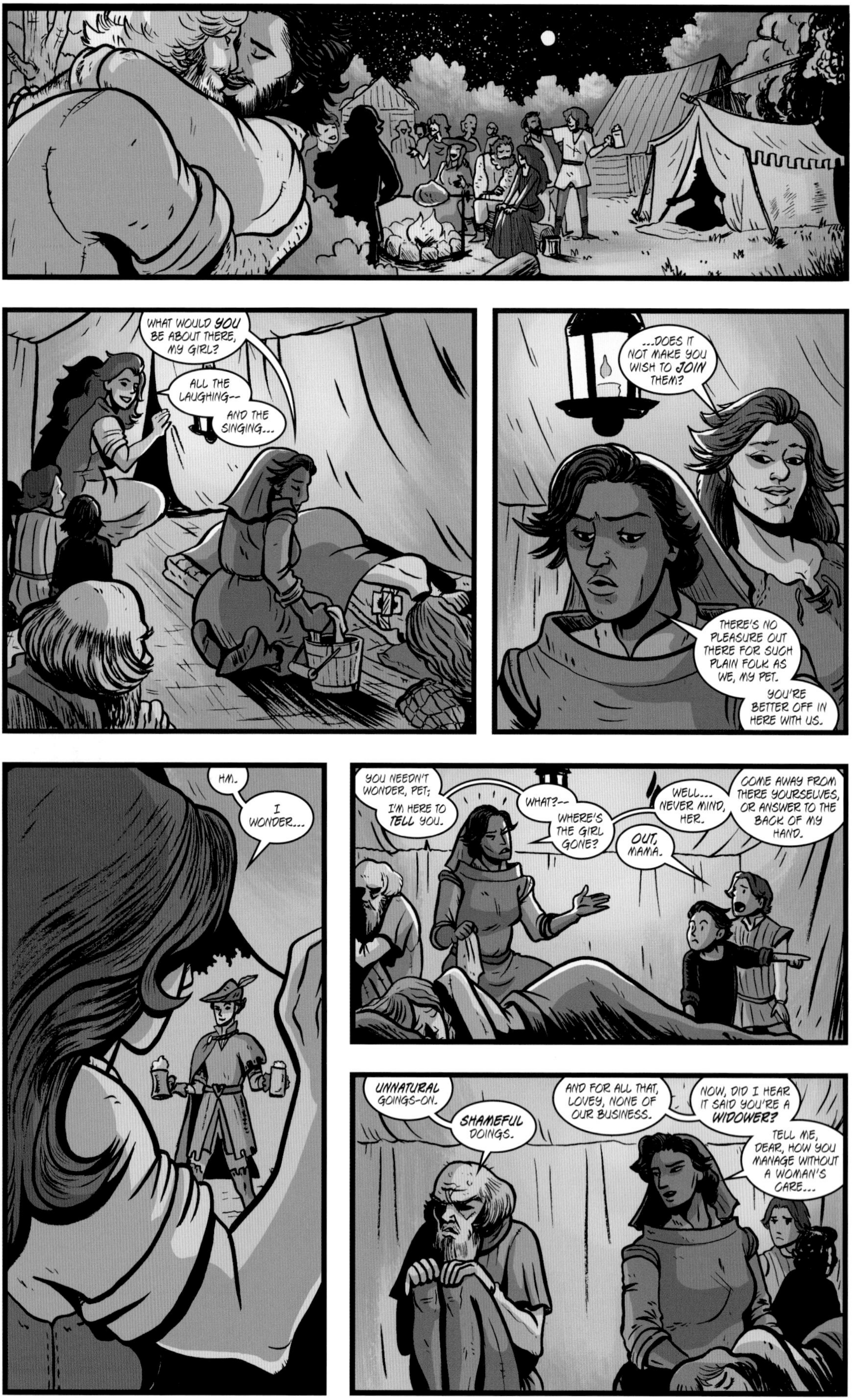

WHAT WOULD YOU BE ABOUT THERE, MY GIRL?
ALL THE LAUGHING--
AND THE SINGING...
...DOES IT NOT MAKE YOU WISH TO JOIN THEM?
THERE'S NO PLEASURE OUT THERE FOR SUCH PLAIN FOLK AS WE, MY PET.
YOU'RE BETTER OFF IN HERE WITH US.
HM.
I WONDER...
YOU NEEDN'T WONDER, PET;
I'M HERE TO TELL YOU.
WHAT?--
WHERE'S THE GIRL GONE?
WELL... NEVER MIND, HER.
OUT, MAMA.
COME AWAY FROM THERE YOURSELVES, OR ANSWER TO THE BACK OF MY HAND.
UNNATURAL GOINGS-ON.
SHAMEFUL DOINGS.
AND FOR ALL THAT, LOVEY, NONE OF OUR BUSINESS.
NOW, DID I HEAR IT SAID YOU'RE A WIDOWER?
TELL ME, DEAR, HOW YOU MANAGE WITHOUT A WOMAN'S CARE...

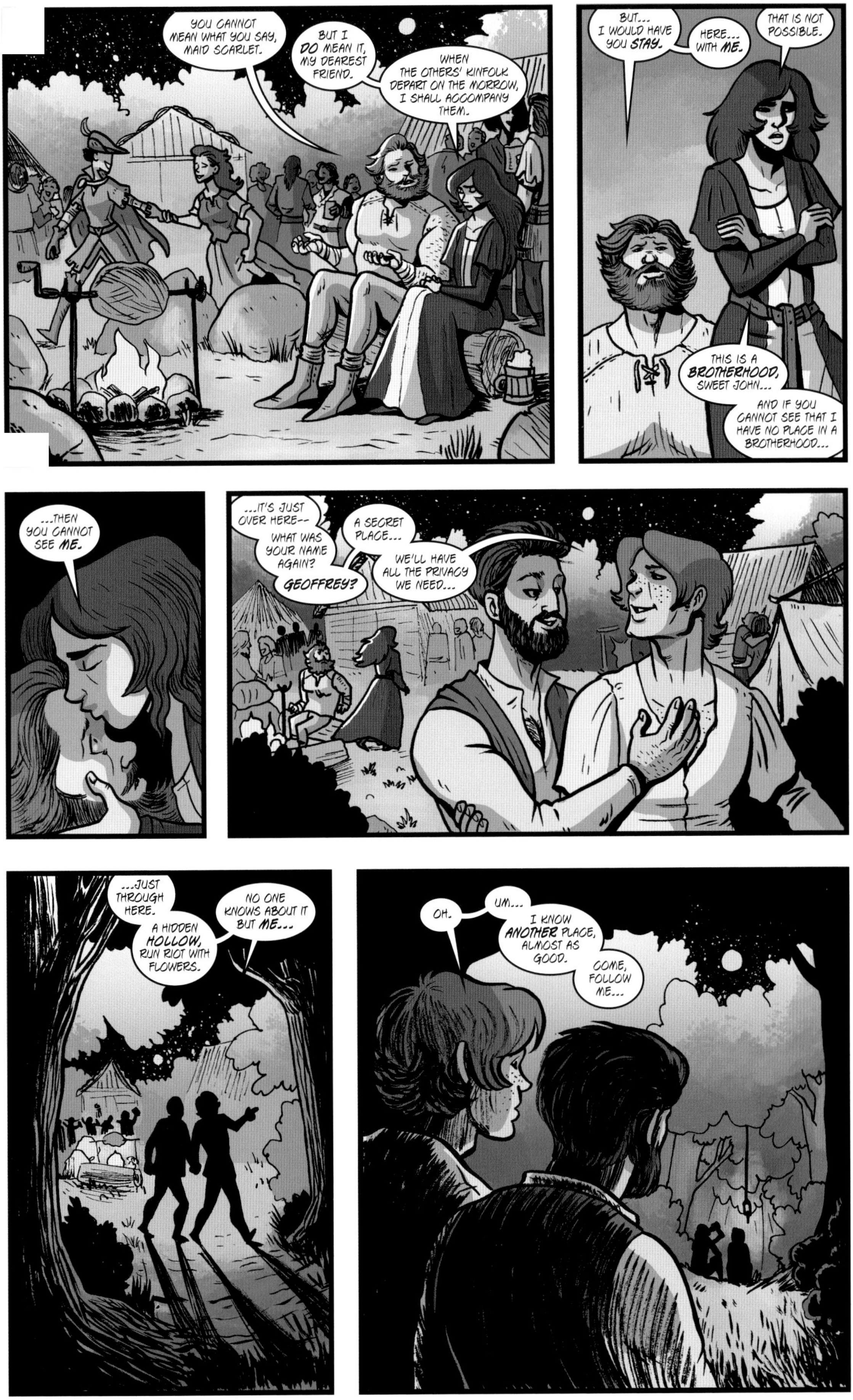
YOU CANNOT MEAN WHAT YOU SAY, MAID SCARLET.
BUT I DO MEAN IT, MY DEAREST FRIEND.
WHEN THE OTHERS' KINFOLK DEPART ON THE MORROW, I SHALL ACCOMPANY THEM.
BUT... I WOULD HAVE YOU STAY.
HERE... WITH ME.
THAT IS NOT POSSIBLE.
THIS IS A BROTHERHOOD, SWEET JOHN...
AND IF YOU CANNOT SEE THAT I HAVE NO PLACE IN A BROTHERHOOD...
...THEN YOU CANNOT SEE ME.
...IT'S JUST OVER HERE--
WHAT WAS YOUR NAME AGAIN?
GEOFFREY?
A SECRET PLACE...
WE'LL HAVE ALL THE PRIVACY WE NEED...
...JUST THROUGH HERE.
A HIDDEN HOLLOW, RUN RIOT WITH FLOWERS.
NO ONE KNOWS ABOUT IT BUT ME...
OH.
UM...
I KNOW ANOTHER PLACE, ALMOST AS GOOD.
COME, FOLLOW ME...

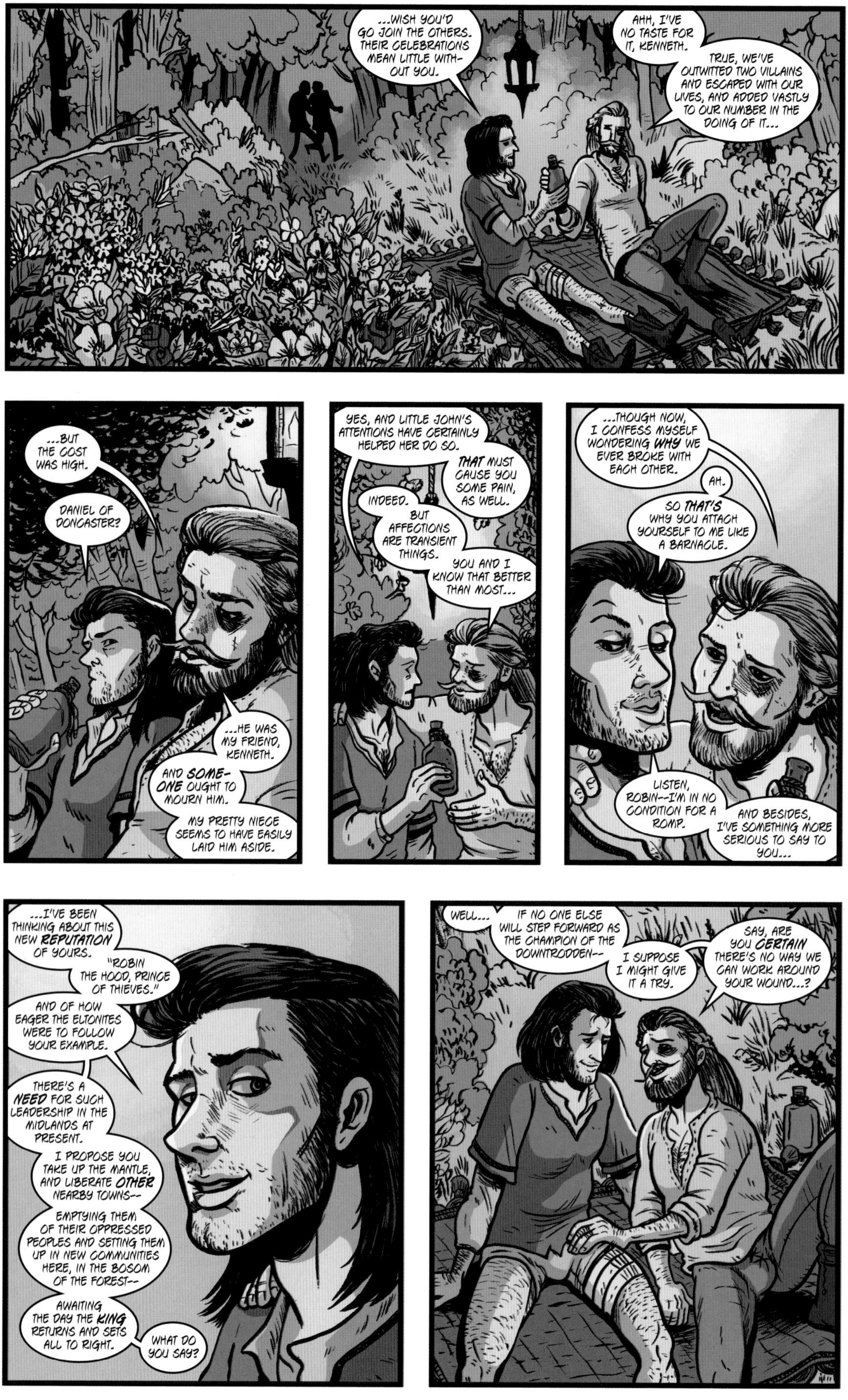
...WISH YOU'D GO JOIN THE OTHERS. THEIR CELEBRATIONS MEAN LITTLE WITH-OUT YOU.
AHH, I'VE NO TASTE FOR IT, KENNETH.
TRUE, WE'VE OUTWITTED TWO VILLAINS AND ESCAPED WITH OUR LIVES, AND ADDED VASTLY TO OUR NUMBER IN THE DOING OF IT...
...BUT THE COST WAS HIGH.
DANIEL OF DONCASTER?
...HE WAS MY FRIEND, KENNETH.
AND SOME-ONE OUGHT TO MOURN HIM.
MY PRETTY NIECE SEEMS TO HAVE EASILY LAID HIM ASIDE.
YES, AND LITTLE JOHN'S ATTENTIONS HAVE CERTAINLY HELPED HER DO SO.
THAT MUST CAUSE YOU SOME PAIN, AS WELL.
INDEED.
BUT AFFECTIONS ARE TRANSIENT THINGS.
YOU AND I KNOW THAT BETTER THAN MOST...
...THOUGH NOW, I CONFESS MYSELF WONDERING WHY WE EVER BROKE WITH EACH OTHER.
AH.
SO THAT'S WHY YOU ATTACH YOURSELF TO ME LIKE A BARNACLE.
LISTEN, ROBIN--I'M IN NO CONDITION FOR A ROMP.
AND BESIDES, I'VE SOMETHING MORE SERIOUS TO SAY TO YOU...
...I'VE BEEN THINKING ABOUT THIS NEW REPUTATION OF YOURS.
"ROBIN THE HOOD, PRINCE OF THIEVES."
AND OF HOW EAGER THE ELTONITES WERE TO FOLLOW YOUR EXAMPLE.
THERE'S A NEED FOR SUCH LEADERSHIP IN THE MIDLANDS AT PRESENT.
I PROPOSE YOU TAKE UP THE MANTLE, AND LIBERATE OTHER NEARBY TOWNS--
EMPTYING THEM OF THEIR OPPRESSED PEOPLES AND SETTING THEM UP IN NEW COMMUNITIES HERE, IN THE BOSOM OF THE FOREST--
AWAITING THE DAY THE KING RETURNS AND SETS ALL TO RIGHT.
WHAT DO YOU SAY?
WELL...
IF NO ONE ELSE WILL STEP FORWARD AS THE CHAMPION OF THE DOWNTRODDEN--
I SUPPOSE I MIGHT GIVE IT A TRY.
SAY, ARE YOU CERTAIN THERE'S NO WAY WE CAN WORK AROUND YOUR WOUND...?

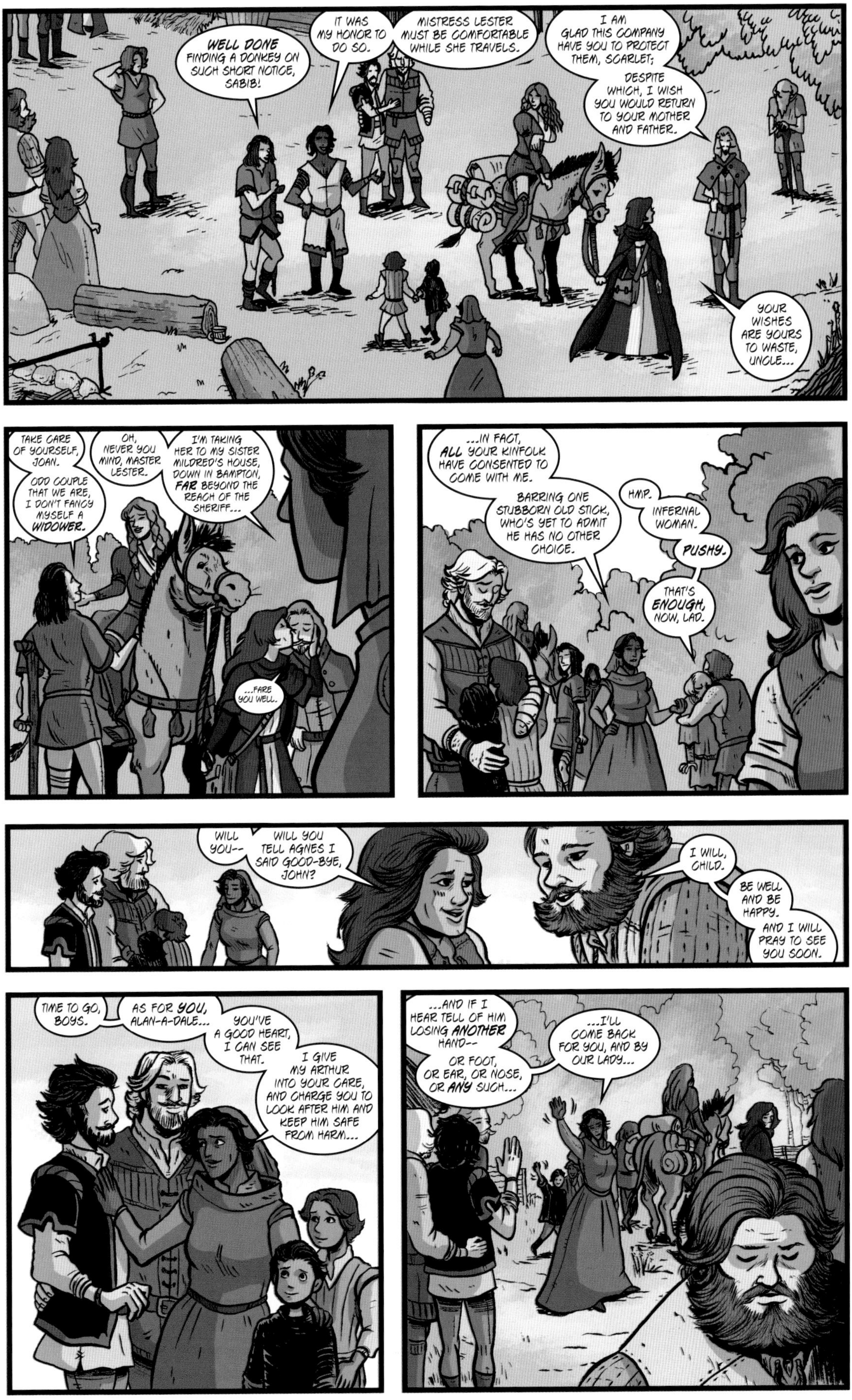
WELL DONE FINDING A DONKEY ON SUCH SHORT NOTICE, SABIB!
IT WAS MY HONOR TO DO SO.
MISTRESS LESTER MUST BE COMFORTABLE WHILE SHE TRAVELS.
I AM GLAD THIS COMPANY HAVE YOU TO PROTECT THEM, SCARLET;
DESPITE WHICH, I WISH YOU WOULD RETURN TO YOUR MOTHER AND FATHER.
YOUR WISHES ARE YOURS TO WASTE, UNCLE...
TAKE CARE OF YOURSELF, JOAN.
ODD COUPLE THAT WE ARE, I DON'T FANCY MYSELF A WIDOWER.
OH, NEVER YOU MIND, MASTER LESTER.
I'M TAKING HER TO MY SISTER MILDRED'S HOUSE, DOWN IN BAMPTON, FAR BEYOND THE REACH OF THE SHERIFF...
...FARE YOU WELL.
...IN FACT, ALL YOUR KINFOLK HAVE CONSENTED TO COME WITH ME.
BARRING ONE STUBBORN OLD STICK, WHO'S YET TO ADMIT HE HAS NO OTHER CHOICE.
HMP.
INFERNAL WOMAN.
PUSHY.
THAT'S ENOUGH, NOW, LAD.
WILL YOU--
WILL YOU TELL AGNES I SAID GOOD-BYE, JOHN?
I WILL, CHILD.
BE WELL AND BE HAPPY.
AND I WILL PRAY TO SEE YOU SOON.
TIME TO GO, BOYS.
AS FOR YOU, ALAN-A-DALE...
YOU'VE A GOOD HEART, I CAN SEE THAT.
I GIVE MY ARTHUR INTO YOUR CARE, AND CHARGE YOU TO LOOK AFTER HIM AND KEEP HIM SAFE FROM HARM...
...AND IF I HEAR TELL OF HIM LOSING ANOTHER HAND--
OR FOOT, OR EAR, OR NOSE, OR ANY SUCH...
...I'LL COME BACK FOR YOU, AND BY OUR LADY...

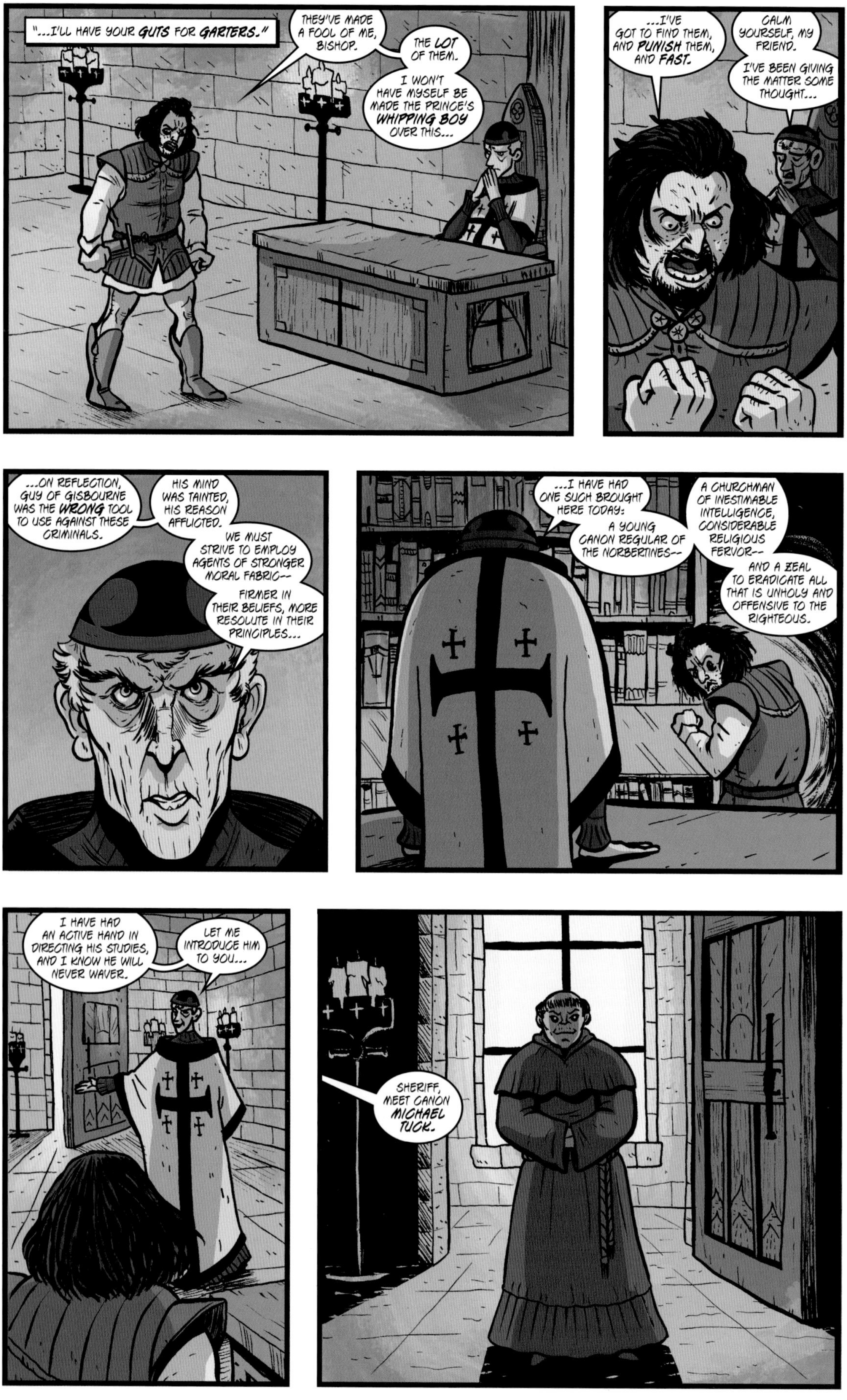
"...I'LL HAVE YOUR GUTS FOR GARTERS."
THEY'VE MADE A FOOL OF ME, BISHOP.
THE LOT OF THEM.
I WON'T HAVE MYSELF BE MADE THE PRINCE'S WHIPPING BOY OVER THIS...
...I'VE GOT TO FIND THEM, AND PUNISH THEM, AND FAST.
CALM YOURSELF, MY FRIEND.
I'VE BEEN GIVING THE MATTER SOME THOUGHT...
...ON REFLECTION, GUY OF GISBOURNE WAS THE WRONG TOOL TO USE AGAINST THESE CRIMINALS.
HIS MIND WAS TAINTED, HIS REASON AFFLICTED.
WE MUST STRIVE TO EMPLOY AGENTS OF STRONGER MORAL FABRIC--
FIRMER IN THEIR BELIEFS, MORE RESOLUTE IN THEIR PRINCIPLES...
...I HAVE HAD ONE SUCH BROUGHT HERE TODAY:
A YOUNG CANON REGULAR OF THE NORBERTINES--
A CHURCHMAN OF INESTIMABLE INTELLIGENCE, CONSIDERABLE RELIGIOUS FERVOR--
AND A ZEAL TO ERADICATE ALL THAT IS UNHOLY AND OFFENSIVE TO THE RIGHTEOUS.
I HAVE HAD AN ACTIVE HAND IN DIRECTING HIS STUDIES, AND I KNOW HE WILL NEVER WAVER.
LET ME INTRODUCE HIM TO YOU...
SHERIFF, MEET CANON MICHAEL TUCK.

A QUEER HISTORY OF ENGLAND

WRITTEN BY ROBERT RODI
WITH ILLUSTRATIONS BY JACKIE LEWIS

A QUEER HISTORY OF ENGLAND
PART 1: ALCUIN OF YORK

bomosexuality as a concept didn't exist in the medieval world; same-sex love was seen as a behavior, not an identity. That said, there were inevitably individuals whose physical, emotional, and romantic inclinations were almost exclusively toward persons of their own gender. Richard the Lionheart appears to have been one of these (and his appearances in Merry Men are in accord with that). But many other queer figures made a mark on English history over the centuries that bridge the Dark Ages and the Renaissance.

The earliest of our subjects is Alcuin, who was born in Northumbria in the year 735 and studied at the Cathedral school of York, where he became a deacon (though there is no evidence he was ever ordained a priest). In 782 he was recruited by no less than Charlemagne to head the king's school for his children in Aachen, Germany. Fourteen years later he was made abbot of Saint Martin at Tours, where he remained until his death in 804.

Alcuin's time in Charlemagne's court is notable for the erotic undercurrent he established with his (exclusively male) pupils, whom he doted on and gave affectionate nicknames to. But his most openly sexual expressions are in verses and letters penned for his contemporaries. As an example, he wrote to one friend—a bishop—of his longing "for that lovely time when I may be able to clutch the neck of your sweetness with the fingers of my desires … how much I would cover, with tightly pressed lips, not only your eyes, your ears and mouth, but also every finger and toe, not once but many a time."

Whether or not he ever acted on such desires, the passionate physicality of these words calls to mind the equally ardent poetry of Walt Whitman, more than a thousand years later. Both men managed to blend homoeroticism with the metaphysical—in Alcuin's case, Christian spirituality; in Whitman's, a more pagan exaltation of the natural world.

A QUEER HISTORY OF ENGLAND PART 2: WILLIAM RUFUS

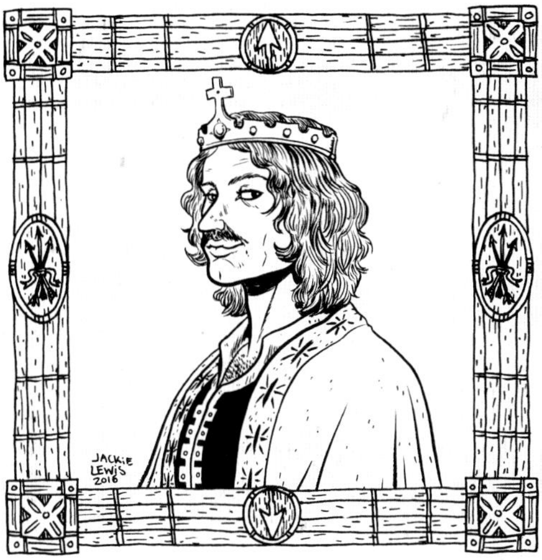
JACKIE LEWIS 2016

Rufus (so called because of his ruddy coloring) was the son of William the Conqueror, who invaded Anglo-Saxon England in 1066 and set up a brutal Norman regime to rule it. When Rufus came to the throne in 1087 (as William II), he proved to be a very different man from his spartan father. He wore his hair long and preferred colorful, stylish clothes (his court introduced the pointed-toe shoes we associate with the middle ages). In fact, Rufus looked more Anglo-Saxon than Norman. The Conqueror's son, it seemed, had gone native.

But only to a point. Rufus completely lacked the piety of such revered Anglo-Saxon kings as Edward the Confessor. He openly consorted with male "favorites" and promoted them based on their looks. Later kings would do the same; but Rufus alone didn't bother to put up a more respectable front by also taking a wife and siring heirs. There were no mistresses or illegitimate children, either, which for a king of his dynasty was basically unheard of. Rufus's flaunting of his affairs with men earned him the ire of the church, and the animosity was entirely mutual. Rufus took every opportunity to antagonize the clergy; for example, he kept several abbacies and bishoprics vacant in order that he, and not they, would profit from their revenues.

Perhaps the biggest mark against him was that he preferred his French holdings to England. This made him popular with his Norman mercenaries (enough for them to overlook his long hair) and very unpopular with his British subjects. In 1100 he was killed in a hunting accident—though the speed with which his brother Henry assumed the throne is evidence that the "accident" was nothing of the kind. Henry, a proper Norman king, made a point of banning long hair at court, and fathered three legitimate and 24 illegitimate children, as if desperate to make up for his scandalous gay predecessor.

A QUEER HISTORY OF ENGLAND PART 3: EDWARD II

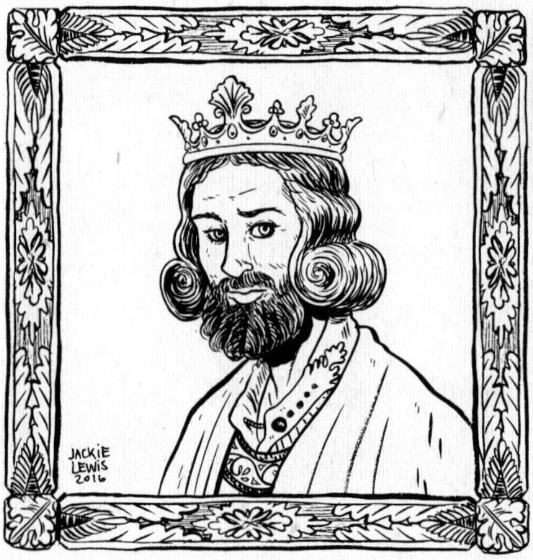
JACKIE
LEWIS
2016

Edward I was one of England's great warrior kings, known by admirer and detractor alike as "the Hammer of the Scots." His heir, Edward II, was bound to be a disappointment; what son could measure up to such a father? But it didn't help that the younger Edward, from almost the moment he came to the throne, was inseparable from a handsome young member of his household, Piers Gaveston, whom he immediately promoted to Earl of Cornwall.

Scholars have debated ever since whether the relationship of Edward and Gaveston was sexual in nature, which in my opinion just shows how far scholars will go to see anything but what's in front of them. Certainly Edward's French wife, Isabella, took the favor her husband showed Gaveston as a direct affront, and she was not a woman who took affronts sitting down (she was known as "the She-Wolf of France," which is not a nickname you get without leaving some serious carnage in your wake). And since Gaveston apparently was the kind of man saw no reason not to flaunt his power and privilege, he earned the deep personal loathing of the nobility, as well. So it wasn't too difficult for the queen and the barons to topple Gaveston and even have him executed.

The king was temporarily held in check; but he soon found solace in another handsome retainer, Hugh Despenser. This time Queen She-Wolf wasn't taking any chances; with the aid of her own lover, Roger Mortimer, she took down not only Despenser, but Edward himself, and put her son on the throne. He became Edward III, another great warrior king. As for our Edward, he did not survive imprisonment; and a story soon gained currency that not only was he murdered, but that the means was especially brutal: rape by a red-hot poker.

Edward II's relationship with Gaveston became the subject of a play by the openly gay Elizabethan playwright (and contemporary of Shakespeare) Christopher Marlowe. In our own era, alas, Edward is best known by the viciously homophobic caricature of him in Mel Gibson's film *Braveheart*.

A QUEER HISTORY OF ENGLAND
PART 4: JOHN RYKENER (A.K.A. ELEANOR)

John Rykener is the earliest known cross-dressing prostitute in British history. He lived in late 14th century London (and also for a time in Oxford), and was arrested in December 1394. The transcript of his questioning survives, and forms the only surviving document to refer to same-sex activity in medieval England…though it seems unlikely to the point of impossibility that Rykener was the only sexual rebel of his kind. What seems far more probable is that his testimony is but a glimpse at a thriving English demimonde that was either considered unworthy of attention by the era's chroniclers, or was something they just weren't aware of.

Under interrogation, Rykener frankly confesses to having sex with men for money while dressed as a woman—including members of the clergy. He even admits to a preference for priests, because they paid better (one Franciscan friar apparently having given him a gold ring, and a Carmelite friar and six "foreigners" are credited with giving him five shillings). It's unclear whether these men knew he was a cross-dresser; but either way, their carnal relations were considered sodomy (as was any non-procreative sex, at that time). Far more transgressive, though—to the point that it was the original reason for Rykener's arrest, not the "unmentionable and ignominious vice" he committed with his clients—was the cross-dressing itself. Sodomy, after all, was just a lewd act; cross-dressing was a disruption of the entire social order.

We learn, through his statement, that Rykener not only posed as a woman to solicit sex; he actually had a fully developed female persona, named Eleanor. We don't know the extent to which he really was Eleanor—he doesn't seem to have adopted her identity on a permanent basis—but he seems to have lived quite contentedly as her at least a part of the time. In Oxford, Eleanor even had a legitimate job as an embroideress, in addition to her more subversive trade (which she plied among students).

The transcription of Rykener's interrogation is all we have of his case; we don't know what eventually happened to him (or to Eleanor). But we can infer from this single document a much larger, more varied, and more nuanced sexual landscape than most histories of medieval urban life begin to hint at.

A QUEER HISTORY OF ENGLAND
PART 5: JOAN OF ARC

Joan was, of course, French; but she is a prominent figure in English history. The so-called Hundred Years' War between France and England (which actually ran 112, plus change), was going badly for France in the 1420s. Joan changed that. When she—a mere peasant girl of seventeen—convinced the French dauphin to give her an army, on the promise that she would see him crowned king, she made good on the vow, leading her troops to liberate the besieged city of Orléans. As a result of this victory, the dauphin was crowned at Reims in 1429, becoming King Charles VII, with Joan in attendance.

This was a tremendous setback for the English, and when Joan later fell into their hands, they famously tried her and burned her at the stake. But that wasn't enough to purge them of their hatred of her; they continued to vilify her for centuries. Shakespeare offers the best illustration of this; his Joan is a lying, scheming sorceress, who consorts with demons and "fiends" until even those abandon her. "My body shall pay recompense, if you will grant my suit," she says, desperately offering them sex in exchange for their unholy aid. They turn her down.

It was easy for the Bard to portray Joan as a demon-consorting witch. By her own admission, she acted at the urging of voices in her head. She claimed they were the voices of angels; the English very much thought otherwise. But there was an even worse indemnification, in their eyes. The Bible (Deuteronomy 22:5) declares, "A woman must not wear men's clothing nor a man wear women's clothing, for the Lord your God detests anyone who does this."

We have no evidence of Joan's sexuality. What we do know is that she cut her hair short, like a boy, and dressed in armor, like a man. For that reason, while we can't call her gay, we can call her queer.

robert rodi (writer)

is an author whose cult-hit novels include *Fag Hag*, *Closet Case* and *Bitch Goddess*; he has also published nonfiction, most recently the travel memoir *Seven Seasons In Siena*. In comics he's best known for his creator-owned series *Codename: Knockout*, but has also written many series for Marvel, including *Loki*, *Elektra* and *Rogue*. In addition he's a journalist, musician and spoken-word performer. He lives in Chicago with his husband, Jeffrey Smith, and a constantly shifting number of dogs.

jackie lewis (Artist)

is a comic book creator from Atlanta. Growing up, she spent most of her time drawing monsters and building forts in the woods. Now, she's thrilled that she gets to draw both of those things professionally. Jackie's published works include *Merry Men*, *The Lion of Rora*, and *Play Ball*.

marissa louise (colorist)

is a colorist living in the woods of Oregon. She is trained in painting, but found her true home in coloring. Look for her work through Oni, Albatross, DC and most major comics publishers.

shari chankhamma (colorist)

is a comic artist living in Thailand. She colored *Sheltered*, *The Fuse*, and *Kill Shakespeare*, among other titles. Her latest work is *Codename Baboushka*, which she both drew and colored. Visit her online at sharii.com, or on twitter or instagram @sharihes.

jon cairns (Letterer)

is a freelance comic creator whose work appears online (*Alpha Flag*, *Untitled SF*) and in print in the *Beyond* (*O-Type Hypergiant*) and *Smut Peddler* (*Love Triangulation*) anthologies. When given carte blanche to create a story, odds are good it'll be set in space—probably featuring hunks and body hair.

try these other great comics from oni press!

PETROGRAD

By Philip Gelatt and
Tyler Crook
264 pages, hardcover,
two-color interiors
ISBN 978-1-934964-44-6

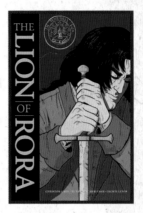

THE LION OF RORA

By Christos Gage,
Ruth Fletcher Gage,
and Jackie Lewis
184 pages, hardcover,
black and white interiors
ISBN 978-1-62010-248-0

NIGHT'S DOMINION, VOLUME ONE

By Ted Naifeh
168 pages, softcover,
color interiors
ISBN 978-1-62010-410-1

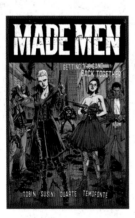

MADE MEN: GETTING THE GANG BACK TOGETHER

By Paul Tobin,
Arjuna Susini,
and Gonzalo Duarte
128 pages, softcover,
color interiors
ISBN 978-1-62010-512-2

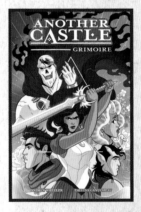

THE LIFE AFTER, VOLUME ONE, SQUARE ONE EDITION

By Joshua Hale
Fialkov and Gabo
136 pages, softcover,
color interiors
ISBN 978-1-62010-389-0

ANOTHER CASTLE: GRIMOIRE

By Andrew Wheeler
and Paulina Ganucheau
152 pages, softcover,
color interiors
ISBN 978-1-62010-311-1